Doing Business in China

Extensively revised, the fifth edition of this successful textbook offers a practical framework for approaching and carrying out business in China.

Building on the strengths of previous editions and the 30-year China business experience of the author, the book provides a guide to market entry, managing operations, and marketing in this unique social and cultural environment, including:

- Why foreign businesses in China need to understand and interact with government in China, both central and local, and how best to do this
- New and revised case studies, including those on successful companies entering and operating in China such as Volkswagen, Hermes, Honeywell, and Diageo
- An in-depth focus on internet marketing in China
- Choosing business partners and negotiating
- Dos and don'ts.

Updated to include information on new government policy on trade partnerships, commercial law, and anti-corruption drives, the fifth edition of *Doing Business in China* will continue to be the preferred text for international students of Chinese business and management studies and for practitioners with an eye on China.

Giles Chance is a former professor of the Tuck School of Business at Dartmouth College, USA, 2011–19, and at the Guanghua School of Management at Peking University, China, 2009–15. He is the author of *China and the Credit Crisis: the Emergence of a New World Order* (2010).

Doing Business in China

Fifth Edition

Giles Chance

Routledge
Taylor & Francis Group

LONDON AND NEW YORK

Cover image: @ Aphotostory/Getty Images

Fifth edition published 2023
by Routledge
4 Park Square, Milton Park, Abingdon, Oxon, OX14 4RN

and by Routledge
605 Third Avenue, New York, NY 10158

*Routledge is an imprint of the Taylor & Francis Group,
an informa business*

First edition published by Routledge 2000
Fourth edition published by Routledge 2016

British Library Cataloguing-in-Publication Data
A catalogue record for this book is available from the British Library

Library of Congress Cataloging-in-Publication Data
A catalog record has been requested for this book

ISBN: 978-1-032-14784-0 (hbk)
ISBN: 978-1-032-14764-2 (pbk)
ISBN: 978-1-003-24116-4 (ebk)

DOI: 10.4324/9781003241164

Typeset in Times New Roman
by SPi Technologies India Pvt Ltd (Straive)

I dedicate this book to the Chinese people, who have succeeded in creating a modern China of which their ancestors would be proud.

Contents

Foreword

By Fang Wenjian
Chairman, The Chinese Chamber of Commerce in UK

China represents a huge opportunity, but for some still a daunting challenge, in terms of developing a business strategy. This updated fifth edition of *Doing Business in China* is a must-read for Western investors who are gearing up to enter the China market.

There is a Chinese idiom (因地制宜), which roughly translates as "adjust measures to local conditions", which is, of course, the key to successful planning and business development internationally.

Recently updated and revised, *Doing Business in China* provides in-depth and relevant, up-to-date advice for Western companies looking to conduct business and making investment decisions there. Giles Chance (and Chao Xi, who wrote the chapter entitled "Business and the Law") have done a wonderful job pointing the way towards a beneficial and effective level of engagement with the business world in China.

Investors in the UK view China, the UK's third largest trading partner, as a critical part of their global strategy. Indeed, according to a recent survey report conducted by the British Chamber of Commerce in China, nearly half of the British companies surveyed plan to increase their investment in business in mainland China in 2022. These companies recognize that China's economic prospects, technological innovation, and clear focus on green development will provide rich opportunities in future. With proper preparation, efforts will be well rewarded.

This year also marks the 50th anniversary of the establishment of China–UK ambassadorial diplomatic relations. The past five decades offer ample evidence of a healthy and flourishing relationship between the two countries, something which is both vital and beneficial to their peoples.

The Chinese and UK business communities will continue to play an important role in promoting the growth of the China–UK economic and trade relationship, and contribute further to maintaining the flow of commerce, to ensure that business ties grow and strengthen.

FANG Wenjian
Chairman of the China Chamber of Commerce in the UK

Foreword
By Sir Sherard Cowper-Coles
Chairman, China-Britain Business Council, London

As geopolitics and the pandemic put enormous stress on relations with China, this fifth edition of *Doing Business in China*, brought up to date by Giles Chance, could not be more timely.

You would expect that there should be no need to suggest that businesses look at China, the world's second largest economy. But China remains, for many, largely unknown and sometimes a step too far. The author has, in this bang up-to-date revision of the ins and outs of the challenging, and often complex and complicated, China market, provided a fantastically useful road map. It is essential for success in doing business in mainland China that companies do their research not only into the obvious areas of law and regulation but, crucially, into a different business culture. Understanding how the state and party engage with the Chinese economy, and therefore the nature of the opportunity for foreign business in China, is also fundamental.

Each of the chapters takes a particular aspect of how to approach and understand the Chinese market and offers invaluable advice and insight from an author with an extraordinary depth of experience on both sides of the equation.

China has a crucial role to play in securing a new and prosperous future for international business. This handbook is the vade mecum for succeeding in that venture, and I cannot recommend it too highly.

Sir Sherard Cowper-Coles
Chair, China-Britain Business Council, London

Abbreviations

ABB	Asea Brown Boveri
AIM	Alternative Investment Market
B&Q	Block & Quayle
B2B	business-to-business
B2C	business-to-consumer
BACC	Beijing Air Catering Company
BYD	Build Your Dreams
CAAC	Civil Aviation Administration of China
CBBC	China-Britain Business Council
CCPIT	China Council for the Promotion of International Trade
CEIBS	China Europe International Business School
CETV	Chinese English Television
CJO	China Judgments Online
CMR	China Market Research
CRE	China Resources Enterprise
E+3Cs	Environment, Consumers, Competitors, own Company
EIU	Economist Intelligence Unit
ESPN	Entertainment & Sports Programming
GDP	Gross Domestic Product
GONGOs	Government-organized non-governmental organizations
H&M	Hennes & Mauritz
HK	Hong Kong
HR	Human Resources
IP	Intellectual property
IPR	Intellectual property rights
JV	Joint venture
KFC	Kentucky Fried Chicken
LM	Lunderskov Mobelfabrik
LV	Louis Vuitton
MNC	Multinational Corporation
MOFERT	Ministry of Foreign Trade
NPC	National People's Congress
NPCSC	National People's Congress Standing Committee
O&M	Ogilvy & Mather

OEM	original equipment manufacturers
P2P	peer-to peer
PKU	Peking University
PLA	People's Liberation Army
PM	Prime Minister
PRC	People's Republic of China
QQ	Tencent texting service
SAIC	Shanghai Automotive International Company
SAML	Shanghai Asset Management Limited
SAR	Special Administrative Region
SASAC	State-owned Assets Supervision and Administration Corporation
SEZ	Special Economic Zones
SKD	Semi knocked-down
SME	Small and Medium-Sized Enterprises
SOE	State-owned enterprises
SPC	Supreme People's Court
SRG	Survey Research Group
SWOT	Strengths, Weaknesses, Opportunities and Threats
TCL	Telephone Communication Limited
UNESCO	United Nations Educational, Scientific and Cultural Organization
US	United States
VIE	variable-interest entity
VW	Volkswagen
WFOE	Wholly Foreign-Owned Enterprise
WTO	World Trade Organization

Introduction

CHINA: a country which conjures up different things to different people. For some, an ancient civilization which dominated east Asia for thousands of years, and a huge and growing market which attracts attention from businesses around the world. For others, a malevolent, ever-surveillant, communist-controlled society set on world domination, and to be avoided.

In recent years, China's growing challenge to the United States as a global superpower has elicited a strong American response, supported by American allies. The more extreme elements of this response have called for a decoupling between China and the West. In response, China has initiated a 'dual-circulation' policy which is aimed at strengthening China's self-reliance and independence from the developed West, especially the United States.

China is often thought of as an economy driven by exports to the United States and other large Western economies. In fact, China's reliance on exports has diminished in recent years. As a percentage of GDP, China's exports rose from 14% in 1990 to 30% in 2006 and declined to 18% in 2020 (World Bank). As China turns inward, the correlation between growth in China and other emerging economies around the world has tumbled from a peak in 2015 of 92% to 32% in 2020 (rolling 5-year quarterly growth, Morgan Stanley).

Yet China, easily the world's largest trading country, remains deeply integrated with the rest of the world. It is the world's largest exporter, and also the largest trade partner of the United States, Germany, and Japan and many other countries, especially those in Asia. China offers the largest fast-growing market in the world for many products and services. From Tesla to General Motors, from Apple to Nike, from L'Oréal to Hermes, from Siemens to Volkswagen, from Ferrari to Ferragamo, and from Diageo to Rolls-Royce, *Doing Business in China* will continue to play a central role in most multinationals' global strategies.

This book's view is that decoupling between China and the developed West is an impossibility. Strong economic and other links between China and its Western partners will continue.

This view is supported by the results from a large recent survey (about 600 respondents) of European multinationals conducted by the consulting company Roland Berger, published as Business Confidence in China Survey 2021, on behalf of the European Chamber of Commerce.

DOI: 10.4324/9781003241164-1

The European Chamber in China has more than 1,700 corporate members, including such industry leaders and household names as ABB, BASF, Bayer, BMW, BNP Paribas, British Petroleum, Deutsche Bank, L'Oréal, KPMG, Maersk, Merck, Michelin, Nokia, Philips, Schneider Electric, Siemens, ThyssenKrupp, Total, and Volkswagen.

A similar picture emerges from the China Business Report issued by the American Chamber of Commerce based in Shanghai, which is based on surveys conducted in June 2021.

The American Chamber of Commerce in China counts among its members all the large American multinationals, including Intel, Honeywell, Hewlett Packard, Pfizer, Coca Cola, Johnson & Johnson, Cargill, Cushman & Wakefield, Boeing, ExxonMobil, General Electric, Goldman Sachs, and many others.

American portfolio holdings of Chinese equity and debt rose from US$ 765 billion in 2017 to US$ 1.2 trillion in 2020, as passive investors followed the increased weighting of Chinese capital markets in global indices. Investors' decision to place more capital in China was probably aided by the 3.5% yield on offer from Chinese Treasury bonds of ten-year maturity, which compared favourably with the 1.5% yield available for the same maturity from US Treasury bonds. An adjustment for inflation, running at 1.5% in China against around 5% in America, made the yield comparison even more compelling in China's favour as the renminbi–dollar exchange rate either held steady or even shifted a little towards the Chinese currency.

Since the last edition of this book was published in 2016, the growing geopolitical separation of China from the United States and its allies, and the parallel increases in Chinese economic self-reliance have introduced an important new element into Chinese business – on-shoring and localization, mostly in China. China business is here to stay, whatever the geopolitical tensions, because it is too big and too important for foreign companies to ignore.

When I became involved in Chinese business in the late 1980s, China was associated by many with extreme poverty, chaos, and violence. It was regarded by most business people as a place they should not spend much time in. But in 1988, when I visited China for the first time, I realized that the Chinese were determined not to go back to the chaos of the Cultural Revolution. The decades of foreign conquest, subservience, and poverty which culminated in the horrors of the Cultural Revolution, had penetrated deep into the Chinese soul. I came to understand that the Chinese people, inspired by their leader Deng Xiaoping, had committed themselves to finding ways to make progress, particularly in an economic and material way. I also realized that, while Mao might have been responsible for the deaths of many millions of Chinese people, at the same time, after the long years of dismemberment, humiliation, and civil war, he had restored to the Chinese their national unity and pride in their country and history. These two perceptions led me to take the view that China would move forwards, and probably be able to overcome the numerous obstacles in its path.

In 1989, we set up an advisory business, with offices in London, Beijing, and Shanghai, because we thought that China was an economy that was set to grow into the future, that there were enormous commercial opportunities to be had, and that we could help foreign companies to realize some of those opportunities. But it was a hard sell to corporate Europe, at least initially. We discovered that, back then, many people did not believe that China had much chance of succeeding.

Today, just over three short decades later, the picture has radically changed. China has developed itself to the point that the country's economy is now the second largest after the United States – and the largest, by some margin, if the economic measurements are adjusted for local price differences. Where 30 years ago, China's presence as a permanent member of the United Nations Security Council, along with the United States, France, Great Britain, and Russia, seemed just an anomaly of post-war reconstruction, today China's position as a global leader seems natural.

Over this short period, obviously the Chinese economy has changed dramatically. As a British soldier based on the Hong Kong border in the mid-1970s, I spent weeks and months observing the fields, farms, and peasants across the border, in what is now Shenzhen, today one of the world's most developed cities. The transformation exceeds the bounds of belief until you see it: hundreds of skyscrapers, the world's third largest container port – another Chinese city, Shanghai, has the world's largest – an extensive metro system, flyovers everywhere you look, and lots of large Mercedes cars, most of them painted the obligatory black, with a chauffeur in front and a millionaire Chinese businessman in the back who has probably made his fortune by establishing one of the many thousands of Chinese factories which export increasingly high-value items to markets all over the world.

The transformation is unbelievable, and indeed, at every point along the way, there has been no shortage of disbelievers and doubters in China's evolution. When we decided to commit ourselves to China in late 1989 – after the events in Tiananmen Square in June – I attended a conference at London's Centrepoint. It was chaired by a prominent British businessman, the late Lord Sharp, a China enthusiast, who led a British company Cable and Wireless, which owned and operated the Hong Kong telephone system. At the end of the conference, Lord Sharp asked the audience to raise their hands if they thought that China represented a good medium and long-term business opportunity. There was not one hand to be seen from the audience of about 300 businesspeople, with a sprinkling of academics, journalists, and government officials. Almost every year since 1989, voices of doubt about China's future have been raised. In recent years, China's excessive debt overload has become a major concern. More recently, to this have been added other reasons for doubt, among them the rapidly ageing Chinese population, water shortages, and a lack of Chinese inventive capability.

But for someone like myself, who has lived and worked through this epic period of remarkable Chinese growth and change, it is my proximity to everyday Chinese business reality which has convinced me of the durability of

China's success and growth path. Even in the early 1990s, when China's economy was still dominated completely by state-owned industries, it was possible to see that beneath the stark and impersonal outlines of a nominally Leninist, centrally planned system, there existed a dynamic, highly commercialized society bursting to get out and express itself. The signposts to this evolution included the competence and shrewdness evident in most Chinese officials and executives, as well as the thriving peasant enterprises which grew enough food to feed China's swelling population, and brought it, in the middle of the night, from the countryside to markets within the main urban centres. From around the late 1990s, this deep well of Chinese enterprise and commercial energy responded to the relaxation of government regulations and social norms like a tropical jungle growing back after a hurricane. The roots of China's successful global emergence since 1980 are to be found not in an under-valued currency and export growth, nor in intellectual property (IP) theft or massive debt accumulation, but in Chinese culture, which emphasizes a high household savings rate, discipline in school, and successful risk taking coupled with persistence, and supported by Confucian family values.

Foreign businesspeople to China sometimes do not stop to think that Chinese society has evolved independently, from its own roots, over thousands of years. It is therefore fundamentally different to Western society. Understanding the origins and evolution of the Chinese ethical and social system is essential to being able to successfully evaluate and conduct business in China, and this book addresses that important topic in Chapter 3 "The Furniture of the Mind". However, the important central fact about China's economy today is that private enterprise, operating within a complex set of rules, codes, and norms maintained by a strong, and recently reinforced central system which calls itself communist, is the main reason why China has been able to achieve the apparently impossible. The same effective mix of centrally imposed structure and free enterprise is the key to China's continued development in the future.

The Chinese Government understands this fundamental truth. You might say that the Chinese Government knows, very well, the Chinese goose which lays the golden egg. That is the reason why concerns over the snuffing-out of Chinese private business by an overweening Chinese Communist Party are wide of the mark. Equally, while some Western authorities have spoken recently of 'peak China' and an expectation of steady Chinese decline from this point on, the likelihood is that in the future, China will continue to develop and grow as it has done fairly steadily since 1980, but at a slower rate.

Where does this spirit of Chinese enterprise come from, and how does it sustain itself? How do private entrepreneurs operate successfully in a centrally planned system which worships communist theorists Marx and Lenin as key influences? How do Chinese Communists interact successfully with people whose only interest is in being commercially successful? And will China continue to provide a fertile environment for foreign enterprise to grow profitably? These interesting and vital questions are all topics for later chapters of this book. Suffice it to say, for the moment, that the answer to the last question is 'yes'. The Chinese are probably the most pragmatic and realistic race on earth. If the system works, use it. If the system cannot be displaced, then live with it. Only if a system or a rule is useless, or if it serves to undermine or diminish Chinese national pride and self-belief will it come under attack. Processes, machines, and people that work are to be respected and used, and things that do not work, however magnificent their construction or aims, are to be discarded. This is one of the golden rules determining Chinese behaviour, and one of the main reasons for China's success in recent decades.

In the succeeding chapters, the book addresses the key elements of a successful Chinese strategy for a Western company. The first part looks at the factors which make Chinese business different to business elsewhere: China's geography, ethnical composition, history, culture, and economy, and its system of government and politics. We examine Chinese beliefs, values, and attitudes, and how these impact on Chinese business practices. We look at the important role played by Chinese Government and officialdom, and why understanding this role is important to success. China has developed a sophisticated body of laws and regulations which govern how foreign businesses set up and operate within China. We consider how foreign businesses should approach China's ever-changing legal and regulatory framework.

The second part of the book is focused on methods and approaches to doing business in China, starting with the internet, which percolates Chinese business activities because China, with its large population and sophisticated mobile internet companies, is by far the largest international user. In 2021, more than half of Chinese retail sales took place online, so the internet will be a big part of the book's discussion of Chinese marketing. How to establish a business in China? Each option is discussed with its pros and cons. The main issues which determine success are analyzed, such as hiring the right staff and relations with the local government, and we examine some of the key management issues, like retaining Chinese staff. Finally, we look at what it all adds up to.

This fifth edition of *Doing Business in China* is based on its predecessors and uses much material and ideas from them. Starting as long ago as 2000, editions one to four were well conceived and ably executed by Tim Ambler, formerly a senior fellow at the London Business School, and Morgen Witzel, a fellow at Exeter Business School. In addition to becoming must-buys at the airport bookshop for China business travellers, these earlier editions have rightfully found a niche in courses around the world which address business in China or Asia. I know this because I taught such a course myself for nine years at the Tuck School of Business at Dartmouth College in the United States, and this book, in different editions, was made into essential reading for my courses. My thanks go to them both, both for proposing me as their successor and in helping me along the way.

Professor Chao Xi, Professor and Outstanding Fellow of the Faculty of Law at the Chinese University of Hong Kong has written a new chapter on "Business and the Law", reflecting current practice in China. I very much appreciate Professor Xi's kind contribution, which adds greatly to the usefulness of this fifth edition.

I must also take this opportunity of thanking Stephanie Rogers, the editor of this book at Routledge, for her help and experience and unfailing good humour in shepherding the project along through its various stages.

I wish to thank also the following people, each with their own many years of China experience, who discussed their ideas and reflections with me during the preparation of this book, namely, Xiang, Lei of Honeywell, Mark Edwards of Diageo China, Cameron Johnson, Bertrand Michaud of Hermes, Jonathan Woetzel of McKinsey, Frans Vandenbosch, John Lehman of NYU Shanghai, and Pierre Cohade.

Finally I should note that Chinese names in the main text have been written using the Western practice, without a comma separating the family name from the Christian or first name. So, Xi, Jinping, as a Chinese would write it, here is written Xi Jinping.

Bibliography

Clissold, Tim (1994) *Mr China*, London: Robinson.
Cradock, Percy (1994) *Experiences of China*, London: John Murray.
Simpfendorfer, Ben (2009) *The New Silk Road: How a Rising Arab World is Turning Away from the West and Rediscovering China*, London: Palgrave MacMillan.
Snow, Edgar (1938, 1961) *Red Star Over China*, New York: Grove Press.
Winchester, Simon (2008) *The Man Who Loved China*, New York: HarperCollins.

1 Business in China
If, when, how, where?

China has become a huge economy and an enormous market: in many prod-uct areas, the world's largest. Most large multinationals regard it as one of their most important future business opportunities. An analysis of the world's leading multinationals indicates China's current importance to their business, either as a manufacturer and supplier (Apple, Ericsson, Tesla, VW) or as a generator of sales and profit (all these, plus many others, for example, Diageo, Reckitt Benckiser, Procter & Gamble, Johnson & Johnson, Qualcomm: the list is long). There is a temptation therefore for any business which lacks a substantial Chinese presence to rush to acquire one for fear of missing out.

This is the wrong reaction. Since 1990, China has transitioned from being a poor society, lacking many things including wealth, to a middle-income country with a prosperous and fast-growing middle class of 400 million peo-ple. In 2021, its car market was about 40% larger than America, the value of Chinese real estate greatly exceeded any other country, and 2020 was the first year that there were more dollar billionaires in China than in America.

China has arrived, and many Chinese consumers have become sophisti-cated, discerning, and often spoiled for choice. The picture of a Chinese fam-ily eagerly buying a Western refrigerator because they believe it must be superior to Chinese fridges is outdated. In white goods, and in many other consumer products – for example, electric cars (BYD, Geely), mobile phones (Xiaomi), outdoor and sports clothes (Anta, Li Ning) – Chinese companies have not only caught up with but overtaken competitors from other coun-tries, be they North America, Europe, Japan, or anywhere else. If the Chinese entrepreneur can see an opportunity, he (or she) will pursue it ruthlessly, cop-ying styles, technology, and marketing approaches and often introducing a Chinese element of design or marketing which may succeed in undermining the foreign competition, because it caters better to Chinese tastes, percep-tions, and habits.

China has become vastly better off, but of course, at the same time it remains China. There may not be, presently, an established market for some products and services which we take for granted in the West.

DOI: 10.4324/9781003241164-2

An example here is Scotch whisky, an important product category which the large British multi-brand drinks company Diageo is relying on for growth in China. The Chinese have their own spirits, collectively called "jiu" in Chinese, of which there are literally hundreds of brands, some with hundreds of years of history, the most famous (and expensive) of which is Maotai, a product of China's poorest province Guizhou. In order to sell Johnnie Walker, J&B, and their portfolio of exclusive single malt whiskies like Talisker and Lagavulin, Diageo have to "build the category". In other words, Diageo have to create a new Chinese market in Scotch whisky, where previously there was none.

This involves answering questions like: "Why should Chinese prefer Scotch whisky to *jiu*?" and "Can whisky be drunk when eating food?", because for Chinese people, the lunch or dinner table is the temple of social and family engagement, and the preparation and consumption of Chinese food is a much-discussed topic of great interest and importance. Therefore, an alcoholic drink which can be consumed at the table stands a much better chance of success in China.

China is a highly competitive market for most products and services. In addition, as China is a completely different society to Western ones (a topic we will delve into in Chapters 2 and 3 in more detail), the needs and wants of Chinese people differ radically from those of Americans, French, or even Japanese. If your products have a market in China, you may find that the market is already well occupied by well-established competitors, both Chinese and non-Chinese. But it is not inevitable that your company's product range will find a market in China. Having absorbed and fully digested these important points, you may decide nevertheless that, like Diageo and others, China is a market that you are prepared to be patient with, where you are prepared to invest over a period of years or even decades, to 'build the category' as Diageo are doing, or else go up against well-established competitors. Or you may decide that it is better, after all, to stay at home.

Here are two stories, from my own experience, of British business leaders who decided not to enter China. One was probably correct to take this approach. The other was almost certainly wrong.

In early 1996 in Shanghai, I hosted the chief executive of a well-known British convenience store chain for a three-day visit. He was considering expanding into Asia and was evaluating which Asian country or countries in which to invest, as well as the methods his company should adopt. During the Shanghai visit, we attended a reception arranged by the Shanghai Government which was well attended by both foreign corporate representatives and Shanghai leaders. At this reception, we fell into conversation with a deputy mayor of Shanghai who had been educated in the United Kingdom and spoke excellent English. The deputy mayor had obviously noticed my client's attendance from the guest list, and went straight to the point, by describing the extensive plans of the Shanghai Government to develop the city with public infrastructure. He identified a need in the planned, yet-to-be-built Shanghai suburbs for convenience stores of the kind that my client's company operated in Britain and encouraged him to consider investing in such a network in Shanghai (which could have course subsequently been extended to other Chinese cities). My client was appreciative and interested but told me later that the number of construction cranes standing idle in the then-new Shanghainese development zone of Pudong gave him cause for serious reservations about China's future. He decided not to take up the offer of the deputy mayor and preferred to invest in Thailand instead.

Here is the second story. About a decade later, I was assisting a China-based mobile phone store chain to list its shares on the London growth market, called AIM, or Alternative Investment Market. We were looking for early-stage investors in the Chinese company, whose business potentially had some common interest with the China mobile phone store network. I approached a similar phone store network in the United Kingdom to see if they were interested in investing as a 'cornerstone' investor in the public share offering. The founder and chief executive of the British network turned down the invitation because he believed that China's mobile phone market was too price competitive to permit any reasonable profitability.

Looking back to the first story, I believe that the British convenience store company was presented with a tremendous opportunity to become established in China early on, and not just in China, but in the most prosperous and liberal city in China, Shanghai, with government backing. The invitation from the deputy mayor of Shanghai to work with local government to establish a convenience store network in suburbs which they were planning to create could have been built, over time, into a huge, profitable, and fast-growing business in China.

Conversely, I think the assessment ten years later of the Chinese mobile phone market by the chief executive of a British phone distributor was perfectly correct.

Shall we invest in China?

The lesson which we can draw from these two contrasting tales is that the decision to invest in China, like any business decision, should be based on a clear and correct assessment of the facts and the market potential, but also, because the future is uncertain, on exercising an educated judgement. Perhaps in 1996 the convenience store executive was surprised by the mayor's invitation. I knew from my three days in Shanghai with him, that he was taken aback by the extent of the rebuilding which he saw around him as we walked through the old part of the city, with entire blocks being pulled down to make away for new roads, flyovers, and a huge extension of the metro system. I know also that he was strongly influenced by the stories then circulating in the media, written by economists and China 'experts', of China's economic instability, and the likelihood of collapse. To be fair, the Asian crisis, which lasted from 1997 until 2002 did seriously impact China, and the country had to dig deep to withstand the negative shockwaves emanating from the collapsed South Korean, Thai, and Indonesian economies around it. But from a longer-term perspective, the rejected invitation was probably a great opportunity missed.

Therefore the question is: how to achieve an educated judgement with respect to China? Hermes, the large French fashion company, starting in 1996, spent five years evaluating if, and how to enter the China market.[1] Once they had decided that China was for Hermes, their first step forward was to build a large three-storey Hermes headquarters-cum-flagship store building in the most fashionable, once-French part of Shanghai. In retrospect, this was a move of genius, because it created, from the beginning, a large Hermes footprint in China's leading fashion city, bringing the company to the attention of the Chinese population in Shanghai and beyond. It also advertised a long-term, multi-decade commitment to China.

The point here that I wish to make is that Hermes developed its judgement in a completely new, completely foreign market by undertaking a long period of investigation, evaluation, and deep reflection. Today, Hermes' business in China is growing in double digits, and underpins the company's stock market valuation of over US$150 billion. Its success in China is rooted in its appreciation of what China consisted of and where the country was headed, in terms of the various dimensions of importance to Hermes, like consumer taste, affordability, market size, and so on.

I do not think it is possible for many companies to follow the example of family-controlled Hermes in taking five years to research and reflect before making (or not making) any commitment. So what are the short cuts? One is to buy in China judgement and expertise, either consultants or experienced local staff, or both, and listen to their advice. A word of warning here: both in the early days of China's attractiveness to foreign investors and today, it was and is common for foreign companies to hire overseas Chinese to lead their China operations. Commonly, these leaders/advisers came or come from Hong Kong, Singapore, or Taiwan. Their English is perfect and they often speak other developed country languages such as German, they are usually trained and experienced in Western business, they speak Mandarin well or adequately, and they can understand and be understood by the foreign company. So, what's not to like?

There is as big a cultural difference between overseas Chinese and mainland Chinese as there is between Americans and the British, or French people from France and French Canadians. Many mainland Chinese dislike the Hong Kong Chinese, because they see Hong Kong as a barren island until it was colonized and developed by the British following the agreement of 1842 which followed the first Opium War between Great Britain and China. They perceive the Hong Kong people as profit-seeking traitors to the Chinese cause. I remember attending a dinner in 1999, hosted in Tianjin, China at which a successful Hong Kong businessman who was trying to create a business, entertained local officials. The officials made comments, to his face, about the Hong Kongers coming in to take advantage of the mainland Chinese and referred to them as "fish-eating peasants". Sure enough, that Hong Kong businessman ended up losing several million dollars in China. This is why the Chinese Government's move in 2020 to annex Hong Kong, apparently in a flagrant disavowal of the 50-year Sino-British agreement of 1984 to create a system of "one country, two systems", was actually supported by many mainland Chinese.

Mainland Chinese feelings towards overseas Chinese from Singapore are less hostile, and their feelings toward Taiwanese Chinese can even be very friendly, but their feelings towards overseas Chinese differ from their feelings towards Chinese who live in mainland China. Similarly, there are often strong feelings in one part of China, say in the world's largest urbanized area Chongqing, about people from other parts of China, say Beijing or Shanghai, or especially Chongqing's competitor Chengdu. I would go as far as saying that if you want to do business in Chongqing, it would be prudent to have a local from the Chongqing area who speaks the local dialect, somewhere near the top of your Chinese organization, and likewise in Beijing, Wuhan, and other cities in China. The exception to this rule is probably Shanghai, because it is a city of immigrants, which developed mainly after the foreign occupation of China in the mid-1800s. People from the rest of China as well as foreigners are all welcomed in Shanghai, provided they bring money or something else of value with them to the city.

So, it may be wise to be careful about relying too much – as many non-Chinese companies have done to their disadvantage – on overseas Chinese to run their operations in mainland China. It is often preferable to have as the local leader in China someone from within the company who is a national of the country in which the company is headquartered, whether it is America, Canada, Mexico, France, Germany, Great Britain, or Spain or wherever, because such a person will probably be respected more by his or her local Chinese counterparts, especially if they can get by in Chinese.

Now to return to my theme of taking decisions about business in China. Every large consulting company, accountancy firm, and law firm has a specialist China operation, and there are also consulting firms which operate only in China. The good China consultants, and there are several of these (I used to run one of these myself, 30 years ago), will provide you with detailed information about the market and competition, and will give you good advice based on their experience. Only you can decide, though, because only you will know whether your business has what it takes to succeed in China (see Chapter 10 for more on this). Obviously, the resources and an appropriate product are essential, but there are other intangibles which are just as important. Two of these are patience and being able to prioritize the Chinese market and its particular needs and characteristics against all the other demands on your business time and energy.

Patience is essential because your timelines are probably different from the Chinese ones. I remember a German client of ours in the 1990s coined the phrase 'hurry up and wait' to describe the Chinese approach to contractual negotiations or to placing an order. The phrase aptly captures an aspect of Chinese behaviour, when the Chinese are either the buying party or an actual or potential partner in a project or joint venture. The Chinese decision-making process is both consensual and autocratic, in that important decisions will be taken by one man or woman, but the process of arriving at that decision involves consultations with colleagues and others, and sometimes even fortune tellers. The process has its own dynamic and the timeline will be affected by the behaviour of competitors, the fortunes of the Chinese company's own business, and even dates and times of year, because some periods, like spring, for example, may be considered to be more auspicious for starting new projects than other times. The period covering Chinese New Year (which follows the Chinese lunar calendar and therefore falls every year on different dates between mid-January and mid-February) including the two weeks prior and three weeks afterwards is off limits to any serious decision-making in China.

It may seem surprising to some, but many foreign companies have failed in China simply because they were not able to place the Chinese priorities and preferences at the same level of importance, or ahead of their own processes and habits. Foreign companies may be doing good business in China in ways which their Chinese partner or the local government may consider to be not in their interests, or undesirable in some other way. In the mid-1980s, when Volkswagen started working with its Chinese partner SAIC in Shanghai to produce cars for the China market, the first step was for the Germans to ship almost-finished VW saloon cars to Shanghai to be finished off and sold by Shanghai Auto. The Germans invoiced the Chinese joint venture for these cars shipped in semi knocked-down (SKD) form. After the mark-up, the Germans made a nice profit, with hardly any risk. After several years of this, the Chinese partner started to object to the lack of momentum, and eventually managed to force VW, after much German foot-dragging and grumbling, to agree to develop a new model for the Chinese market – known as the Santana 2000 – which would be manufactured increasingly in China.

Volkswagen wisely listened to, and eventually accommodated their Chinese partners. Conversely, in a different case in the 1990s, a major British clothing retail company was not prepared to change its Britain-based sourcing strategy to accommodate Chinese interests. As it always placed its own interests and the rest of its business ahead of Chinese interests, its attempts to establish a retailing operation in China never got off the ground.

There are many other examples of foreign companies who were not prepared to overturn well-established in-house habits or rules, to accommodate Chinese requirements or interests. The consultant will probably give you well-informed advice, but only you know if flexibility and patience are qualities that your company can adopt in its Chinese operations. If patience, flexibility, and long-term commitment are likely to be a big challenge for your company, then perhaps the Chinese market is not for you.

Obviously, the best way to start to develop your judgement about China is to go there yourself. China is a continent-sized country. Assuming that you have two weeks available for a first visit, where should you go? I suggest that on your visit, you need to do the following:

- Visit Beijing and Shanghai
- Meet one or several Chinese Government officials
- Visit several businesses operating in your sector, one of which should be a Sino-foreign joint venture
- Meet several experienced expatriates who live and work in China
- Visit two or three of the following cities: Guangzhou or Shenzhen, Chongqing or Chengdu, Wuhan, Xian, and Shenyang.

From this agenda, you will gain a sense of the following:

- The variety, scale, and profound difference of China
- Some of the opportunities on offer, and the competition
- The attitude of the Chinese Government towards foreign investment and operations in your area of interest
- The main difficulties confronting foreign companies in China, and ideas for dealing with them
- Whether forming a joint venture with a Chinese partner is necessary and desirable
- The most promising locations for your business to operate in China.

Planning and conducting an efficient and productive fortnight of visits in China is made much easier (or even possible) with help from an experienced, on-the-ground adviser or consultant. Here, you may find that the chain of local offices operated by your government's China trade body (in Britain, this is the China-Britain Business Council), plus advice from the staff in the home country headquarters, may be enough. Or you may prefer to hire a local consultant to help you plan and execute the trip. If the latter, do not forget that on-the-ground advisers in China may have their own reasons for introducing you to certain people, places, or companies.

Broadly speaking, there are four types of first visits:

- Trade missions, led by Chambers of Commerce, trade bodies, or trade associations
- Co-operative missions, with perhaps 3–5 people from different companies sharing costs
- Fairs, exhibitions, and trade shows
- Individual (as described above), using local advice.

Trade missions

Trade missions are a specialism of the dedicated trade bodies we discussed above and offer several advantages, including both the opportunity to network like-minded businesses from your own country, and access to a wider variety of Chinese contacts than might otherwise be possible. Costs will be lower and may well be subsidized by your own government. Most of the hassle involved in setting up meetings, accommodation, and travel is taken care of by the sponsoring body. More importantly, tuition about China is, in effect, provided as one goes along.

Missions have an advantage in that, because of the scale of the mission which may include representatives from 50 or 60 different foreign companies, Chinese hosts may tend to react a bit more positively and 'push the boat out' to help delegates. An official delegation has a reassuring cohesion and substantive image, particularly if the sponsoring body has good relationships and a good reputation. Meeting the group's needs becomes a matter of (keeping) face and, in general, more effort will be made to help with requests for meetings and introductions. Groups tend to have established seniority rankings and go-betweens. This enables the hosts to understand who is who within a group context and to make judgements as to which members are most valuable.

Not as good is the fact that time may have to be given to activities and subjects one would rather avoid. As groups are becoming more regional and specialized, the difficulty of keeping distance from direct competitors (welcomed by China of course) increases. A group always travels more slowly than an individual. This will partly depend on the balance of initiative and interest on the Chinese and UK sides. Missions may be organized by trade sector or geographic destination(s). To minimize these problems, schedules are generally tailor-made. In the UK, the China-Britain Business Council usually meets with companies joining a trade mission for a couple of hours, well before the mission departs for China. The company's entry strategy is discussed (and possibly challenged), and then personal appointments are made in line with that. The group travels together and meets up in the evenings, but each individual may pursue his/her own agenda.

A trade mission is perhaps best seen as reconnaissance rather than expecting to find the right partner, still less finalize a deal. On the other hand, as the mission sponsor's local offices organize the local arrangements, sensitive briefing can help to line up reasonable prospects. Trade missions are usually only a first step, but they can help open doors and establish relationships that could bloom in the future.

These missions are opportunities for people watching, as well as business finding. Try to develop the 'golden eye', the origins of which expression lie in the ancient story of the Monkey King. In essence, the 'golden eye' allows you to distinguish real people from ghosts. Most bureaucracies in any country are filled with 'ghosts'. Of the huge number of people you will meet on a mission, only some will be 'real' and only some of those may become friends and partners. The ability to use the 'golden eye' is probably more likely to determine market entry success than any economic analysis.

As China's market economy has developed, these group missions have become less fashionable. Nevertheless, they do retain value for those who really have no experience of China. The alternative is to go on your own and simply travel as a business tourist (we will address this in a moment), but trade missions still offer superior opportunities to make contacts, providing you can afford the time and cost.

Co-operative missions

Co-operative missions are similar to trade missions but are more tailored. This means less time spent on boring activities, but probably less access to top officials. It is unlikely that you will know compatible businesses wanting to visit China at the same time, but some consultants will put interested businesses together and help with the administration. Some of these specialize in working with smaller firms and will generally do their best to help keep costs down. Again, although these are becoming less common, they still have a role to play.

Fairs, exhibitions, and trade shows

Fairs and exhibitions are the modern equivalent of the markets along the silk road in Marco Polo's day. Handled skilfully, they are not just places to exchange goods or services for money but centres of information and the beginnings of friendships. They can also go horribly wrong; there are plenty of tales of sitting in a cavernous hall for a week, surrounded by people who do not want to know, with nothing to fill in the time, except to calculate how much this experience is costing. However, a little advance spadework can avoid this fate. As one tactic, consider organizing a reception (perhaps jointly to spread costs) for other compatible exhibitors and potential customers. Send out personal invitations ahead of time, using local business directories. Telephone first to try to learn personal names, rather than just inviting 'The Marketing Director'. A formal personal invitation card is highly regarded. Guests will also be favourably impressed if the attention they receive on arrival is personal, intensive, and enjoyable for them. It should be like an invitation to one's own home.

In more high-tech sectors, the technical seminar has replaced the fair. Travel is simplified since, in theory, the customers come to you. Government agencies may be able to help defray some of the costs in these cases, as most Western governments are keen to support anything connected with high-tech. Another advantage of technical seminars is the involvement of the ubiquitous Chinese research institutes. These bodies are a bridge between Chinese industry and academia, and provide much of the leading thinking for Chinese commerce. Here, a successful approach in making contacts may be to stress knowledge transfer rather than commerce; this approach is more likely to succeed in getting the more senior and/or more technical brains of the institute to attend. Of course, the potential downside is that one may end up transferring knowledge without generating business for oneself.

The Canton (Guangzhou) Import and Export Fair, also known as the Canton Trade Fair (www.cantonfair.org.cn) is the grandfather of them all and also the largest. Founded in 1957, it is held once or twice a year. There are national and international pavilions, the latter devoted to goods that China exports, and a multinational sourcing service which helps overseas companies find outsourcing partners in China. Many other regional or sector-specific trade fairs have sprung up since the mid-1980s (organizations like Euromonitor provide lists of these, and some also advertise directly on the World Wide Web).

Sources of advice, data, and information on China have proliferated enormously in recent years. Where finding reliable statistical data and analysis about China used 30 years ago to be a real problem, today the problem is deciding which of the multiple sources to use and which to trust.

Complaints have been made, over the years, about the veracity and reliability of Chinese-produced economic and other data. However, I have found that Chinese statistical data is as accurate as you could expect in a rapidly changing country with 1.4 billion people, and I have often used it successfully. The only health warning I would issue about Chinese statistical data is about anything which directly concerns the Chinese Communist Party, which either bans publicity about itself, or changes it to emphasize the elements it likes.

Sources of information about China can be found from the following:

- Specialist information providers
- Home government such as, in the UK, the China-Britain Business Council (CBBC), or in the US, the US-China Business Council, and the European Chamber of Commerce
- Home embassy in China
- Home country professionals and businesses
- Dedicated trade bodies
- Chinese embassies abroad
- Think tanks, like the Mercator Institute for China Studies in Europe, or the Asia Society in New York
- The internet.

Specialist information providers

Specialist information providers include businesses and organizations such as the Economist Intelligence Unit (EIU) and Euromonitor. "Access China" is an EIU service which provides quarterly data and analysis on China's 31 provinces and 40 largest cities. Euromonitor offers up-to-date statistics and a number of reports, for example:

- Industry-specific reports offer insight into market size and share in China; as well as industry trends in each specific industry
- China Country Briefings and China Country Factfile provide Chinese statistical data, and in-depth medium-term economic and consumer trend data and analysis, or a self-described national SWOT analysis
- A multiplicity of reports into many specialized consumer sectors. The titles of a few recent reports give a good indication of the level of detail:
  - Wound Care
  - Weight Management and Well-being
  - Sleep Aids
  - Eye Care.

and there are hundreds of others.

The EIU and Euromonitor will probably be all you need for up-to-date, detailed Chinese national, provincial, and urban data, plus useful, extremely detailed analysis. I have found the Chinese-produced statistical bible, published annually, the *Chinese Statistical Yearbook*, invaluable for very detailed, accurate, and up-to-date facts on a full range of Chinese economic and social data. The China statistical bureau publishes a lot of data online.

For day-to-day news and illuminating opinion pieces, the *Financial Times* and the *Wall Street Journal* both provide an excellent service. Other major national newspapers, like *Le Figaro, Der Spiegel, the New York Times, The Times* in London, and *The Guardian* all operate large Chinese news bureaux which provide regular Chinese news and analysis.

There is a range of magazines and journals covering China; many are highly academic but others such as *Far Eastern Economic Review* or *China Economic Review* can be helpful.

Home country support

Most governments of countries that actively trade with China will provide information and assistance to exporters. The US Department of Commerce offers facilities, as do trade ministries in most Western major trading countries. As well as advice within Australia, Austrade has approximately ten offices in China. The European Chamber of Commerce operates chapters in Shenyang, Beijing, Shanghai, Shenzhen and Guangzhou, Nanjing, Chongqing, and Chengdu.

The most important helpers in this category are the specialist trade bodies which may be wholly or partly components of national governments. These include both government-sponsored groups such as the CBBC, the US-China Business Council, and private bodies such as the American Chamber of Commerce in China.

China-Britain Business Council

Helping our Members grow Trade and Investment between the UK and China since 1954

The China-Britain Business Council (CBBC) is the UK's national business network promoting trade and investment with China. Since 1954 we have acted as the independent voice of business located at the heart of the action, engaging across both countries in every sector and region. We support our Members and partners by delivering the advice, analysis, and access which they need to seize the China opportunity.

Through our presence across the UK and our network of nine offices in China, we are uniquely positioned to serve our Members' interests in the UK and China. Our team of experienced in-market specialists are dedicated to guiding and advising our Members through our wide range of professional services.

Our diverse Membership includes some of the UK's leading companies and universities, many of the most dynamic UK SMEs, and an ever-increasing number of Chinese companies exporting to and investing in the UK.

CBBC plays an important role in helping shape bilateral relations between the UK and China through our close links to the UK Government and the Devolved Administrations; the Chinese Government at national, provincial, and municipal levels; and the British and Chinese Embassies.

Website: www.cbbc.org
Email: enquiries@cbbc.org

The US-China Business Council performs a similar service for American companies seeking Chinese information and contacts.

Home embassy in China

Embassies conduct government relations. The main reason for contacting the local embassy is if relationships with Chinese Government entities are involved or are sought. If the People's Republic of China (PRC) government ministerial visits or major contracts are involved, you will want your embassy to be involved too, and you will get their attention. Otherwise, look to trade bodies such as, in Britain, the CBBC to provide advice, information, and Chinese contacts.

The Chinese abroad

The reciprocal to these Western bodies is the China Council for the Promotion of International Trade (CCPIT), formerly largely an export body, but now much more interested in companies seeking to invest in China. It has a good website (https://en.ccpit.org), and numerous links to local chambers of commerce, industry bodies, and the like in China. The principal Chinese office for British companies wishing to contact Chinese businesses overseas is the Chinese Chamber of Commerce, which has its headquarters in London.

Similar Chinese Chambers of Commerce exist in the countries where Chinese companies have operations and investments, which means all the countries of North America, Europe, and Australasia. It is worth contacting the local Chinese Chamber of Commerce to find out what information and contacts in China they can provide. At the least, they may direct you to an official in Beijing who could prove to be a useful connection.

The Bank of China operates large offices in all the capital cities of the developed world. These can also be useful first points of contact, because the Bank of China is one of the world's largest trade financers and intermediaries. I am privileged to have the Chief Executive of the Bank of China in London write a foreword to this book. His name is Fang Wenjian, and he can be contacted by post at the Bank of China office in London.

Think tanks

The numerous think tanks or institutes which have sprung up in the Western world in the last three decades all cover China (to a greater or lesser extent), and some cover it in great detail. The views they express tend to reflect the country and the city in which they are based, partly because many receive funding from their governments, or have been funded by successful businessmen with particular views. Some of the American think tanks, like the Heritage Foundation, are unashamedly conservative American organizations, with perspectives to match. Out of the dozens in America, the most prominent and reputable are the Council for Foreign Affairs, the Brookings Institute, and the Peterson Institute in Washington DC, the Hoover Institution at Stanford University in California, and the Asia Society in New York. From the dozens in Europe, we mention here the Royal Institute for International Affairs in London, the Breughel Institute and the European Institute for Asia Studies in Brussels, the German Council on Foreign Studies and the Mercator Institute for China Studies. All of these organizations host talks and seminars, which are usually published as videos online (mostly on YouTube), and they publish papers on the Chinese economy, geopolitics, Chinese politics, and a range of Chinese business issues.

General knowledge and sensibilities

Such is China's prominence in the global economy, today Chinese hosts justifiably expect foreign visitors to have some knowledge of:

- Chinese geography, recent history and economic reform
- Chinese culture and etiquette, notably on matters of the table
- How Chinese society works, especially at the top, that is, the major players in organizations, governments, and ministries, as distinct from politics
- Doing business in China.

Under Mao, Chinese politics and business – such as they were – were closely intertwined, in fact often indistinguishable. But for many years after the opening up of China in 1980, Chinese politics and Chinese business became increasingly separated.

However, since around 2013, this trend towards greater independence of Chinese business has reversed. The question increasingly asked today of Chinese business is: "Are your business activities socially useful? Do they promote the well-being of Chinese people, and do they support the objectives of the Chinese state?" All Chinese businesses which have contact with foreign companies, whether privately or state-owned, openly subscribe to China's political line. China's deep economic integration with the rest of the world, including Europe and America, is explicitly acknowledged by the Chinese Government. But it is impossible for Chinese business to involve itself in activities which could be construed by government officials as damaging to the Chinese state. These prohibited activities might include giving foreigners access to important defence-related information or technology, or even making foreigners aware of the true state of China's progress in important technological fields like microchip or missile design. Chinese companies doing business with foreigners are carefully monitored, and often contain managers who make regular reports to Chinese intelligence about foreign business.

This should not worry or deter foreign business from engaging with Chinese customers or partners, but it is something about which they need to be aware. Obviously, companies which operate in business fields like microchips or defence which are of prime importance to China's own national development can expect their products, marketing, and organizations to be subjected to very strong interest. They may also find that attractive offers are made to company personnel visiting China to join a Chinese company, in order to share their experience and know-how.

The Chinese Government is extremely well informed about all aspects of foreign countries, especially the major players like the United States, Britain, and other members of the G7. Do not be surprised to find your opposite number at a Chinese dinner commenting accurately and knowledgeably on some aspect of European or American government policy. Some aspects of the Western press can irritate the Chinese, and so media coverage provides a good list of topics to avoid. This does not just refer to government and

Communist Party officials; as noted above, many ordinary Chinese find Western reportage of events in China one-sided and biased. This particularly applies to Western press coverage of issues such as human rights, where many Chinese believe the Western media are hypocritical.

Geopolitics and human rights are subjects which are best avoided altogether at any kind of social or business meeting with Chinese people. Victorian dining room etiquette forbade discussion of religion, sex, or politics. That is no bad rule for visitors to China today.

There is a very large number of books on Chinese history, geopolitics, and business. Here I mention five. *A Brief History of the Dynasties of China*, by Bamber Gascoigne gives a short but insightful picture of Chinese history. For anyone wishing to understand the Chinese Communist revolution and the life and work of Deng Xiaoping, who laid the foundations for today's China, I recommend the classic, if idealized *Red Star over China* by Edgar Snow, and *Deng Xiaoping and the Transformation of China* by Harvard professor Ezra Vogel. Richard McGregor, for many years a journalist for the *Financial Times* in China, wrote in 2010 an excellent account of the Communist Party, and how it works in *The Party*. For a clear guide to the often-confusing Chinese economy, I suggest *Cracking the China Conundrum* by Yukon Huang, a former World Bank official of mainland Chinese origin.

Food plays an important role in Chinese culture, and it is probably worth acquiring some familiarity with it. No restaurants in any non-Chinese Chinatown will prepare the visitor for food in China, though they may provide some idea of the regional variation. They will also help provide dexterity with chopsticks, which is worth acquiring if weight loss during the first visit is to be minimized.

In France and most other European countries, opening a bottle of good wine is regarded as a normal way of enjoying food. But traditionally it is normal for Chinese people to enjoy one or other of the many kinds of Chinese food without any alcohol. Beer or wine may be drunk, but it is the exception in China, not the rule, and a glass will usually suffice. Chinese people do like alcohol, but they usually drink late, after dinner, and focus as much on Chinese spirits *jiu* as on wine. Foreign companies (such as Diageo, mentioned earlier) are anxious to introduce Western drinking habits to China, to stimulate the consumption of wine, whisky, and brandy. They are having some success. However, foregoing the consumption of alcohol at a Chinese meal in China is usually a wise move.

In the past, recognizing the difficulties and differences of Chinese names and language, many Chinese people wishing to interact frequently with foreigners adopted foreign names. Some still do. We all know that Chinese traditionally put family names first and Westerners put them last. But the Chinese sometimes, in an effort to be polite or to conform to expectations, reverse the order. Thus in Chinese, Xi, Chao (Mr Xi) becomes, in English, Chao Xi. However, please note that in this book the Western usage is employed, without a comma to separate the family name (first) and the Christian name (second).

Finally, a health warning: briefings and books like this one usually provide long lists stating how much executives must learn before visiting China, to the point of inducing total paralysis. There can never be enough time in a busy manager's schedule to absorb all this material before departing. There is no need to be over prepared; natural courtesy will nearly always suffice. Most important is to be friendly, alert, and above all, keep an open mind. There are plenty of differences between Western and Chinese people, but there are plenty of common features too, notably a sense of humour.

Individual visits

A small firm may decide it cannot afford professional advice and that it has confidence in its own skills. That's fine: get on a plane and go but it would still be wise to read something before arriving.

Solo travel in China is now easier than in many parts of the world, and the traveller to the big cities of eastern China will find that hotels and other facilities are as good as, or better than those at home. If all you want to do is to go and look around, a tourist visa (depending on where you come from) is the best and cheapest option. Most Western travel companies have relationships with private Chinese agents. If all else fails, the state-owned China International Travel Service will book packages and organize tourist visas for solo travellers. Solo travellers can also contact consultancies or organizations like the CBBC whose local offices will, for a fee, organize a translator and a schedule of meetings with their contacts. This costs more, but can be very helpful for collecting knowledge.

China offers sixteen kinds of visa, from tourist and student visas to work, study, and VIP visas. Bona fide foreign business visitors will be welcomed, and obtaining a visa should not present a problem. The L visa is for tourists, the M visa is for commercial trade activities, and there is also an F visa for exchanges, visits, study tours or 'other relevant activities'. People wishing to visit China to investigate or confirm the business opportunities would normally qualify for an L or M visa. People based in China and working there would receive a Z visa. The application process is internet-based and efficient, and usually requires the following (at a minimum):

- A written visa application, containing a digital photo
- An invitation letter issued by a Chinese business or trade partner, the official 'host'. This should clearly indicate the purpose of the visit and its term, it should be stamped with the Chinese organization's official stamp, and signed over the stamp by an accredited representative of the Chinese company. The visa application is always made in person at the Chinese consulate. Travel companies can be authorized to make visa applications and to collect processed passports.
- A payment of about £100, plus more for emergency delivery. Visa payment is normally made at the time of visa collection, which is about three or four business days after the application has been made and accepted.

While you are in China, the government will regard the host company, or organization, as responsible for you. If the host is genuinely interested in your mission and provides substantive help, life then becomes much easier.

Finding a host can sometimes be an adventure in its own right. One of the problems is that, unless you have been properly introduced by suitable intermediaries, often you simply do not exist in the minds of Chinese companies. Someone answering a ringing phone in a Chinese office will not necessarily feel any obligation to pass on a message or do a favour for an unknown voice. Letters, messages, and faxes are unlikely to get any response unless contact has already been initiated. To complicate life, a letter/fax about a future event may not be deemed worth a response until immediately before that event. Silence probably means 'no'; but it may also mean that a reply is not yet necessary. At all events, plan meetings before you go to China; cold calling is not appreciated and you are unlikely to be invited in.

If introductions can be made from the home country and if appointments have been confirmed, then the individual visit may prove the most direct (and the most cost-effective) mode of entry. Certainly, it is the most flexible.

Finding business partners

It will be obvious by now that some sort of partnership arrangement with a respectable Chinese entity is well-nigh essential in the first instance. As we will discuss later in the book, business in China functions primarily on a relationship basis, whether we are talking about customers, suppliers, joint venture partners, or even local government officials.

What about finding a partner before going to China? As we have seen, desk research and producing lists of potential contacts is easier than actually getting to discuss business with them. Make use of go-betweens wherever possible, such as the China-Britain Business Council or other organizations described above. They have the local knowledge, reputation, and *guanxi* to be taken seriously, whereas the visitor is just a ghost.

Ultimately, though, the job has to be done in the field. The first meetings with go-betweens, hosts, and other contacts may not yield anything more than a few names. Track these down, using existing relationships to build new ones. Exploit the system: contacts lead to contacts. This will take time, and it will be hard work, but a few days in China will equate to several weeks of research at home. With these new relationships, depth matters more than quantity. You will find that partner search works both ways: often, Chinese entities are as anxious to find reputable foreign partners as you are to find them. Email has made all this much easier, and almost all Chinese companies have English-speaking staff, if the principals do not themselves speak English.

Establishing a base in China is not done overnight. It takes time to build personal relationships with clients, partners, and others with whom mutual trust can grow. Trust is not an on/off switch. The Chinese use small matters (punctuality, for example) to test commitment. As the tests get bigger and are satisfactorily met, trust grows. The visitor's behaviour and actions on almost every level will be scrutinized by Chinese hosts in an attempt to determine trustworthiness. If suitable relationships are proving elusive, one should consider pulling back and rethinking one's approach. What is putting out the bad vibes? Get help from a Chinese expert.

Finally, a programme of visits needs a clear and realistic set of desired outcomes. Colleagues need a shared view of the minimum conditions for entry; in other words, what results constitute 'go' and 'no go'. Benchmarks for a visit make it possible to assess whether it has been successful. On the other hand, serendipity must be given a chance. One Western firm went to China to sell cheese-making equipment (optimistic in a non-cheese-eating society), and came back with orders for a bean curd plant, which turned out to require similar equipment. Amazing things turn up if one is alert to them. Be prepared to seize chances as they come.

Often, the difference between a big success and only moderate success or failure in China is the quality of the relations made in China. Solid Chinese relationships at the levels of government and business make an enormous, often critical difference to the prospects of success there. The Chinese people you meet will evaluate you as someone they can trust, like, and do business with, or not. For visitors, speaking Chinese is not essential (although a few words will help); but being friendly, helpful, and pleasant will take you a long way. Chinese people love humour, but they are also very serious and shrewd. You will be surprised at how thoroughly your character and intent will be worked out during the course of a business meeting or social occasion in China by people in the meeting who do not appear to be paying attention or even to be able to understand English.

Similarly, your success will depend on the good faith and quality of the Chinese people with whom you choose to do business. A direct relationship between your Chinese partners and the local government is usually a good sign, and similarly, the absence of such a relationship is often a bad sign. Developing a personal relationship is as important to you as it will be to your Chinese counterparts. If this proves difficult to do, then it may be a sign to look elsewhere.

Success is never guaranteed, but should be more likely with the following:

- Do your homework before the visit
- Never accept any piece of information about your own prospective market in China at face value
- Work out in advance where to go and what to achieve
- Pick a suitable visit type, whether as part of a trade mission or larger group, or as a solo venture
- Trivial as they may seem, worry about the diplomatic niceties. Pack samples, literature, and small gifts. Your contacts will want to take something tangible from your meetings. Get your business cards ('name cards') printed on the back in Chinese – PRC Chinese, not the traditional characters still used by overseas Chinese. Take a whole box, or two. Business cards are a 'must' in China.
- Be prepared for the process to take time and be patient.

Be friendly, but do not be afraid of being serious. Most importantly, no matter what the provocation, never shout or lose your temper in China.

Note

1 Author's discussion with M. Bertrand Michaud, former General Manager, Hermes China. 21 July 2021.

Bibliography

Gascoigne, B. (2003) *A Brief History of the Dynasties of China*, London: Robinson.
Huang, Yukon (2017) *Cracking the China Conundrum*, Oxford: Oxford University Press.
McGregor, Richard (2010) *The Party*, London: Allen Lane.
Vogel, Ezra F. (2011) *Deng Xiaoping and the Transformation of China*, Cambridge, MA: Belknap Press.

2 "Through a glass darkly"

China from a Western perspective

To visit China is to place yourself in a different world, a vast space geographically, with several thousand years of partially recorded history which spring, almost entirely, from China's own roots. There are not many other countries in the world which owe so little to external culture and influence as China. Japan might be one, although the American occupation of Japan from 1945 thoroughly changed Japanese governance and heavily influenced the country's society and culture. Where else? Parts of Russia perhaps, especially Siberia. But the point here is that the first and succeeding impressions of China are of a country with its own ways of thinking and of doing, many of which are profoundly different to Western ways of thinking and doing. Where foreign influences like Buddhism, Christianity, or Judaism have entered the country, they have always acquired especially Chinese characteristics, and even today, there are calls for such traditional Chinese cultural influence to be brought to today's foreign ideas and beliefs.

Twice, Chinese ruling dynasties were established by barbarians from north of the Great Wall, once in 1368, and again in 1644, when the last Ming emperor enlisted military support from the north, only for the Manchus, who entered as servants, to become China's masters by seizing the imperial throne. Two hundred years later, in 1840, the British Government followed its traders and entrepreneurs (like opium trader William Jardine) to southern China, followed by Britain's European competitors, anxious to share the booty: France in Shanghai, Japan in Manchuria, and Germany in Shandong. Then, between 1933 and 1945, Japan invaded and conquered much of eastern and northern China. Eventually though, China repulsed both the Europeans and the Japanese, and under communism and Mao Tse Tung emphasized the country's separateness from the rest of the world for a decade or so in the 1960s and 70s, by becoming an international recluse, entirely closed to foreigners.

Mao died in 1976, the Cultural Revolution ended with him, and China started opening itself to the outside world again at the end of the 1970s. Its integration since into the global economy has been spectacular. Today, a million or two non-Chinese live, work, or study in China. Yet China retains its strong national character. China's sense of itself as a unique and special entity has been reinforced by the policies of President Xi Jinping's

DOI: 10.4324/9781003241164-3

government, which emphasize China's territorial and national integrity. China's enormous size and long history of greatness in east Asia give its people a sense of invulnerability against any external threat.

China is open to the outside world, but today, unlike in the nineteenth century, such openness is on China's terms. To be successful, foreign businesses have to learn what those terms are, and understand how to work with them.

In this chapter, I describe the basic characteristics of China as a country and society. In the next chapter, I turn to Chinese values and modes of behaviour and the philosophies and ideas that inspire and underpin them, without an understanding of which no foreign business can succeed in China.

We start by addressing the following:

- The *geography* of China (where things are)
- The *history* of China (why things are)
- The *ethnic make-up* of China (who the Chinese are)
- The *culture* of China, with reference to particularly important points such as language, food, literature, and the arts
- The current government of China and the *political situation*
- The Chinese *economy* and its future prospects
- Chinese *attitudes* to the West (both official and unofficial).

Geography

In the south and centre of China, the Pearl and Yangtze are massive rivers flowing west–east, whose river basins provide the bulk of China's fertile soil, and hence its population. The important Chinese cities of Shanghai, Nanjing, Wuhan, and Chongqing owe their prominence in part to their location on the Yangtze, while Guangzhou stands on the Pearl River near its exit to the sea near Hong Kong. Further north, the historic cities of Luoyang and Xian stand on the mighty Yellow River, whose dusty, eroding soil provides a modest means of cultivation, as well as regular natural catastrophes caused by its flooding. North of Harbin, the Amur River marks China's northern border with Mongolia. Moving west from the river-plains of the country's east and centre, the landscape climbs steadily to hills and mountains, culminating in the mighty Himalayas. The country's main rivers, which flow south and east from these huge mountains, provided China's people from the earliest times with a means of irrigation and hence with food, as well as a means of communication between east and west, by boat. It is also worth remembering that the Red River (which flows through Hanoi), the Mekong, the Salween, and the Irrawaddy, which between them irrigate and partially demarcate Vietnam, Laos, Cambodia, Myanmar, and Bangladesh, all spring from the part of the Himalayas which lies in Tibet, under Chinese control.

North to south, from extremely cold to warm, wet winters; west to east, from mountainous and land-locked to flat and well-watered, with maritime access, are two ways of analyzing the variety and change which China's geography gives to its culture and society. North to south, and west to east – both parameters are significant. Historically, China's imperial cities have been in the north of the country because the northerners have possessed the military practices and traditions necessary for conquest and expansion. Western land-locked cities like Xian and Chongqing have developed their economies by way of river borne trade, and Nanjing, Shanghai, and Guangzhou have all achieved greatness partly because of their situations at or near the mouth of the Yangtze and Pearl rivers.

Foreign companies have tended to base themselves in the east of China, with headquarters in Shanghai – regarded as China's commercial capital – or Beijing, where the major political and legal decisions are made which profoundly affect economic and commercial life in China (and beyond). Any significant foreign business targeting China business will need at least a foothold in both cities. For companies selling retail or industrial products into China, Shanghai and Beijing could form the centre of a network of offices spread in cities throughout China, starting in the south with Shenzhen, Guangzhou, Nanning, and Changsha; Wuhan, Hangzhou, Chongqing, and Chengdu in the centre; and Xian, Shenyang, and Harbin in the north. We discuss office location further as part of business set-up in Chapter 6.

The following regions of China can be considered 'key' for business purposes (a more detailed breakdown of the regions is given in the appendix at the end of this chapter):

1 *Beijing, Tianjin, and north-central China.* Beijing is the centre of government and the wealthiest city in China. Highly populous and relatively well off, it is the centre of political power.

2 *Shanghai and the Yangtze Basin.* About 30% of China's population live in the eastern Yangtze basin. Shanghai is famous in China for leading in matters of commerce and urban development.

3 *Guangdong and the south* A different climate, language, and cuisine, and the heart of China's world-leading export industry. Shenzhen, next to Hong Kong, is a leader in innovation and finance.

4 *The Wuhan region.* The central heartland of the Yangtze valley, well-populated and industrialized, and catching up with the better-off coastal provinces such as Guangdong, Fujian, Shanghai, and Shandong.

5 *The west.* Chongqing became the largest city in China when several million people were moved there two decades ago to make way for the world's largest dam, the mighty Three Gorges Dam. Sichuan, separated by mountains from China's east, is distinctive for its sub-tropical climate and fiery cooking. Chengdu, one of China's former imperial cities, competes with numerically larger Chongqing for regional leadership. Further north, Xian has emerged an important hub for China's less populated but strategically significant north-west.

6 *Northeast China.* Often overlooked by Western investors, perhaps because of its reputation as a 'smokestack' industrial centre and its cold

climate, but rich in raw resources and talent. Shenyang and Harbin are populous and prosperous.

7   *The rest.* The highlands, mountains, and deserts, often empty and desolate, but with some large population centres; many non-Chinese ethnic groups inhabit these regions, especially in the south-west near to Myanmar, Laos, Cambodia, and Vietnam.

All these classifications have their utility, but for the first-time businessperson they can still be a bit daunting. After all, we are dealing with a huge country, any one of whose provinces is equivalent to a fair-sized European state (Italy, Spain, France, or Great Britain, for example).

Most foreign companies enter China by addressing the eastern provinces, between Guangdong in the south, north to Shanghai, Nanjing, and Shandong, west to Beijing and down to Wuhan in the centre. Here, one finds about two-thirds of China's population and about three-quarters of China's disposable income, and it's where a large proportion of China's more sophisticated, internationally oriented people live. However, China offers a wide choice to the enterprising foreign company, and large markets exist outside of this east-central region: in the north-east, where about 110 million people live; in the west, population about 200 million, and in the north-west, about 100 million people. These three latter regions are separate from each other and each has its own, very different culture, history, and taste. Each can comprise, on its own, a worthwhile market within China.

History

History is near the top of Chinese peoples' daily discussion agenda (together with what they had for lunch or dinner), because they like to compare current political developments in China with some or other item from 3,000 years of recorded Chinese history. Understanding something of Chinese history is useful for any business person wishing to become involved in China, and is therefore worth spending some time on. The best short account of Chinese history that I have found is *The Dynasties of China* by Bamber Gascoigne. In 200 pages, it covers the period from the earliest recorded times, around 1600 BC, up until the year 2000, and can be easily read on a long flight, for example, from London to Beijing, or from Los Angeles to Shanghai.

Gascoigne's little book uses an insightful, brief account of China's imperial evolution, through eight separate dynastic families between 1600 BC and 1912, to describe the evolution of Chinese society, and the impact of the most important ideas which have affected and formed China's customs and collective thought processes. Any businessman or woman considering China for the first time could do no better than to study its pages to get a broad and useful picture of the background to China's society today.

There is, of course, also a substantial recent Chinese history to be considered. The most important aspects of the recent two decades are as follows:

- Continued Chinese economic growth, allowing China to surpass Germany and Japan in size since 2003, to become today the second largest global economy, with all the geopolitical influence which that position brings with it, with the possible prospect of surpassing the United States in economic size by around 2030.
- A shift from the position of an American follower adopted by Chinese leader Deng Xiaoping in 1980, to a leadership position in Asia, and beyond. President Xi Jinping has promoted the concept of a unique Chinese economic and social model which is different to that of America and other G7 countries, and better suited to Asian conditions.
- Evidence of rapid demographic ageing, aggravated by the effects of China's 40-year-old one-child policy. Since 2013 we have seen a fall in the size of the domestic Chinese labour force. This has been followed by a decrease, since 2017, in the absolute size of the Chinese population.
- The deadly COVID virus which spread from Wuhan, central China throughout the world in early 2020. This has changed the general perception of China around the world from enthusiastic curiosity and a desire to engage and know more about the country, to widespread suspicion and a wish to disengage from China. This change of perception of China has merged with a separate element: an increasing American fear that in the future, China may not just match, but overtake the United States in economic and even military terms. The merging of these two sentiments has seen a significant heightening of anti-China rhetoric, especially in the United States. However, so far this increased rhetoric has not been matched by any desire by Western business in China to decouple from China. Since 2020, no foreign business has relocated to the United States, and only one or two, out of thousands, have moved production away from China. Such is the attraction and pull of the huge Chinese market for companies from countries around the world.

Following are some recurrent themes from Chinese history which play a part even today in the thoughts of the Chinese, consciously or subconsciously.

The integrity of China

Most Chinese believe implicitly in the territorial integrity of China. They are often rather hazier about exactly where the Chinese boundaries should be drawn. The Han heartland of north China has been the core of Chinese and political entities for millennia, and the Amur River clearly marks China's northern boundary with Russia (although an area of Siberia to the north and east, including today's city of Vladivostok, was annexed by Russia from China in 1868 at a time when the Qing dynasty was in terminal decline). The south and the west, with their large non-Han populations, entered the Chinese fold only later. Other south-eastern areas once under Chinese rule, like Vietnam and Mongolia, are independent today. The present limits of China's territory are generally accepted, with the obvious exception of the small island of Taiwan which lies off China's south-eastern coast, to which at the end of China's civil war in 1949, Chiang Kai-shek and the defeated supporters of the Guomindang retreated after their defeat by the communists. For China, Taiwan is an essential component of Chinese territorial and national integrity, and President Xi has made its 'reunification' with the Chinese mainland an important part of his programme of national rejuvenation. Taiwan's prosperity, and its burgeoning democracy make the island very unwilling to become part of the mainland. But given China's massive military build-up and increasing focus on cross-straits amphibious operations, Taiwan's continued independence depends more than ever on its support by the United States. The American Taiwan Relations Act of 1979, which immediately followed America's recognition of Beijing as the capital of China, instead of Taipei, provides a modest but non-binding guarantee of American support for Taiwanese independence. Since then, America has pursued a policy of vague non-committal towards Taiwan's status, in order to keep its options open. A Chinese invasion of Taiwan cannot be ruled out.

The threat from the outside world

Textbooks on business, politics, or economics in China sometimes comment that many Chinese dislike and mistrust foreigners, referring to them as 'barbarians' or 'foreign devils'. Certainly, between 1840 and 1945, when a weak China was being occupied and plundered by the British, French, Japanese, and Germans, foreigners went through a period of unpopularity and were often blamed for the poor situation in which China found itself at the time. For example, the failure of the post-World War One Versailles Peace Treaty in 1919 to give Japanese-occupied Shandong Province back to China occasioned a furious outburst of Chinese xenophobia. China's integration with and acceptance of other countries has varied throughout its long history, but there have been long periods of international interchange, in which not only goods but people and ideas were imported and found a place in Chinese society. In former centuries, Buddhism, Christianity, and Islam were imported along these lines. In the nineteenth century, some Chinese perceived their county as relatively weak, and concluded that its best strategy was to learn from the West and became more like it (a view reinforced by the success of Japan, which did exactly this, starting from the Meiji restoration in 1860). The revolution that toppled the Qing dynasty was motivated by the desire of its leader Sun Yat-sen to make China more 'Western'. Later, the communists also recognized the need for contact with the West. It was Mao who opined that China should learn from the West, apply that knowledge which seemed relevant to the Chinese situation, and discard the rest. Even during the height of the Cultural Revolution, some Western companies traded quietly with China to supply vital commodities like oil.

The major concern of most Chinese is not the presence of foreigners in China, but the impact they may have on Chinese culture and society. It is important to recognize that China's views of the outside world have been formed over centuries of often unhappy history. In the early centuries, China's primary external contacts were with Turkish, Mongol, and Tibetan nomad raiders from the north and west and Japanese pirates to the east. These forces brought disorder and chaos; at times, the invaders even occupied China and ruled it. In fact, for more than half of the last thousand years, part or all of China has been ruled by a foreign power. The Manchus of the Qing dynasty adopted much of Chinese culture but remained a distinct ethnic group which controlled the country. In 1912 with the fall of the Qing dynasty, there were massacres of Manchus in the south, where local Chinese took revenge for what they saw as two and a half centuries of foreign oppression.

More recently, contacts with the West have often been equally unhappy. The Ming dynasty restricted foreign traders to a narrow point of entry around Guangzhou, where they had to do business with local middlemen. This state of affairs lasted for hundreds of years, until a combination of opium and modern artillery blasted open the doors of China in the 1830s and 40s, and the Western nations began to impose their authority. The damage opium did to Chinese society in the nineteenth century has never been properly assessed, but the memory of the opium trade remains vivid today. The Westerners also spread ideas, which could be just as dangerous as drugs. In the 1850s Hong Xiuquan, a young Hakka man from the south who had just failed his civil service exams, had a nervous breakdown and became convinced that he was the younger brother of Jesus Christ. Armed with a partial Chinese translation of the Old Testament and a series of prophetic visions, he began converting his fellows. The result was the Taiping Rebellion (1853–64), which laid waste to central China and cost at least 20 million lives.

In the twentieth century, foreign meddling in China continued; American, and other Western backing for Chiang Kai-shek and the Guomindang (Chinese Nationalist Party) was bitterly resented by many Chinese. Then came the Japanese invasion with its immense destruction and loss of life. The Rape of Nanjing, which may have resulted in 100,000 deaths, was but the best publicized of many such incidents which occurred in China in the 1930s and 40s. The memory of these brutalities make Chinese nationalism and territorial integrity winning cards for China's government to play.

And yet, the foreigner going to China is usually treated hospitably and with great politeness, because the Chinese culture supports politeness and a warm welcome to strangers. The Chinese, as a nation, do not hate or fear foreigners. Genuine xenophobia is rare, and Chinese tolerance for different attitudes and ways of life is no less than the tolerance of many Americans and British people for foreign perspectives. But China is aware of the jealousy felt by other great powers (or former great powers) of burgeoning Chinese economic and military strength, and they are determined to not allow their national renaissance to be stalled or reversed.

There are, of course, generational differences within China itself. Older people, who remember the years of isolation, austerity, and occasional confrontation with China's neighbours, may be somewhat more conservative in their views. But China's millennials, growing up when economic reform and the open-door policy were already accomplished facts, view the outside world in a different light. Millions of Chinese born since 1990 have studied or travelled overseas and have been exposed to Western culture and mores. In fact, the hundreds of thousands of Chinese students who attend European and American schools and universities have today become essential sources of revenue to institutions of higher education in the West. In 2022, for instance, it is estimated at the time of writing (early 2022) that about 29,000 mainland Chinese will attend British universities as undergraduates. One research project has found that young Chinese and young Canadians share more common values and beliefs with each other than either group does with their own parents' generation. This probably tells us more about the attitudes of youth than it does about either Canada or China.

The fear of chaos

China's history provides plenty of evidence that the size and ethnic variety of the country gives ample scope for internal strife, which brings destruction and poverty. Around 220, at the end of the Han dynasty period, the population of China was about 60 million. By the end of the wars of the Three Kingdoms period, 60 years later, the population had fallen by a half. By the time the Ming dynasty took power, in 1368, the population was still only 60 million; all the natural increase in numbers had been swallowed up in the bloody cycle of war, invasion, earthquake, and flood. Small wonder that in classical Chinese thought, Heaven is populated by a celestial bureaucracy, which attempts to maintain order and keep out the demons who bring chaos.

Order is a primary social and political goal in China; it may even be the most important goal. Government policy on the economy – and many other things – can look inconsistent and changeable without this simple truth: one of the government's chief policy goals is the promotion of social stability. Steadily rising levels of household income are perceived as a vital plank of social stability in China. The economic reform programme began with this in mind, and economic growth and diversification continue to be focused on it. No organization – least of all a foreign business – whose activities seriously threaten stability will be tolerated for long. Even though China has relaxed many of the former restrictions on how and where foreign firms operate, both central and local governments take a keen interest in the economic and business environment, and intervene in a manner quite unknown in most Western countries. For example, government can and does terminate the licences of those businesses – foreign as well as domestic – that are perceived as behaving against the interests of the state. No evidence is required for government to do this and there is no recourse once the decision to terminate has been made.

I discuss the essential relationship of business with local Chinese Government in a later chapter.

The authority of the state

To defend against chaos, on Earth as in Heaven, China has erected formidable government and administrative structures. The Qin emperor, bringing order and unity to China after the chaos of the Warring States period, set the pattern followed by every ruler of China since, including the communists: a strong, authoritarian administration and bureaucracy, pyramidal in structure, with the emperor himself at its head. In neo-Confucian society (see Chapter 3), the state had a structure similar to that of the family; the emperor/father owed a duty of care to his subjects, who in turn owed him unquestioning obedience. Only through this mutual bond could order be maintained.

With some modifications, this theory has stood the test of time. Incoming dynasties, or most recently the Communist Party, usually assumed power with a great deal of moral credit, as they were perceived to have the power to clean up corruption, unite the country, oust foreign invaders, and bring stability, prosperity, and peace. Over time, of course, people start to become more cynical about their rulers and the bonds grow weaker. Yet criticism of rulers in China almost never means that people want to change the system by which they are governed; what they usually want is the same system but a change of ruler. Sun Yat-sen got this badly wrong in 1912 when he tried to replace the empire with a republic; the experiment lasted just a year before authoritarian rule returned under Yuan Shikai, and later Chiang Kai-shek and the Guomindang. Today, some Western observers interpret growing criticism of the Communist Party in China as a desire for democracy. This seems unlikely; what the average Chinese wants is a strong, honest leader who will guarantee stability, peace, and prosperity. Interestingly, this desire is just as strong among millennials as in the older generations.

The just revolutionary

Paradoxically, despite the fear of chaos and desire for stability, Chinese history is full of revolutionary movements and secret societies, from the Red Eyebrows rebel movement which overthrew the usurper Wang Mang and restored the Han dynasty in the first century AD, to the Buddhist-influenced White Lotus Society which rebelled repeatedly against the Qing in the eighteenth century. As dynasties grew weaker, such groups proliferated; the end of the nineteenth century saw hundreds of such groups springing up around China, the most famous of whom were the Boxers, whose objective was to drive foreigners out of China.

With very few exceptions – such as the special case of the Taiping, who were a religious movement apparently seeking radical change – these movements were all conservative. They did not want to change the system but wanted to remove rulers who were perceived to be incapable of ruling. Most had roots in ancient Chinese systems of belief such as Buddhism, Taoism, and Confucian thought. There are strong similarities in ideology/theology, at least, between the White Lotus Society and the Falun Gong, a sect banned in China in mid-1999, and persecuted by the then-president, Jiang Zemin.

The most successful of the 'just revolutionaries' were, of course, the communists. Their programme included a radical revision of the structures by which China was governed and ruled, and they were quick to distinguish their form of authoritarian rule from that of the empire. Nevertheless, their goals were largely the same as earlier movements; to restore stability and stop the forces of anarchy.

The presence of these movements serves to remind us that although stability is desired in China, it cannot always be guaranteed. Any weakening of central power is nearly always accompanied by local unrest, the purpose of which is usually, and paradoxically, to restore order.

Ten key figures in Chinese history

1 *Duke of Zhou.* The ancient sage-king of China, widely referred to by Confucius as a fount of moral authority.

2 *Confucius.* The greatest philosopher of the East, he constructed a moral and social system which continues to serve as the foundation for Chinese society.

3 *Qin Shi Huangdi.* The first true emperor of China, he founded the Chinese bureaucracy and established its long-lasting system of government.

4 *Zhuge Liang.* A counsellor in one of the warring states of the Three Kingdoms era, he has become a legend for his cunning strategy and statecraft harnessed to a strong moral purpose and sense of duties of the state.

5 *Zhu Xi.* One of the greatest of the later philosophers, his neo-Confucian synthesis of earlier thought was the basis of the moral and political regeneration of China by the Song and then the Ming, and remains the basis of modern Chinese philosophy and education.

6 *Qianlong.* Probably the last truly great Chinese emperor: a warrior, poet, and builder, who received the first British embassy to China in 1798.

7 *Cixi.* Imperial concubine and later dowager empress who held China together after the Taiping Rebellion and in the face of Western invasions and internal unrest. Her death was the signal for the empire's collapse.

8   *Sun Yat-Sen*. Chinese Christian, with a Chinese-American wife, he admired the West and attempted to make China into a republic. Many of his followers in the Guomindang movement were descendants of Taiping rebels.

9   *Mao Tse Tung*. The most important figure in modern China, one of the founders of the Chinese Communist Party and its leader until his death in 1976. He established the modern Chinese state.

10 *Deng Xiaoping*. Mao's successor and architect of the economic reforms that began in 1979. He has been demonized by many in the West as an authoritarian and repressive ruler. On the other hand, in China his economic reforms have lifted half a billion people out of poverty. It remains to be seen how history will judge him.

Ethnicity and language

China is dominated by the Han ethnic group, both culturally and in terms of numbers, but the country is fairly heterogeneous, and there are dozens of other distinctive ethnic groups. Most are dispersed around the periphery of the country, though there are exceptions such as the Hakka, who still live in central and southern China. The Hakka may be descendants of the original inhabitants of south China before the Han conquest.

Another Chinese ethnic group worth mentioning are the Hui, a generic name for Chinese Muslims (as distinct from the Muslim Turkish population of Xinjiang). Most of the 8–9 million ethnic Chinese Muslims live in the Ningxia autonomous region, but there are several hundred thousand living in their own district in south-west Beijing. (You know you have entered the Muslim quarter when the butcher shops begin displaying beef instead of pork in their windows). Huo Da's novel *The Jade King* (1992) is an excellent introduction to the lives of the Beijing Muslims.

Ethnicity in China expresses itself most obviously in terms of language. According to UNESCO, there are 205 living languages in China – more than in Europe – although admittedly some of these are only spoken by a few thousand people. Mandarin, or more correctly Putonghua ('the people's language'), has been the standard dialect of Beijing and lower Yangtze regions since the Manchu conquest. It was adopted in the late nineteenth century as the lingua franca for the administration and the elite. Hu, spoken in Shanghai and the eastern regions, and Yue, commonly known as Cantonese and spoken in the south, are very prevalent, but Minbei (spoken in Fujian), Xiang, Gan, and Hakka are also common in some regions. Taiwan also has its own language, Minnan (a variant of Minbei), and most overseas Chinese communities speak either Minbei or Yue as their first language. Some of these languages have more in common than others. There is considerable difference between Mandarin with its four tones and Yue/Cantonese with six tones; the difference has been described as greater than that between Spanish and French.

There have been attempts to standardize spoken language. In the imperial period, *wenyan*, a very formal and ornate spoken language directly related to the written language, was used by bureaucrats and scholars, but was unintelligible to ordinary Chinese. Late in the nineteenth century *wenyan* was abandoned in favour of *baihua*, literally "plain speech", and it was at this point that Mandarin was adopted as the *guoyu*, or national language. The use of Mandarin as a standard language was continued under the Guomindang and the communists, and is spoken by nearly all well-educated people. Virtually all Chinese speak and read Mandarin Chinese, or Putonghua, but for many, it is a second language.

Mandarin is the language of daily use in business in China, but those with a command of a second language have an additional card in their hands. A few years ago, the author of this book was at dinner with a party of business-people from Shanghai, in a restaurant where the waiter was from Beijing. The customers were not very impressed with the waiter, and proceeded to be rude about him in their own Shanghai dialect, which the waiter of course could not understand. This was a trivial incident, but its importance in areas such as business negotiations should be apparent. We might think our Mandarin interpreter is reporting faithfully all that the other parties are saying; but if they then break off and begin talking in their own language or dialect, then the interpreter becomes as deaf as we are.

In terms of *written* language, all Chinese use almost the same characters. Thus a Putonghua speaker and a Yue speaker may not be able to understand what the other is saying, but they can communicate in writing. This has obvious implications for business, particularly in areas such as advertising.

Culture

The Han Chinese culture is an ancient one, and nearly all Chinese, including many who are not themselves of Han ethnic descent, are extremely proud of it. Unlike in the West, where we see our history as marked by distinctive breaks – the fall of Rome, the Protestant Reformation, the American Declaration of Independence – the Chinese see their history as a continuous process, disrupted but never entirely interrupted by foreign occupation and conquest. The emphasis on stability means that some things such as food and styles of art and architecture have evolved only slowly over thousands of years.

China has a scientific, artistic, and literary tradition that is as old as its civilisation. Bronze working, carving of jade and ivory, silk weaving and embroidery, painting, and calligraphy go back 3,000 years, and more.

Ceremonial vases and wine vessels survive from the Shang period (1600 BC) and a few even before. Chinese literary traditions also span 3,000 years, from the ancient classics such as the *Yijing*, the *Daodejing*, the *Analects* of Confucius, the *Spring and Autumn Annals* and the works of Sunzi, through to the great poets and novelists of the past millennium. Luo Guanzhong's *The Three Kingdoms* (fourteenth century) is an epic tale of the fragmentation of China after the fall of the Han dynasty, focusing on the heroic figures of counsellor Zhuge Liang and his rival the great general Cao Cao. *Flowers in the Mirror*, by Li Ruzhen (nineteenth century), is a satire which compares to *Gulliver's Travels*. Other literary classics include *The Water Margin, Outlaws of the Marsh*, and *Journey to the West* (all available in English translation). Most famous of all, the *Dream of the Red Chamber* by Cao Xueqin in the seventeenth century recounts how a great family falls into decay and declines in fortune. Cao has been compared with Tolstoy and Proust, and has the same power as they, both as writer and social commentator. The book has remained popular since its publication – in the late nineteenth century, the dowager empress Cixi had several rooms in the Forbidden City decorated with scenes from it – partly because its story has been seen as a metaphor for China's own imperial decline.

The Chinese, or at least those in mainland China, tend to think of all Chinese, including the *huaqiao* (overseas Chinese), as being part of the same cultural family. Feelings among the *huaqiao* themselves are a little more mixed, but the majority in East and South Asia, at least, feel a strong kinship with the Chinese of the mainland, even if they have no wish to be politically associated with the country.

Yet again, Chinese culture itself is heterogeneous. There are great regional differences, not only in the various ethnic groups mainly in the south and south-west, but among the Han themselves. The regions are very proud of their distinctive local cultures, evidenced in different cuisine types, hairstyle and clothes, behaviour, accents, and attitudes to life.

Interestingly, and this may be a sign of increasing confidence in the country's stability, China's leaders have shown themselves more ready to accept and even promote diversity in recent years. Tourism, an important contributor to many local Chinese economies led by Beijing, Shanghai, and Xian (where Emperor Qin's famous terracotta army can be seen), trades on regional and ethnic differences. Museums have begun opening galleries dedicated to different ethnic minorities and their history and traditions.

At the same time, though, Chinese governments – and Chinese people – are fiercely proud and protective of their culture, however it may be defined. One of the great fears expressed during the opening up of China was that this ancient and proud culture would somehow be corrupted by exposure to foreign influences. To some extent, that fear remains.

Food for Thought

Food is an important part of Chinese culture, so much so that cuisine is sometimes called the ninth art. Eight traditional styles of Chinese cuisine survive, each named after its home region:

- *Shandong*: from the north-east, this style features seafood and emphasizes stir-frying and deep-frying
- *Guangdong*: emphasizes fresh ingredients and rapid cooking to seal in flavour
- *Sichuan*: this complex style uses many different pungent spices and can be very hot
- *Jiangsu*: the cooking of the Shanghai region, it emphasizes salty and sweet flavours, with many stocks, sauces, and thick soups
- *Zhejiang*: features seafood and is noted for its slow-cooked stews
- *Hunan*: slow cooking, stewing, or steaming, with food often heavily spiced
- *Anhui*: deep-fried, heavy sauces
- *Fujian*: seafood, with dishes marinated in wine to achieve sweet and sour flavours

We should add the Beijing style, which derives from the imperial kitchens rather than from thousands of years of Chinese peasant life. Beijing duck is a delicious delicacy much enjoyed by foreign visitors to China's capital.

Government and the political situation

Since 1949, China has been a one-party state, governed by the Communist Party of China. The central government is in Beijing, but there are 23 provinces, four self-governing municipalities and five autonomous regions – Guangxi, Nei Mongol, Ningxia, Xinjiang Uygur, and Xizang (Tibet) – directly under it and two special administrative regions (Hong Kong and Macau). Guangxi and Ningxia were created out of former provinces in 1958, around two major ethnic groups, the Chuang (Zhuang) and the Hui, or Chinese Muslims. Below the level of the provinces there are more tiers of government, at county, township and village level in rural areas, and city, district, and neighbourhood levels in cities.

Government enters into every aspect of life in China, especially including private business. The remit of the local government office and its officials, usually led by a mayor, extends very widely, and it is the job of local government to know about everything that goes in in their area and, where appropriate, report on it to central government. Often this interest in everything turns out to be helpful to foreign businesses, provided that their products or technology is perceived as being beneficial to China and its economy. The point is that foreign business in China cannot expect to be able to proceed without the local government knowing everything about them, often from company employees who have been told to make reports to local officials. It is extremely important for foreign business leaders in China to develop and maintain close working relations with their local government office.

The organizational structure of government is largely the same as it has been for centuries. At the level of the provinces, there was some cutting and pasting in the 1950s and 60s: Chinese majority areas of Mongolia were added to the Manchurian provinces, and several old provinces in the heartland were abolished. Otherwise, the hierarchy of administration is much as it has been since the country was unified 2,000 years ago.

Before 1911, China was ruled centrally from its northern capital (since 1260, Beijing) by the emperor, whose will was done by the civil service bureaucracy which ran China. The bureaucrats were selected through competitive examinations and were relatively widely sourced, although only wealthier families could afford the education needed to pass the exams. Only about one in every two million Chinese succeeded in joining the privileged ranks of the bureaucracy. The short-lived republic of Sun Yat-sen attempted to create a Western-style, two-house government, but this collapsed as, in the absence of a strong central system of control, China reverted to local strongmen. Sun Yat-sen's heir, Republican Chiang Kai-shek governed the parts of China which he controlled on the back of the old bureaucracy and his personal network. The result was largely ineffective and highly corrupt.

Against many odds, and using China's war with the invading Japanese to weaken Chiang Kai-shek, after 1945 the communists were able to defeat Chiang Kai-shek's exhausted soldiers in the field. What was left of the Guomindang retreated to Taiwan, and Mao brought the communists to power in Beijing, like virtually every revolutionary movement in China before them, promising to restore order via effective government and administration. By and large, they succeeded. Most unbiased studies of China after 1949 have concluded that, except for short periods of time such as during the Cultural Revolution, China has been well run. The things that have been important to the Chinese people – peace, safety in their own homes, freedom from crime, enough to eat and, since 1985, rising economic prosperity – have for the most part been delivered.

The economic reform movement set in train events that loosened the ties between the people and the state. Opening up the labour market, for example, meant greater freedom of movement. The agricultural reforms of 1978 leased farmland to the farmers. The central planning system which was beloved of Mao's regime has been gradually augmented by market mechanisms. The reforms of 1997 allowed Chinese people to own property, and real estate and private business has boomed. Today China boasts a real estate market which, admittedly overvalued, is at today's writing date worth twice that of the United States. Chinese private business accounts for about two-thirds of the economy, and almost all new employment.

As China grew and boomed, concerns in government and more conservative Chinese circles over the growth and unaccountability of private business in China started to emerge. This came to a head with the 2008 Western financial crisis which shocked the Chinese and served to persuade them that American systems of economic and social organization carried with them unacceptable risks for Chinese social stability. After 2012, Xi Jinping's administration started to make an about-turn in the trend of steady liberalization and increasing government weakness. He started by using a widely popular anti-corruption drive to neutralize his many opponents (including former President Jiang Zemin), and continued by restructuring the Chinese Army, in the process bringing a number of top Chinese generals to book for corruption, thereby 'encouraging' the others to toe the line. Xi has used his power to extend (or re-extend) the government's control over every aspect of the Chinese economy and social activity in order to promote a nationalistic strategy of Chinese strength and independence which is projected through Asia and the South China Sea to America and the rest of the world. Since October 2020 the Government has moved to place restrictions on, and regulations around the activities of China's huge internet companies – Tencent, Alibaba, Didi, and others. The most recent evidence of this was the introduction on 1 November 2021 of a personal information protection law aimed at denying social media companies free access to the private financial, health, biometric, and other data of individuals in China. This law and its predecessors – the Cybersecurity Law of 2017 and the Data Security Law of 2021 – carry sentences of heavy fines and imprisonment against non-complying individuals. Xi has also made it illegal for Chinese private tuition companies to operate as profit centres.

Many have identified these recent actions as anti-business and anti-foreigner, and as the beginning of a new Chinese era of statism. However, the Chinese Government has stated firmly that it remains strongly in favour of private enterprise which promotes social ends regarded as useful and beneficial. In fact, with private enterprise playing such a central and important role in China's economic life, it would be impossible for China to turn its back on its private businessmen and women without destroying its economy and way of life. Such a backward step is unthinkable, and the more extreme and lurid descriptions of China's recent regulatory actions are misplaced. China remains pro-business and pro-enterprise. However, Xi's regime has marked a change from the recent past. It has become even more important for foreign companies operating in China to develop and maintain close connections with the Chinese Government (whether local or central, or both), to understand government's motivations and direction of travel, and to ensure that their company's identity and purpose is well understood and supported by government. The interaction of private business with government in China is not just a matter of paying tax and obeying the law, although these are important. Strong mutual understanding is critical to success.

Economy

> It doesn't matter if the cat is black or white, so long as it catches mice.
> (Deng Xiaoping)

Most books on China devote large sections, even whole chapters, to the Chinese economy. I do not, for three basic reasons:

1   There are already plenty of sources on this subject, and for those who want to know, statistics on the gross industrial output of Anhui province can almost certainly be found somewhere on the internet, if not in print
2   Much economic forecasting concerning China is little more than guess-work, and even Chinese economists will cheerfully tell you that the margin of error in their figures could be anything up to 10%
3   China may not be changing fundamentally, but the economy is still changing quickly. Economic analysis is likely to be out of date within a year or two.

During its first growth phase, between 1985 and 2005, the Chinese economy was regarded as an interesting but local phenomenon which would run out of steam, probably quite soon. In fact, from the early 1990s, largely unobserved, Chinese exporters started playing an increasingly important role in world trade. The addition of the huge Chinese population to the global labour force, via trade and China's accession to the World Trade Organization in 2001 became the major factor in the globalization of the early 2000s, which drove down consumer prices worldwide. If price deflation around this period (or dis-inflation) did in fact create a need for bankers and investors in New York to search for yield in American real estate markets – a search which ended in catastrophe – then it might be said that China's economic emergence from the 1990s helped (unwittingly) to create the environment for the 2008 credit crisis.

In any case, by 2008, China had already become an important global eco-nomic force. Its continued fast growth after the credit crisis, in the face of many doubters, made it between 2009 and 2020 the primary single country engine of growth, employment, and profits worldwide. Foreign companies with Chinese operations invested in them, and most of those that did not have a Chinese presence went about developing one.

Today, the Chinese economy has grown from obscurity 30 years ago to become not only the world's second largest economy but the world's largest buyer and user of most commodities, of energy, and of many industrial and consumer products. Looking forward over the next decade or two, for large global multinational corporations like Volkswagen, General Motors, Toyota, Siemens, Nike, and many others, China is their most important single mar-ket. Annual Chinese economic growth, which ran for two decades near to

10% or more, has moderated today to around 5% or 6%. But this is 5% or 6% of a large number, and such growth ensures that China still continues to be the world's most significant single growth engine.

Will the Chinese economy continue to expand? Or will the China doomsayers be proved to be correct, at last? Our view is that China contains enough dynamic, forward-looking businesses, all of which are privately owned and managed, to provide forward economic momentum in the years ahead. The determination and capacity of the Chinese Government to maintain China's progress will underwrite this. Investment in real estate and infrastructure, one of the historic motors of Chinese growth, is cooling because now much of China is over-built with residential accommodation, and the country's road, rail, and airport networks are now the world's largest and most modern. Nevertheless, export growth is strong and will continue. The Government hopes that private Chinese household spending will take over as a main economic driver from heavy government-led investment. Doubtless private Chinese consumption will become a more significant growth driver than it is now, but it is uncertain how quickly this will happen, and the future Chinese economic growth rate may be closer to 3–5% per annum than 6–8%. Even then, because of its size, the economy is going to continue to present a compelling proposition to foreign companies and investors.

China continues to be presented with large economic obstacles, including the need to raise productivity in its large state-owned sector, an ageing population, and a labour force which is decreasing in size. However, the determination, hard work, and ingenuity which have driven the China economic miracle for 40 years will likely not suddenly desert the country.

Chinese attitudes to the West

As China slowly emerged from the nightmare of the Cultural Revolution in the 1980s, and started to look outwards, the West, particularly the United States, provided a model for many Chinese policymakers and business people. But the 2008 financial crisis fundamentally changed the way that China perceived the West. Ten years of President Xi Jinping's rule over China since 2012 have seen a complete change in China's attitude to the West. Today, the Western-oriented Chinese perspective of former times has changed into a vision driven by national pride in China's achievements, and by an acknowledgement that China has now grown well beyond the comfort level of its G7 partners, especially America which, at a national level, sees China as more of a threat than an opportunity. As the West fumbles to find the correct posture towards the resurgent Chinese giant, China itself is preparing for Western disengagement and hostility by emphasizing its own self-reliance. But make no mistake: China remains deeply integrated economically with the rest of the world. It is the major trading partner of most of its G7 partners, including America, and everyone knows that no important progress can be made on halting climate change (or on any other global issue) without close cooperation with China, the world's largest polluter.

Why all of this matters

We come back to the question posed at the beginning of the chapter: what does the businessperson of today need to know about China? Will an understanding of culture and history be of any assistance when doing business? Will a knowledge of the works of Confucius or Mao's *Little Red Book* be useful when negotiating a joint venture?

The answer, as with most knowledge, is that it depends on how it is used. Culture is not an exact science; it is a set of frameworks, which are often intuitive and emotional, within which people operate. As we discuss in the next chapter, we are often affected by culture without being aware of it. Our attitudes to hierarchy, the way we make decisions (including purchasing decisions), our attitudes to others, ethics, and personal tastes are all to some extent shaped by our inheritance.

This does not mean that culture is a predictor. Within the parameters of a given culture, vast allowances must be made for variations in the behaviour of individuals. With 1.3 billion people in the PRC, and another 55 million overseas Chinese, the variations are large.

Nevertheless, a study of culture as an environmental factor makes sound economic sense. Some firms seem to approach the world as if all humanity were universally the same. In the face of reality, that position is soon modified. The next level of simplification is racial, or national, stereotypes. Politically correct commentators are appalled by this but, for most international travellers, they are useful first approximations. The Chinese use them when they meet people from other parts of China. Marketers the world over are trying to get through these superficialities to understand the real people behind them.

By looking at Chinese culture and asking how it differs from our own, we are forced to start looking at our own culture in more depth. Why do *we* think and behave as we do? Are there any lessons to be learned from this? We can, if we are careful, use China as a mirror. Although we are looking through a glass darkly, we can nonetheless see something of our own reflection.

To reach a correct understanding of China is to start from a point of humility, as the French company Hermes did when it began to examine the opportunities and possibilities for its luxury business in China. Rid yourself of the idea that your own country's ways or Western ways are always the best. Look with an open mind at the way that Chinese people think about everything: about their past, about their own lives and opportunities, and about you. I promise you that you will discover this process to be enormously enriching personally, as well as an essential starting point for comprehending and evaluating your opportunities in the Chinese market.

A Appendix

(a) The regions of China

1   *The north*, including Beijing and Tianjin cities and Hebei, Shandong, and part of Henan provinces. Population: *c.* 260 million (2019). This is the

second most densely populated area of China and contains several major cities (including the capital), much rich agricultural land, and a lot of heavy and light industry. The climate is temperate, though the winters can be cold and harsh.

2   *The Yellow River valley and the north-west*, including Shanxi, Shaanxi, and part of Henan provinces, the eastern part of Gansu province and the Ningxia autonomous region. Population: *c*. 140 million. This is the ancient heartland of China, including in its bounds the 'yellow earth' country where the first Chinese civilisation emerged. The western part of this area has some minority Turkish ethnic groups, and Ningxia is home to a large proportion of China's Hui (Muslim) people. The climate consists of cold harsh winters and hot dry summers.

3   *The east coast*, including the city of Shanghai, Jiangsu, and northern Zhejiang provinces. Population: *c*. 130 million. This is the most densely populated area of the country, with some of its richest agricultural land, particularly in the delta of the Chang Jiang (Yangtze) river. Apart from Shanghai, there are also a number of large urban manufacturing centres, including Nanjing, Wuxi, Suzhou, and Hangzhou. The cities are growing rapidly, encroaching on agricultural land as they do so. The climate is generally moderate, though the winters can be very wet.

4   *The Dongting Hu and the lower Yangtze valley*, including Anhui, Hubei, Jiangxi, and Hunan provinces. Population: *c*. 240 million people. This is rich agricultural land studded with industrial centres, the largest of which is Wuhan. This area was largely overlooked in the first wave of economic growth, but is now receiving increasing levels of investment. The climate is comparatively moderate.

5   *The upper Yangtze*, including the province of Sichuan. Population: *c*. 110 million. Cut off from the lower valley by the Daba Shan mountains, Sichuan was once the poor relation among China's provinces, but is now growing again. Sichuan has a distinctive subculture, history, and cuisine of its own.

6   *The Pearl River basin and the south-east coast*, including Guangdong, Fujian, and southern Zhejiang. Population: *c*. 180 million. This heavily mountainous region faces the sea, and until 1990, Fujian and Guangdong were almost entirely dependent on shipping, agriculture, and fishing. It too has its own regional subculture. Some of the first Special Economic Zones were located here, because it is far from China's heartland and therefore suitable for experimentation, and its people have hundreds of years' experience of contact and trade with foreigners. Parts of Fujian near to Taiwan are heavily militarized. The economy is booming, thanks in large part to the presence of Hong Kong and some early Special Economic Zones like Shenzhen, Shantou, and Hainan. Guangdong is the centre of the Yue (Cantonese) language region and has its own subculture and cuisine. The climate is sub-tropical with heavy rains in the monsoon season.

7   *The south-west*, including Hainan provinces, the Guangxi autonomous region and the provinces of Guizhou and Yunnan. Population: *c.* 140 million. This area, almost cut off from the rest of China by the Nan Shan (Southern Mountains), is sometimes referred to collectively as Lingnan (South of the Mountains). Guangxi is the home of the Zhuang ethnic group. This region is very mountainous, ranging from the lower mountains along the Vietnamese border south of Nanning to the high ranges bordering Tibet to the west. Timber and mining are major industries, and agriculture is also important in the deep valleys around Guiyang and Kunming. Tobacco is grown here in large quantities, and the region is also suitable for the cultivation of the opium poppy which provides the basis for a large drug trade with China's neighbours, and drug smuggling through Hong Kong and its neighbouring points of access to the sea. The area, being contiguous or close to Vietnam, Laos, Cambodia, Myanmar, and India has considerable strategic importance in Chinese military planning. The population includes about 50 different ethnic groups. The climate is sub-tropical in the valleys, harsh in the high mountains.

8   *Manchuria* (the northeast), including Liaoning, Jilin, and Heilongjiang provinces. Population: *c.* 110 million. An industrial powerhouse, Manchuria has China's largest oilfields and a number of major manufacturing centres including Harbin, Jilin, Changchun, Shenyang, Fushun, Anshan, and Dalian. The Manchu and Han Chinese ethnic groups are effectively intermingled, but there are Mongolian groups in the west and several hundred thousand Russians, descended from White Russian refugees, around Harbin; these retain their own language, restaurants, and even vodka distilleries. The climate is harsh and cold in winter, dry in summer.

9   *Mongolia*, encompassed by the Nei Mongol autonomous region. Population: *c.* 20 million. The major centre is the capital, Hohhot; elsewhere, there are scattered towns and mining, but most of the area is given over to pastoral herding, much as it has always been. There is a Han Chinese majority, most of whom are comparatively recent emigrants; the rest are of Mongol descent. Hot dry summers give way to bitterly cold winters.

10   *Turkestan*, as the West still sometimes calls it, including most of Qinghai and Gansu provinces and the Xinjiang Uighur autonomous region. Population: *c.* 40 million. As in Mongolia, the majority of the population are now Han Chinese, but these are concentrated in cities such as Urumqi. The rural population are largely Turkish. Much of this vast area is almost entirely uninhabited, such as the Tarim Basin and the Taklamakan Desert. Again, the climate ranges from hot dry summers to cold hard winters.

11   *Tibet*, including the Xizang autonomous region and part of Qinghai province. Population: *c.* 3 million. High mountains, bleak, and largely uninhabited. Tibet has its own culture and history, and was largely independent until occupied by China in the 1950s; its status continues to be the subject of dispute and protest both inside Tibet and internationally.

(b) Chinese history in a nutshell

Chinese history is a story, over more than 3,000 years, of periods of unity and progress under a strong central government, interspersed with regime collapse followed by fragmentation and regression, in which regional local strongmen control parts of China, occasionally fighting each other with much loss of life and destruction. Hence the devout Chinese wish for the unity and stability on which their prosperity and progress depends. Much of the appeal of the Chinese Communist Party today to the Chinese people consists of the Party's success since 1949, and especially since 1980, in stabilizing, unifying, and enriching the country.

- *Ancient period.* Chinese civilisation was established along the Yellow River; the legendary King Huangdi (Yellow Emperor) probably flourished around the 25th century BC.
- *Xia dynasty, c.* 21st to *c.* 16th centuries BC. A mythical, fabled state.
- *Shang dynasty, c.*16th to 11th centuries BC. The first archaeological evidence comes from the Shang dynasty. Bronze working and horse-drawn chariots were introduced.
- *Western Zhou dynasty, c.* 11th century to 770 BC. This is the era of the fabled sage-kings of ancient China who so influenced Confucius, King Wen, and the Duke of Zhou.
- *Spring and Autumn period,* 770–481 BC. This period saw China politically divided but culturally rich, with many competing artistic and philosophical schools. Confucius, Mengzi (Mencius), Laozi (Lao Tzu) and Xunzi (Guan Tzu) were all active, and many classics of Chinese literature date from this time.
- *Warring States period,* 403–221 BC. The rich and powerful states of north China fought each other for supremacy almost continuously for two centuries. The master strategist Sunzi (Sun Tzu) was active in this period.
- *Qin dynasty,* 221–207 BC. The civil wars ended with the unification of China by its first true emperor, the powerful Qin Shi Huangdi who, over a period of just thirteen years, suppressed dissent, reformed society, expanded imperial rule into southern China, and began major works such as the Great Wall. He has been described by some historians as a bloodthirsty tyrant, but modern China still shows many influences of his rule.
- *Western Han dynasty,* 206 BC to 24 AD. Qin's heirs were not able to keep the throne, and the strong monarch of the Han dynasty consolidated the empire. This was a period of economic prosperity and cultural greatness.
- *Eastern Han dynasty,* 25–220 AD. After the brief usurpation of Wang Mang, the Han resumed their rule, but their power was much weakened. Ultimately the empire slid into chaos and broke apart.
- *Three Kingdoms period,* 220–65. As in the earlier Warring States period, the country was fragmented and several states fought each other for control.

- *Jin dynasty*, 265–420. China was briefly reunited under the dynasty of Western Jin (265–316) before breaking apart again under the Eastern Jin dynasty.
- *Southern and Northern dynasties*, 420–589. Several emperors built their dynasties, but could not last. China was fragmented with much conflict and many smaller states attempting to break away.
- *Sui dynasty*, 581–618. This dynasty reunited China, but collapsed when the Emperor Wen was defeated by the Koreans and the Turks.
- *Tang dynasty*, 618–907. Picking up the pieces after the Sui, the Tang dynasty restored order, and its emperors expanded China's power and prestige.
- *Five Dynasties and Ten Kingdoms*, 907–79. When the Tang dynasty collapsed, China fragmented into more warring states. Foreign invaders, mainly Turkish and Mongol tribes from the north, increased the pressure.
- *Song dynasty*, 960–1279. The Song were able to reunite China for a time, but the pressure from the northern invaders was becoming intense, and the Jurchen tribe ultimately drove the Song into the south in 1127. China was divided once more.
- *Yuan dynasty*, 1271–1368. Kublai Khan's Mongols conquered all of China and united it. This was actually a time of some prosperity, with China opened up to foreign trade.
- *Ming dynasty*, 1368–1644. After the Mongol empire disintegrated, the Ming dynasty took control and swiftly reunited China. Culturally and economically, China reached a high level during the Ming dynasty.
- *Qing dynasty*, 1644–1911. The Ming dynasty gradually fell into decay and was replaced by the Manchu tribes from the north-east, who conquered all of China in a series of military campaigns lasting about 20 years. The Manchu emperors Kangxi and his grandson Qianlong were great figures who between them ruled China for 135 years (1661–1796). Kangxi was a warrior and conqueror, and under his rule China reached its greatest extent, occupying its ancient enemies in Mongolia, Turkestan, and Tibet. The Tibetans were singled out as they had been allies of the Mongols and remained implacable enemies of China. Qianlong was a poet, artist and builder; in Beijing, many of the buildings in the Forbidden City and the Bei Hai park were built to his direction.
- *Republic of China*, 1912–49. Established by Sun Yat-sen, it quickly collapsed into a familiar Chinese pattern of feuding provinces ruled by warlords, until Chiang Kai-shek was able to impose peace and some unity in the late 1920s by doing deals with local strongmen. Disunity returned with the Japanese invasion (1933–45). After the success of the Communist Revolution of 1949, the government of the Republic of China went into exile on Taiwan.
- *People's Republic of China*, 1949–. Established by Mao Tse Tung and the victorious communists in 1949, the PRC has undergone many changes, including the Cultural Revolution of the 1960s and 70s, and the

economic reform process, which began in 1978. But the country has remained united, and its prosperity and influence have increased vastly.

Bibliography

Bond, M. H. (ed.) (1986) *The Psychology of the Chinese People*, Oxford: Oxford University Press.

Keay, J. (2009) *China: A History*, London: HarperPress.

Kissinger, Henry (2011) *On China*, New York: Penguin Press.

Kroeber, A. R. (2016) *China's Economy: What Everyone Needs to Know*, Oxford: Oxford University Press.

Moise, E. E. (1984) *Modern China: A History*, London: Longman.

Naughton, Barry (2017) *The Chinese Economy: Adaptation and Growth*, Boston, MA: MIT Press.

Quangyu, H., J. Leonard and C. Tong (1997) *Business Decision Making in China*, London: Haworth Press.

Wang, J. (ed.) (1990) *Westerners through Chinese Eyes*, Beijing: Foreign Languages Press.

Wang, Huiyao and Lu Miao (ed.) (2019) *Handbook on China and Globalization*, Cheltenham, UK: Edward Elgar.

3   The furniture of the mind

A comprehensive coverage of the roots of contemporary Chinese business thinking would take a thousand scholars a thousand days. Here, I seek merely to open the door into a room, one that is full of furniture that the occupants of the room themselves have, for much of the time, long ceased to notice. The 'room', that is, the Chinese mind, is dimly lit. When the Westerner enters it, some pieces seem the same as at home; some are strange, some are old, inherited from ancestors long dead, and some are new. Some may not be noticed in the half light and blundered into, perhaps causing damage.

The Western mind has its own furniture that we likewise rarely notice. The way we think is inherited from Greek, Jewish, and Christian patterns of analysis dating back two thousand years or more. Whether we now go to church or synagogue is no reflection of their influence on our thinking today. With more powerful means of mass communication and a missionary zeal for which there is no apparent explanation except, perhaps, Western arrogance, patterns of Western thinking have been more exposed to the Chinese than theirs to us. The lighting, in this metaphor, is thus brighter for the Chinese entrant.

The first focus of this chapter is on philosophies and how they affect the psychology of today's businessperson. Whether the inheritor of the culture is in PRC, Singapore, or the USA matters about as much as whether the inheritor of European culture is in Europe, Argentina, or Australia. But location does make some difference and younger generations feel, as they always have, that they are very different from their parents' age group. Why, if every generation is so different, do ways of thinking survive for centuries?

The line between philosophy and a particular school of thought and religion is not as clear as in the West. Confucianism is not a religion in the sense of believing in deities. Buddhism is not strictly a religion either, but the ancestor cult may be. Frankly, their classification is immaterial; we are concerned with their impact on modern thinking. This leads to a review of values.

China's two most important belief systems, Daoism and Confucianism, were both home-grown. Other important ideas and beliefs arrived in China over the centuries: Buddhism, Manichaean-ism (from Persia), Hinduism,

DOI: 10.4324/9781003241164-4

Zoroastrianism, and Christianity. In Quanzhou, a seaside town in Fujian, western China, which rose to fame as a trading port between the tenth and fourteenth centuries, one can see the altars, temples, and statues which the followers of all these beliefs erected. Where imported ideas spread, they were invariably mingled with Chinese ideas, so that after a few years, they had evolved into something different, merging with Chinese ideas of nature, ancestor worship, and balance.

The discussion of philosophy and values progresses to strategy, and China has its fair share of great and influential strategists who have been influenced by traditional beliefs. Sunzi, or Sun Tzu as he is more familiarly known in the West, could be called the greatest strategist of all time. His book *The Art of War* has had a profound effect on military thinking, especially guerrilla warfare. (*The Art of War* as we know it today was heavily rewritten in the third century AD by the general Cao Cao, one of the key figures of the Three Kingdoms period, who adopted it as a manual of strategy for his own officers. The end result is no less valid for all that). Today, the thirteen chapters provide guidance to businesspeople and generals alike and are too well known to need more than the briefest of recaps here. Another famous text, *The Thirty-Six Stratagems*, has also had much influence, as has the novel *Romance of the Three Kingdoms* which chronicles the struggle between the master strategist Zhuge Liang and his rival Cao Cao.

Philosophy

In broadly chronological order, let us look at:

- Ancestor cult
- Daoism (or Taoism)
- Confucianism
- Confucian disciples
- Legalism
- Buddhism
- Neo-Confucianism
- Christianity
- Communism.

Chronology is not necessarily the most accurate way of looking at these concepts since they moved in and out of fashion in no particular order. Confucius may have lived before and/or after the early Daoist philosophers, but their thinking seems to have preceded his. Confucianism, however, did not dominate until it was adopted by the Han emperors about 300 years or so later. Typically, it was followed by Daoism's resurgence. The two, very different, thought systems today comprise the two most important influences on Chinese thought processes and ways of doing things.

It is curious that so much philosophy originated in a relatively brief period around 400 BC, right across the world from Greece to China: Daoism and

Indian Yoga are not just contemporary but very similar. It is certainly possible, if not likely, that some of these philosophies inspired each other, or were inspired separately by some common source.

Ancestor cult

This is both the oldest belief system, and the core of Chinese religious observance. For perhaps four thousand years, all classes of society from emperors to serfs, intelligentsia to peasants, have swept out tombs and left food, drink, and lights for their fathers and forefathers, particularly at the Qing Ming Festival (5 April) which is dedicated to this purpose. The beliefs seem to be traceable to Shang times (sixteenth to eleventh centuries BC). At that time, the worship of royal ancestors was central to maintenance of the dynasty. Certain ancestors were worshipped on certain days, and the pattern of associations of days and observances built up.

The same period seems to have seen the birth of many of the Chinese equivalents of Western superstitions concerning numbers (such as Friday the thirteenth) and practices (such as walking under ladders), though the origins of these may be far older. Whether such things are rational is beside the point; they deeply affect doing business in China today. Eight and scarlet are still 'lucky'. There are right times to do things, such as to start a business, or there are right, or 'lucky' directions for buildings to face. Fortune telling remains strong in parts of China, just as the West has an undiminished appetite for astrology. Feng shui – literally "wind, water" – is still taken very seriously by many: the series of fatal accidents that attended the construction of the Jinmao Building in Shanghai were attributed by senior project managers not to shoddy construction methods, but to the fact that "the building is too high and too aggressive. It disturbs the dragons in the clouds". Feng shui practitioners were also called in to advise on construction of buildings for the Beijing Olympics in 2008. Popular beliefs of whatever type often exercise more influence over popular culture than does formal religion.

Daoism (c. 500 BC)

Dao (Tao in older texts) is usually translated as The Way, although there are many other connotations as well. Daoism is not a religion as such (though there are religious movements based on Daoist principles), but rather a way of thinking based on what occurs in nature that will bring harmony and wisdom. The instigator was one Laozi, (*Lao* = old, *zi* = master), supposedly the author of the immortal classic *Daodejing*. The title *Daodejing* was applied to the work subsequently; the title has been translated as "the old or classic book of integrity and the way" (the middle word, *de*, means integrity, or virtue). It began possibly as a collection of oral stories developed over the great period for Chinese philosophy between 600 and 300 BC. Zhuangzi, the greatest of the Daoist writers whose existence can be verified, lived towards the end of that period.

We cannot overstress the importance of Daoist thinking in 'pairs of opposites'. For black to be black, it needs white. For strength to be strength, it needs weakness. And so on. Every characteristic has its opposite, and every action has an opposite reaction. For example, it is natural for a Chinese person influenced by Daoism to think that a period of national unification will naturally be followed by a period of national disunity, because every movement has its natural opposite.

For those unfamiliar with the *Daodejing*, it is worth at least dipping into to get the flavour; it can be very enjoyable. Daoism expresses itself in the need for consensus and balance, as is found in nature. Decisions in China always require discussion and a degree of consensus. If consensus is not found, often the decision is postponed, sometimes indefinitely. This important Chinese characteristic can be traced directly to the influence, often subconscious, of Daoism. China's interest in the environment is also linked to Daoism's ancient roots in the natural order.

We have looked here at Daoism before turning to Confucianism, whatever the precise chronology, because it provides many underpinnings of Chinese thinking which so differentiate it from the West. Specifically, there are the concepts of balance and paradox. The *dao* is the 'non-being' (*wu*) within which any 'being' (*you*) exists, and vice versa. The *dao* is the source of all being and non-being, so to speak, the natural laws of the universe from which we spring, to which we return, and with which we should be in harmony in the meantime. *Yang* and *yin* are essential Daoist concepts which we define later. They are not polar opposites so much as complementary halves of the same whole. Even, for example, the selection of a balanced meal uses these two powerful concepts. Food and drink are functional such as red wine (*yang*) being perceived as good for the blood (which it probably is) whereas white wine (*yin*) is more gentle and romantic (no comment). Thus choosing the dinner wine can have unintended overtones.

One of the most important concepts in Daoism is *wu-wei*. This translates literally as 'non-action', but should not be thought to imply 'inaction'. Rather, *wu-wei* is the process by which a leader causes things to happen by providing an essential state of harmony wherein action happens spontaneously or naturally. This concept found its way to the West in the eighteenth century via the Jesuit missionaries in China, who were rather taken with Daoism and thought they glimpsed similarities with Christianity. A number of Daoist texts were translated into French and were widely read by French philosophers and intellectuals of the period. One of these, the economist François Quesnay, translated the term as 'laissez-faire' and used it to justify free markets and non-intervention by the state in the economy, on the grounds that unregulated markets would function naturally to produce the greatest possible good. Today, the idea of unregulated behaviour producing the best possible outcome is near to the heart of every right-wing economist working for the Heritage Foundation today in the United States, and it is often cited as a reason for not trying to regulate the so-called 'tech' companies in America. Ironically, a fundamental element of modern capitalism, which the West has exported to China in recent years, actually came from China in the first place.

Confucianism (551–479 BC)

This later period when philosophy flowered, was also marked by continuous warfare around much of the globe, notably the period of Warring States in China (403–221 BC). Interstate rivalry changed the selection of senior advisers to leaders from hereditary to the most (intellectually) competent, albeit from within the *shi* (gentleman) class, and Confucius was one of these. As a result there was considerable social and intellectual movement. It was also a time of rich cultural flowering, when the Hundred Schools of Thought debated amongst themselves. Only a few of these ideas, including Daoism, survived; others like the Mohists were later suppressed, and of others, such as the Agriculturalists and the Story Tellers, only their names survive; we have little idea as to what their beliefs were.

While Confucius, a member of the *shi* class and a senior civil servant, was certainly affected by the war-ravaged times in which he lived, his philosophy did not become official orthodoxy for China until about 300 years later during the Han dynasty. The following traditional Chinese story is used to introduce a discussion of Confucian social philosophy, which is central to efforts to explain and predict Chinese social interaction.

The protagonist, Xue Ren-gui, is an accomplished soldier who left his pregnant wife eighteen years earlier to fight a distant campaign for the emperor. Returning home, he notices a young man shooting wild geese with great skill. Provoked, he challenges the youth to a test of marksmanship. The rival readily accepts, whereupon Xue immediately puts an arrow through his heart, saying, "a soldier like me could not let another live if he was a superior in marksmanship with the weapons in which I excel".

Of course, it turns out the youth is Xue's son, whom he has never seen. The remorse of the father is tempered by the fact that the son has violated two cultural imperatives. First, he did not recognize his father: so strong are the bonds of family and the imperatives of filial piety that a son should know his father regardless of any factors that may disguise his identity. Second, the son has committed the cardinal sin in the Chinese tradition: he has challenged his father and thereby affronted social order. In the words of a Chinese proverb, "In a family of a thousand, only one is the master", a threat to the family is a threat to the body politic and a violation of Heaven's mandate. It must therefore be ruthlessly suppressed. This idea is important in a one-party state like China, which sometimes employs harsh measures to maintain order.

Confucianism has been guiding the behaviour of people of all classes since the Han dynasty, irrespective of the criticisms. In the time of Confucius, the great problems were how to govern, how to maintain order in society and how to guarantee happiness and prosperity for the people (*plus ça change…*). Confucius's solution was that both the rulers and the ruled should be educated. Governing is in the first place education and training, and the ruler should first educate himself and then govern with the help of 'virtues', meaning something close to the Daoist 'integrity' (the word does not have the overtone of religious morality that it may carry in the Middle East and in the West).

In this sense, there are five constant virtues: humanity, righteousness, propriety, wisdom, and faithfulness. These virtues are expressed in five cardinal relations: sovereign and subject, parent and child, elder and younger brothers, husband and wife, and friend and friend. Of these five relationships, the first two are the most important in Confucianism. The last quality, faithfulness, is still seen as necessary, especially in business. Constancy is, as we shall see, a key part of *guanxi* (relationships).

Confucius held that all men were alike in nature. He suggested that good and capable people should be appointed to official posts, a proposal that was different to the prevailing hereditary rule. Yet he also defended the hierarchy of the nobility. He advocated the elevation of good and capable people, but never opposed the hereditary system and advised people to accept their lot. Confucius saw a world in which harmony could best be achieved by everyone recognizing his or her place in the world. Confucius thus legitimized the strong hierarchical order which dominated the family and the society of his time and throughout much of Chinese history. This is in interesting and important contrast to Western thinking, where the realization of personal freedom has often been associated with the overthrow of the current governance: for example, in the French Revolution.

Confucius distinguished two kinds of individuals: *jun zi* (gentleman, prince, great man, or proper man) and *xiao ren* (literally; petty man or small man):

- Great man, being universal in his outlook, is impartial; petty man, being partial, is not universal in outlook (Confucius, Book 2)
- He (great man) sets the good examples and then invites others to follow them (Confucius, Book 2)
- Great man cherishes excellence; petty man, his own comfort. Great man cherishes the rules and regulations; petty man, special favour (Confucius, Book 4)
- Great man is conscious only of justice; petty man only of self-interest (Confucius, Book 4).

Leadership belongs to the great man; he need not be of noble birth, but should have the five constant virtues.

Confucius defined filial duty as:

While his father lives, observe a man's purposes; when the father dies, observe his actions. If for three years (of mourning) a man does not change from the ways of his father, he may be called filial.

(Confucius, Book 1)

Both the subject and filial relationships lead to a predominantly vertical structure of relationships. In modern business, a paternalistic management style is thought by some to be a direct consequence in both China and Japan.

In essence, Confucianism sets out a framework for interpersonal relationships of all kinds.

Confucian disciples (Mozi, 5th century BC; Mencius, c. 371–289 BC; Xunzi, c. 298–238 BC)

Confucian thinking was the standard against which others pitted their wits. Mohism advocated universal love, which was an extension of the idea of humanity. Mozi, the movement's leading thinker, believed that people with 'virtue' and ability should be elevated and was opposed to inherited wealth or nobility.

Mencius developed a theory of government by benevolence, believing that man was born with goodness. In his view, man possessed inherent qualities of benevolence, righteousness, propriety, and wisdom, which some people were able to preserve and others not. In Mencius's view, every sovereign was able to rule by a policy of benevolence and every citizen was able to accept it.

Xunzi thought that man was born with evil, but education could change man's nature. Further, he emphasized self-improvement, and self-fulfilment. This view that study can lead to self-improvement remains current.

Confucianism was adopted officially by successive imperial regimes, and it has profoundly influenced Chinese thought patterns. Under Mao, Confucianism was officially out of favour, even though Confucian thought patterns were too well entrenched to be much affected (and Mao himself was imbued with them). In 1985, a special institute was founded in Beijing for the study of Confucian thought. Since then, China has established Confucius institutes around the world. Interest in Confucianism has increased steadily, and the works of Confucius and his school are being studied in the light of today's social and economic problems. Today, it is important for foreign visitors to appreciate that the Chinese readily embrace Confucius and his ideas as both an essential historical fact and as part of their national heritage.

Legalism (c. 220 BC)

Legalists believed, quite simply, in law and order. Furthermore, they believed that the law possessed a virtue that set it above any other human principle; everyone had to obey the law in every circumstance. This was law applied exactly, without exception. Unlike Confucius, (but like Thomas Hobbes, the English philosopher of the seventeenth century), the Legalists believed that man is fundamentally amoral and is guided purely by self-interest and the future, not by tradition or the desire to do good: he must therefore be coerced by law into doing right. Otherwise, man had to be punished.

Han Feizi, the most prominent exponent of Legalism, rejected the Confucian notion that most men tend towards the good and can be relied upon to behave ethically through a social system that exerts pressure on people to conform. For him, the only way to achieve conformity was through the rule of law. His system of thought was based on three important principles. The first of these was *fa*, meaning roughly 'prescriptive standards', but also with connotations of law and punishment. People should comply with *fa* so that their behaviour conforms with the public good, or be punished as a result. The second was *shi*, meaning 'authority' or 'power'. The exercise of *shi* is necessary to ensure compliance with *fa*; but conversely, *shi* should also be governed by the dictates of *fa* to prevent abuses of power. The third was *shu*, the technique of controlling the bureaucracy by comparing 'word' with 'deed' (or more generally, potential performance with the actuality). The emperor Qin Shi Huangdi adopted Han's views and became the guiding force behind the Qin empire.

Legalism was, and is, perceived as being excessively harsh and inhumane; all human relationships are subordinated to the rule of law. When the Qin dynasty was replaced by the Han dynasty, Confucian thinking replaced Legalism as the official doctrine. But elements of Legalism can still be seen today in Chinese thinking, particularly concerning the authority held by the state over the individual, and in the importance of structure and hierarchy not just in the family, but in administration and governance: the Chinese bureaucratic system on which the Han and later dynasties relied, elements of which arguably still exist today, has both Legalist, and Confucian elements. Influences of Legalism can also be found in some of Mao's writings. On the whole, though, Legalism did *not* prevail over Confucian thinking. This helps to explain why *guanxi* remains so important, and why most Chinese prefer to solve problems through mediation rather than resorting to legal process.

Buddhism (c. Fourth century AD)

By the 3rd century AD, Confucianism was discarded by the then governing class, just as the Han dynasty also began to fail. Social elites were looking for something new and, as often in China, this meant that they turned to the past to resurrect older, purer forms of thinking. Daoism enjoyed a resurgence. At the same time, Buddhism arrived from India.

Buddhism's official arrival dates to about 70 AD when the Han emperor Ming Ti had a dream of a golden flying deity. Buddhism's popularity spread in China, probably because the ideas of balance and nature-inspired harmony which are found in Buddhism were already present in Daoism. Within a few decades, as so often with foreign importations into China, Chinese Buddhism had started to develop its own characteristics, and to evolve away from its Indian roots. Although Indian classics like the *Awakening of Faith in Mahayana* were widely read and studied, within a few generations Chinese Buddhist scholars like Fazang and Linji were establishing 'Buddhism with Chinese characteristics'.

By the sixth century, the monasteries, largely thanks to imperial patronage, had obtained substantial economic power (as they did hundreds of years later in Europe). Inevitably, excess power led to corruption, and in 845 the Tang emperor Wuzong began a persecution, destroying monasteries, works of art, and scholarship. Over 250,000 monks and nuns returned to the laity. Later, the Cheng brothers and Zhu Xi built many elements of Buddhist thinking into their neo-Confucian synthesis (see below). Today, thanks to neo-Confucianism (see below), Chinese Buddhism is so intertwined with Confucianism and Daoism that it is difficult to separate them. Buddhism was largely suppressed after 1949 and many temples closed, but reopened in the 1990s, both as tourist centres and for their traditional purposes.

Neo-Confucianism

Neo-Confucianism appears in the period of imperial revival in the Sung and Tang dynasties. Like many reform movements in China, it sought to make China strong again by ridding the country of foreign and corrupt influences and adopting a purely Chinese philosophy. A group of scholars set out to resolve the apparent contradictions between Confucianism, Daoism, and Buddhism and create a unified system of thought. Much of the early work was done by the brothers Cheng Hao and Cheng Yi; the exposition of the final product was the work of the most important late Chinese philosopher, Zhu Xi.

By building a single thought-system which embraced all the different aspects of Chinese philosophy and thinking, the neo-Confucians (the name is a later tag) set a framework for thinking in China. Highly conservative, looking back to the masters (Confucius, Laozi et al.), the neo-Confucians reinforced views on education, self-development, and interpersonal relations along largely Confucian lines. This system has persisted to this day.

Christianity (1583 AD)

Exactly when Christianity arrived in China is not known, but there was a Nestorian Christian community in the west of China from at least the eighth century, and in 1289–90 a Chinese Christian called Rabban Sauma visited England and France as an envoy of one of the Mongol rulers. He must have caused a sensation.

Franciscan missionaries followed (or maybe preceded) Marco Polo into China; an archdiocese of Beijing was created, but converts never numbered more than a few hundred. Matteo Ricci pioneered a Jesuit presence in 1583, even though the Ming emperors had closed China to foreigners. He was well trained in language and Confucian thinking by Chinese in Europe. With modern echoes, the Jesuits' market entry strategy was to make themselves valuable to the Ming emperors through technology transfer (including cannon manufacture) and thus earn import rights for Christianity. Ricci determined that the ancestor cult and Confucianism were 'social' rites, and could thus be incorporated within Christianity (just as Saturnalia had become Christmas).

Initially the strategy worked well, and by the end of the Ming dynasty a substantial foothold and converts had been achieved in Beijing and some cities further south. In the eighteenth century, however, other Catholic orders, perhaps jealous of the Jesuits' Chinese exclusivity, challenged Ricci's acceptance of ancestor cult and Confucianism. One thing led to another, the missionaries were forced to leave and Christians were persecuted.

As the Qing dynasty weakened in the nineteenth century, fresh waves of missionaries of all denominations appeared. Undoubtedly heroic, they made various contributions to health and education at local levels and achieved many converts. Nevertheless the impact on China, and Chinese thinking, overall was minimal. During the conservative Boxer Rebellion in 1900, the rebels killed many Christian missionaries.

Christianity had a low profile in China through much of the twentieth century, although several Chinese warlords, and other prominent people, like the Wellesley College-educated wife of Chinese wartime leader Chiang Kai-shek, were baptized and attended church regularly. But, by 2000 there were perhaps two million Christians in China with little or no influence. Since then, though, the number of Christians in China has increased dramatically. In 2015 it was estimated that there were nearly 60 million Christians living in the country, the majority being recent Protestant converts. Although various theories have been advanced, no one is quite sure why Christianity has experienced this sudden upsurge. As noted in the previous chapter, the authorities have taken notice and are now attempting to co-opt Christianity into Chinese culture and social structures. In spite of its recent surge, Christianity remains quite marginal in China. If it showed strong popularity across a broad part of the country, the Government would probably be alarmed and would take steps to limit or reverse its spread. Christianity is likely therefore to remain quiescent in China. Unlike Buddhism, it has not had widespread influence on the Chinese mind.

Communism (c. 1920s)

The history of Communism in China has been well covered in a variety of other books, and does not need repetition here. As a *philosophy*, communism never really put down roots in China. Mao ruled in much the same way that the emperors had, and so did Deng. Today it operates as the ruling *party*, which is a good enough reason to join. Communist ideology – Marxism and Leninism – has adjusted to accommodate market pragmatism, but Xi's government has tried to prevent a complete capitalist takeover in China by underlining the relevance of traditional communist thought to China. The cynical might think that acceptance of the ideology was convenient in providing a rationale for revolution and to get support from Russia. That would be unfair. Mao and his contemporaries had a genuine desire to reform China, and to distribute wealth from the rich to the poor. Corruption, and the abuse of power in the 30 years either side of 1900, had advanced to the point where some puritanical doctrine was essential to clean the stables. Confucianism, which respected the inherited order, was banned; yet many of the precepts of the two systems (such as the idea that government is for the benefit of the people) coincide, and Confucian ideas continued to infuse practice. Mao's doctrines on education and (early) concepts of government owe as much to Confucius as to Marx.

The Cultural Revolution declared war on traditional Chinese thoughts and beliefs, and attempted to repopulate Chinese minds with Mao's version of Leninism. But by the time Mao died in 1976, most Chinese were too hungry and exhausted to think of much except their own survival. When the reform and growth years arrived in the 1980s and 90s, it was easy for Chinese, who had had their heads emptied of many traditional ideas, to relate to China's version of capitalism, without much thought of what the Communist Party was supposed to stand for. Today almost every Chinese person believes strongly in China, and most support the Chinese Communist Party, because it is successful, but often without believing in or paying much attention to communist thought and ideology, in spite of the efforts of Xi Jinping's government to elevate their importance.

Eight key concepts in Chinese thinking

- *Dao*: the Way; something akin to the Western concept of the natural order of things, or natural law.
- *De*: virtue; a key Daoist concept which guides people to correct behaviour and away from narrow self-interest.
- *Li*: rituals or rites; sets out the correct form of behaviour in a given situation so as to preserve harmony and face.
- *Mianzi*: face; including one's self-respect and public dignity. Preserving *mianzi* is a key goal in most interpersonal relations. Having a 'thick face' means that one is impervious to face issues, that is, thick-skinned in English, probably because public respect is already eroded.
- *Ren*: literally 'benevolence'; but in fact covers the traditional ethical code of how one should treat other people. Not to be confused with the same (pinyin but not Chinese) word for a person.
- *Yi*: rightness or righteousness; the knowledge of what is correct in any given situation.
- *Yin–yang*: the two halves of a whole, often in reference to *dao*. Treated as complementary, rather than polar opposites, *yang* and *yin* describe two halves of the same whole; they are, so to speak,

the sunny and shady sides of the same mountain, but one needs to be careful with analogies. *Yang*, which also means the sun, is associated with positiveness and masculinity; *yin* (the moon) is negative and feminine.

- *Zhi*: knowing or knowledge, but procedural rather than factual. In other words, knowing *how*, not knowing *what*.

Values

Chinese beliefs and values stem directly from the philosophies mentioned earlier in this chapter. Here we focus on a few of the most important, including:

- Age, hierarchy, and authority, strongly linked to each other and to Confucianism
- 'Face' or personal reputation and dignity
- Cultural dimensions.

I have taught Chinese undergraduates and graduate students in Peking University and Sun Yat-Sen Universities in China, and I can testify that, as one would expect, Chinese millennials think differently to their parents and grandparents. But if you place a few Chinese students in a room with people from other parts of the world, they will immediately be recognizable as mainland Chinese people who hate confrontation, embrace consensus, say what they believe others want to hear for fear of upsetting them (keeping their real thoughts private), and prefer to keep a low profile.

Age, hierarchy, and authority

Respect for tradition, ancestors, and age, stemming from Confucius, and perhaps also from earlier traditions, was among the main values of people in old China. The respect for age was manifested especially in family life, which had a profound effect upon other parts of social life. The hierarchical relations of a Chinese family were determined by age. The names of sisters and brothers followed the age-order of the family members. For example, an older brother was addressed as 'older brother' (*gege*) and a younger sister likewise (*meimei*). Only parents called their children by their given names.

Similarly, industrial workers in old China did not typically question higher authority or seek authority themselves, thus reinforcing the subordinates' subservience and dependence on superiors. Authority in industry and business was viewed as an absolute right of owners and the managers in control. Superior–subordinate relationships were typically personal, subjective, and viewed as father–son or master–servant relationships. No two persons were equal in relation to each other. An older person had more authority than a younger one, and a man had more authority than a woman.

These attitudes are obviously out of date, but their habit still persists.

The Qin dynasty (221–207 BC) held the family responsible for the public acts of its members as part of their social pressure on each individual, inculcating obedience to the Government and to the social order through the family. In a sense, this still operates. The one-child rule, for example, is enforced more through family and local community pressures than any legal system. Recently, the one-child rule was relaxed, and families are encouraged to have more than one child. But many do not, because it is expensive.

'Face' (miànzi), *or personal reputation and dignity*

The pervasive Chinese concept of gaining, giving or losing 'face', or being made to look clever or stupid in front of others, focuses on questions of prestige and dignity, and reflects surprising vulnerability in self-esteem. The Chinese are acutely sensitive to the regard in which they are held by others or the light in which they appear to other people. Giving 'face' in public to others is extremely important in China. It is seen as an essential form of politeness. Conversely, causing someone to lose 'face', or look foolish in front of others will not be overlooked or forgotten, and can have severe consequences: at the very least, co-operation will cease, and retaliation may ensue.

Losing and saving face are well understood in the West. Less so is the concept of giving face; that is, doing something to enhance someone else's reputation or prestige. The heavy use of shame as a social control mechanism from the time of early childhood tends to cause feelings of dependency and anxieties about self-esteem, which produce self-consciousness about most social relationships. As a result, a great deal can be gained by helping the Chinese to win face and a great deal will be lost by any affront or slight, no matter how unintended, especially for older, and/or more senior people.

The Chinese concept of sincerity is the opposite of the Anglo-American, in that the Chinese believe that they can manifest sincerity only by adhering carefully to prescribed etiquette, whereas many Westerners believe that etiquette obscures truth.

Giving face is also closely connected with *guanxi* (see Chapter 4). We are more likely to establish good relationships with those who always give us face and vice versa; thus it accumulates. If *guanxi* already exists, then 'giving face' or giving status increases the opportunity for rewards. Flattery, in short, may be helpful. It is always better to conceal the truth if the truth involves blaming or criticizing a Chinese person in front of other people.

Cultural dimensions

The Chinese are not *either* individualist *or* collective, but both at the same time. Five groups of differences between Chinese tradition and features of Western decision theory have been identified: motivation and consequence, unity and diversity, circle and sequence, harmony and self-interest, and certainty and uncertainty. Elements from Chinese culture that impact on decision-making include 'face', the individual–collective dichotomy, hierarchy, equality, self and social role, and personal modesty.

Motivation and consequence

According to Western theory, the manager assembles the possible outcomes from alternative actions, judges the probability of each outcome, and then chooses the action most likely to have favourable consequences. In contrast, the Confucianist evaluates the motives and intention of the manager, taking ethical or moral principles as the criteria. The consequences examined are those that arose in the past, facts about past decisions, and not estimates about the future. In other words, if the principles worked before, continue with them and do not speculate about the future.

Unity and diversity

Chinese tradition emphasizes synthesis and unitary principle, from which problem-solving attributes are deduced, while the Western approach is to focus on the specific characteristics of the problem, permitting a wide variety of objectives. An example of this thinking is found in the ancient Chinese classic, the *Yijing* (The Book of Changes), which deals with knowledge of the universe as a whole. Minor principles can be deduced from a few major ones, instead of working Western-style from the observation of reality. Having said that, Chinese thinking, obviously, also includes the observation of reality.

Circle and sequence

Chinese think of nature in terms of closed, spiral, or circular systems of interrelated elements, whereas Western decision theory is sequential (for example, with linear, exponential, or repeated patterns such as economic cycles). In traditional Chinese thinking, consequence derives from many interrelated factors. A circular network is used to highlight the effects as a whole. The more linear Western approach can be presented as a sequence of decisions, such as a 'decision tree', each analyzing the problem more narrowly.

Harmony and self-interest

When determining the optimal decision, Chinese tradition is to emphasize harmony and the group, but Western decision theory presumes that the decision-maker will optimize self-interest or maximize subjective expected utility. There are many Chinese sayings which reinforce the idea that a person who stands out from the group will be criticized and may be prevented from reaching his/her goal: "The tree growing high above the others will be blown down by the wind" and "The gun fires at the first bird in the flock". Similarly, the Confucian Doctrine of the Mean is, "Take the mean of the two, remain neutral without bias" and the Daoist doctrine states, "Strive for no fault rather than merit, retreat for the purpose of advancing". Of course business-people, in search of first-mover advantage, will quite often seek to be first. A Chinese businessperson may well be embarrassed by being innovative, whereas a similar partner in the West would be proud of it. Being first in China may carry profound cultural and social difficulties. Imitation, however, may give 'face'.

Certainty and uncertainty

Chinese tradition is oriented towards certainty, not the evaluation of uncer-tainty that is emphasized in Western decision theory. In their struggle for existence against numerous dangers and disasters, the Chinese felt that the future was very hard to face. As luck and misfortune came from the supernat-ural, divination played (and still plays) an important role in making deci-sions. The Chinese value past experiences more highly, depending on these for future action; again, note the importance of history and historical think-ing. Past experiences are the guarantee and premise for success (just as they are for many Wall Street analysts, come to that). This view is reflected in sayings like, "The old finger is hottest" and "One will pay for it if one does not follow an old man's words".

Economics

Ancient Chinese contained no word for 'economics'; the modern term, *jing ji*, is a Japanese loan word and does not appear until the end of the nineteenth century. There is, however, a very ancient term, 'administering wealth', which appears in the Daoist text the *Yijing*, and this gives some clues as to how the Chinese approached the concept of economics. Unlike rationalist Western theories, Confucian thinking sees human agency as an essential feature of economics. Chen Huan-chang, a Chinese mandarin who later studied Western political economy, argued in his book *The Economic Principles of Confucius and His School* that Confucian writings mention three factors of production: land, capital, and the virtuous man. Of these three, it is the last, he wrote, that is by far the most important.

But whatever the tenets of ancient Chinese philosophy, modern Chinese economics has been very strongly influenced by Western economic theory. Many senior Chinese government ministers who have economic responsibili-ties today hold degrees in economics or business studies from respected Western institutions like Oxford, Harvard, Yale, MIT, or Berkeley. The long-serving head of China's Central Bank, Dr Yi Gang, even served for a time as an associate professor in economics at an American university, before returning to China as an academic at Peking University. He then joined the People's Bank of China in 1997. The Chinese Government has shown itself since 1990 to be remarkably skilful at managing a fast-growing and often unbalanced economy without a serious mishap. This success is due in part to the prevalence of the best Western education at high levels of the Chinese administration, as well as to accurate observation of China's many micro-economies, from Shanghai to Chongqing, and from Guangzhou to Harbin and Xian.

Strategy

In China, the idea that one can look far into the future and lay out strategic moves, step by step, in some pre-planned sequence is even more unlikely than it is elsewhere. So does that mean that Chinese businesses do not think strategically? Quite the reverse.

Business strategy as warfare

As mentioned above, the period of Warring States (403–221 BC) provided plenty of material for strategist theorists, chief amongst whom was Sun Zi (pronounced Soon Zer). As the people who led the army during war and the government administration during peace were frequently the same people or drawn from the same circle, the same strategic management principles were applied in peace and war. According to Sun Zi, the supreme aim of war was "not to win one hundred victories in one hundred battles" but to "subdue the enemy without fighting". In competition either in politics or business, strategy should be aimed at disposing one's resources in such an overwhelming fashion that the outcome of the contest is determined before it gets started.

To convert Sun's ancient thoughts to modern marketing terms, the equivalent might be:

* What kind of business we are/should be in
* Analysis of the competitive environment
* Competitive positioning
* Motivational factors
* Implementation.

Strategists study these five factors to assess the chances of success, and calculate their strengths, and weaknesses vis-à-vis that of their opponents. Deception, speed, and concentration of forces are the rules of war.

Of the various military metaphors, guerrilla warfare is the most appealing, both because marketers usually have too few resources for the task and because it is not just Army A versus Army B: the surrounding population (that is, end consumers) is usually decisive. Guerrilla warfare, if successful, proceeds through three phases: invisibility, evasion, and concentration. In the first, the guerrillas maintain the lowest possible profile and set up their infrastructure and relationships with the surrounding population. In the second, battles/skirmishes are fought only to increase resources at the enemy's expense. The third stage, only conducted when the organization has grown strong enough to overwhelm its opposition, is akin to classic warfare.

Whether it is in the small wins early or the large, pitched battles later, all Chinese writers point to the importance of focusing energy onto the point of contact so that, in that place, and at that time, the enemy is outnumbered, encircled, and suppressed. Failing that, at least ensure your positioning occupies 'the high ground', whatever that may be in consumer terms. It may well be as simple as a higher price, it may be relying on the strength of a brand to carry the business through hard times and into new markets.

Mao was also fond of saying that his two main mistakes were over-estimating and under-estimating the enemy. That this recent Chinese history echoes Sun Zi is no surprise. Mao studied Chinese history closely. He was not just a master general but a master guerrilla and, in another time, might have been a master marketer or business executive. Brand names and business reputations in China live as long as anywhere else. In this long-term game, Chinese players will have learned from these histories, and the application of military game-playing to business is both a major and conscious part of their planning.

Shanghai Volkswagen

When people think of joint ventures (JVs) in China, they often think first of SAIC Volkswagen, the early (1984) JV between the Shanghai Automotive Industrial Company (SAIC) and VW. A second JV was established with First Automotive Works in 1987 in the city of Changchun. Between them, these two JVs gave Shanghai Volkswagen a powerful presence in the market. Growth was slow at first, as there were few roads, few petrol stations, and few people with the disposable income to buy a private car.

Initially, Shanghai VW's managers concentrated on two markets; government car fleets and taxis. Both were highly successful. The red Volkswagen Santana became a feature of Shanghai's streets, and there were sales in other cities too. In 2000, Shanghai VW manufactured 53% of all the cars sold in China.

However, the newly affluent 60 million middle class in China could now afford private cars, and initially they did not want a brand that had associations with either taxis or cars used by civil servants. However, the Santana soldiered on and remains in production. Other competitors were crowding in. General Motors launched a joint venture in Shanghai in 1997, and its Buick brand became popular almost at once. Honda, Toyota, and Peugeot were also on the scene with JVs or subsidiaries of their own.

More critically, the domestic car industry was surging, and local brands like Chery, Lifan, and Geely were cheaper than cars made by the joint ventures. Chery's QQ micro-car, costing the equivalent of around US$ 4,000, saw sales increase by 130% in 2006. Altogether, the Chinese brands had taken 28% of the market by 2006, and Japanese imports another 27%. Meanwhile, Shanghai VW had seen its market share slide from over 50% in 2000 to just 15% in 2005.

In October 2005 Shanghai VW announced a programme aimed at recovering its previously dominant position. The plan was to roll out at least ten new models, aimed specifically at Chinese consumers, with the first to go on show by the opening of the Beijing Olympics in 2008. At the same time there would be a radical shake-up of its cost structures and supply-chain operations, including renegotiating the two JV contracts to reflect the realities of the new situation. In particular, Shanghai VW wanted its two JV partners to collaborate more closely with each other in order to achieve 'synergy'.

Importantly, Shanghai VW persuaded its foreign parts suppliers to set up their own JVs in China. By 1993, it already had 85% local content.

The year 2012 saw a big increase in capacity with plants in Ningbo (January), Urumqi (May) and Yizheng (July) starting production. Over 30 years, Shanghai VW has had its ups and downs, but its original city taxi market has held firm due to various municipal incentives, thus providing a bedrock for the business.

Despite a slowdown in China's auto market, Shanghai Volkswagen's sales surged 24.4% in 2011 whereas China's auto sales as a whole had their slowest growth in 13 years, with output and sales of passenger cars up by only 4.23% and 5.19%, respectively, according to data from the China Association of Automobile Manufacturers.

In 2015 Shanghai VW produced six brands of cars under the Skoda label and 11 VW variants, including the Santana and Gran Santana. Although sales were down in 2015, the previous years saw strong growth.

Trickery/ cleverness

There is a semantic problem here: no one, including the Chinese, likes a word like 'trickery', loaded as it is with negative connotations. At the same time cleverness (better) does not quite convey the legitimate role of disinformation. Context affects meaning: we like to be tricked by a magician at a party, but are angry if we are tricked out of our money by a fraudster. In this section, I refer to business practices that are legitimate but likely to mislead, and thereby outwit, other players. We are not talking about cheating.

I will call it 'cleverness' to avoid offence. The Chinese tolerance of cleverness in this sense is greater than that in the West. As ever, it is limited by relationships (you do not outwit your own father) and it is also reciprocal (the West is *expected* to be devious even when it is not). The cunning entrepreneur, the crafty businessman who is 'eight sides all wide and slippery', is an admired figure in many circles.

The view of cleverness or trickery is invariably one-sided. Here is a Chinese view of Western businesspeople, written in a handbook for Chinese managers in 1990:

> We have to know the tactics needed for the struggle, know the opponents and ourselves, and be able to see through their tricks. The foreign capitalists will always try to cheat money out of us by using every possible means including deception.

Overseas Chinese

Most of this chapter applies equally to the overseas Chinese communities, though with some small differences. Most importantly, although most of them had some Maoist sympathizers and many left China during Maoist rule, especially in the 1950s and 60s, Maoism was never put into practice in these overseas Chinese communities (Singapore or Hong Kong, for example). Therefore, Maoism does not really figure strongly in their furniture of the mind, although Daoism, and Confucianism certainly do. There has also been greater penetration of Western ideas in many cases; there are far larger numbers of Chinese Christians overseas than in China, for example. Finally, through education and the media, many overseas Chinese have accepted some Western modes of thinking, and these are married, in some form, with their own Chinese habits of thought and behaviour. (This is one of the reasons why many mainland Chinese might regard the overseas Chinese with some reserve).

Conclusions

The purpose of this chapter has been to explore, and to some extent compare, mental furniture. No two single individuals, still less 1.3 billion people, think exactly alike, nor would anyone expect that. For the purpose of contrasting differences, I have tended to compare China with the West and have ignored other parts of the world. Obviously, the closer the cultural and historical links – for example, with Japan, Korea, and Vietnam – the more furniture is shared or similar; yet it does not do to ignore the great differences between modes of thinking in these countries as well. The main point is that China's very long and unique history has generated particular beliefs and ways of thinking which strongly influence today the thought processes and actions of Chinese people, often unconsciously. Non-Chinese business people doing business in China will benefit greatly from trying to understand these special influences.

Bibliography

O'Balance, E. (1962) *The Red Army of China*, London: Faber & Faber.

Wing, R. L. (1988) *The Art of Strategy: A New Translation of Sun Tzu's Classic, The Art of War*, New York: Doubleday.

4   Relationships and regulations

The rules are fixed; the people are flexible.

(Chinese proverb)

Since the 4th edition of this book was published in 2017, we have seen the United States, under President Trump, conduct a campaign aimed at 'punishing' China for practices alleged to be illegal and harmful to the interests of the United States (and, by extension, to much of the rest of the world). The Trump-led US-China trade war of 2018–20 was intended to initiate a process of economic decoupling from China, reducing the West's reliance on China.

This campaign made a large impact on China's attitude to its global role and to the West, and consequently China has started to turn inwards. This reverses the trend started by Deng Xiaoping in 1980 of looking outwards, and learning from, and developing with the developed West. The new Chinese concept of 'dual-circulation' puts a heavy weight on increasing Chinese self-reliance via internally generated economic growth.

But China's leaders still recognize China's deep integration through trade with the rest of the world because this is a constant and, for the foreseeable future, here to stay. So, at the same time as stressing the strength of its domestic economy and society, China has continued to open up previously restricted sectors of its economy to foreign investors. The rules for foreign investment into China in key sectors have been relaxed. In the automotive and banking sectors, it is now possible for foreign multinationals, like Volkswagen, and Toyota, JP Morgan, and Goldman Sachs to establish and operate wholly owned entities in China. Such opening, bringing much-needed foreign expertise, is well understood by the Chinese to bring beneficial results to the Chinese economy.

At the same time, government controls have been tightened, for example, over the independence of Chinese schools and media. The position of the Chinese state-owned sector as the champion of the Chinese economy has been reinforced. Since November 2020, a series of regulations have been issued which closely control the activities of so-called Chinese 'tech' companies. These affect the management and use of data, especially personal information. Online Chinese companies which provide private tutoring services for profit were outlawed in 2021.

DOI: 10.4324/9781003241164-5

The Chinese Government has begun to assert itself strongly as a proactive regulator in fields where it believes that regulatory intervention is able to prevent erosion of government control and the impoverishment of the Chinese household in economic or privacy terms. This new trend, a clean break with the more liberal, laissez-faire pattern established since 1990, is clearly underway. At the time of this writing in late 2021, it is not known what further steps the Chinese Government may decide to take in this direction, and it is important for foreign companies to try to understand the Chinese Government's aim, so that the correct policies can be adopted.

The Chinese Government sees the contribution made by foreign companies, their people, investment, and their technology to Chinese society as essential, and it intends to continue encouraging foreign involvement in the Chinese economy. However, it is determined to re-establish the pre-eminent position of the Government, and especially of the Chinese Communist Party in China. The joint impact of increased Chinese affluence, and the huge Chinese 'tech' companies like Alibaba and Tencent together threatened to undermine the prestige of the Party and the Government. A series of policy moves since late 2020 has been aimed at reversing that perceived undermining.

It is clear that the Chinese Communist Party will continue to try and dominate the Chinese Government and the country and will likely succeed in doing so. It is even more important than it was for foreign companies to be perceived in China as good and useful Chinese citizens. Foreign companies operating in China must pay close attention to the rules which govern their conduct, as well as to the key government personnel in their operating regions, such as the mayor and the Party Secretary.

At the same time, personal relationships and personal networking in China remain as important as they have always been. Foreign businesses in China need local partners in much the same way that they do in any world market. One of those partners, for any foreign business in China, is the local government. Relationships also have to be cultivated with distributors, suppliers, customers, and the community in general.

Relationships, however, are more important in China than in most other countries for three reasons: first, the government plays a much more direct role in the economy in China than do most Western countries or even many developing economies. In China, the economy is seen as being at the service of the state and 'the people', and the state does not hesitate to intervene when it thinks the economy is going in an undesirable direction. This applies to local as well as central government in the People's Republic of China and, to a greater or lesser degree, to every government in the region. Cultivating good relationships with government is always a critical factor in assuring the success of a Chinese venture.

Second, there are sharply differing attitudes to law – particularly to its aims and purposes – in China compared with the West. In the West, we tend to see the law as an essential and fair set of rules of conduct governing our society, and also as our primary form of redress if things go wrong. In China, the ethics and standards of behaviour required in a Confucian society play as large a role in setting rules of behaviour as does the law in Western societies. China has moved fast to start catching up with the established legal frameworks of developed Western societies (see Chapter 5 "Business and the Law"), but social pressures based on Chinese traditions of behaviour are – and have always been – an important way of ensuring compliance. Therefore, as we discuss below, some of the issues that Westerners tend to think of as legal are better seen in China as relationship issues.

Third, and related to the above, there is the fact that much of Chinese society – including its huge business sector – is, and always has been organized on relationship principles. There are three key principles which can be added to the box in the previous chapter:

- *Qingmian*, or 'human feelings'; respect for the feelings of others is of great importance, particularly in relationship management.
- *He*, or 'harmony' is a very powerful concept which stresses the smooth running of a group or a society. Harmony is seen as good, and conflict as bad. *He* can also mean gentleness or friendliness.
- *Guanxi*, which is usually translated simply as 'relationships' or 'connections'. It is no exaggeration to say that relationships are the modus operandi of Chinese business. They are how things get done.

After looking more closely at this last concept, this chapter and the next apply it in three contexts – government, legal/contractual, and commercial. In all three, relationships are essential for doing business in China and around the region. They need to be considered and developed *simultaneously*. Some types of relationships will, in given circumstances, be more important than others; but over the long term, all three have to be maintained.

Guanxi

There are almost as many definitions of *guanxi* as there are people who have observed and written about it. "A network of interpersonal relationships and exchanges of favours established for the purpose of conducting business activities", is as good a definition as any. The idea of favours is particularly important. Implicit in the concept of *guanxi* is the expectation that, at some point in time, favours given will probably be returned. Nevertheless, *guanxi* is not some form of bank account where 'net favour indebtedness' can be measured. The whole system, *guanxiwang*, is a web of subtle, and not so subtle, intangible obligations or recognitions (not rights). Some businesspeople, especially younger ones, dismiss *guanxi* as old-fashioned, to be replaced by modern Western methods. That is unwise; the two will co-exist, and the newer concept may evolve into the older, with time. *Guanxi* is a comparatively new word, entering the vocabulary only in the twentieth century, but the practice goes back to antiquity. *Guan*, from which it derives, means a customs house, gate, or barrier. Thus, without *guanxi*, the door to business is firmly barred.

Westerners have difficulty with the concept of obligations or recognitions unmatched by rights. Conversely, the Chinese had no word for (and thus no concept of) 'rights' until they had to import *quan li*, via Japan, for Western translation purposes. Rights are rooted in law, and *guanxi* is rooted in Confucianism. In China, the individual is defined in part by his or her family and social context, as distinct from the Western view in which the individual defines his or her context.

Guanxi is not an accounting concept, but a description of feelings in which a very small favour may mean a lot, and a big one count for less. Feelings are not subject to double-entry bookkeeping. The concept is also pragmatic: if doing a favour, whether in reciprocation or not, can fit in with what one plans to do anyway, so much the better. But it may not be presented to the recipient in those terms! The important point is that business in China, however much influenced by Western theory and practice, can be expected to depend on relationships.

The Chinese classify *guanxi* capital (*ziben*) according to its efficacy (*ling*). The key features are:

* Durability (*naiyong*), meaning unconditionality. Thus the more certain you are that support will be reciprocated, the longer it can be deferred
* Hardness (*ying*) *guanxi* refers to the relative importance of the other party: the more senior the 'harder'
* Connectivity (*linghuo*) refers to the onward *guanxi* in relevant networks; however strong the relationship may be with someone who is a dead end, he or she is still a dead end.

The last idiom seems to live somewhere between consanguinity and the degree of obligation. The sub-components are 'endowed' (*tiansheng*) by birth, whether immediate family (*zhixi qinshu*) or father's relations (*nanfang*). The weaker non-birth varieties are seen as personal savings (*jilei*) which may be utilized (*laguolai*) for business. Feelings (*ganqing*) built up from shared experience accumulate: the longer (ideally since childhood), the better. Relationships formed within the family are, for the purpose of business, the weakest, and seen, to some extent, as instrumental (*liyong*), self-interest (*liyi*), and money (*jinqian*) *guanxi*.

Durability is similar perhaps to trust, and connectivity to identity (of interest). This shared identification is sometimes called the *guanxi* base. Each of us is an amalgam of nature (genes) and nurture (experience) and this last idiom directly mirrors that of *tianzi* and *ganqing*. It is interesting, but not surprising, that expatriate Chinese are more likely to deal with other expatriates originating from the same part of China.

It is important to note that not all *guanxi* relationships are equal, and two people having a *guanxi* relationship does not imply an absolute bond between them. Either or both may have still stronger *guanxi* relationships with others, perhaps depending on the degree of kinship, as noted above. *Guanxi* has been described as existing in concentric circles around each person. First there are *guanxi* relationships with members of one's own family and kin-group. These they describe as 'obligatory' relationships. Kinship means obligation, and this is the strongest form of *guanxi* because, in theory, you must perform any favour asked of you. The second, middle circle they term 'reciprocal' relationships. There are lasting, long-term relationships with old friends, classmates, close colleagues, and peers. People exchange favours here as a matter of course, but there is always a sense of balance; you must not ask too much of someone, or at least, not unless you are prepared to give an equal or greater amount back at a future date. The outer ring the authors term 'utilitarian' relationships. These relationships are with people one knows through association but perhaps not well. At the same time, they are not exactly strangers, and so if person A needs something, he or she might well think of approaching person B and asking for a favour. The favour might or might not be granted; there is no necessity for person B to do so. Nor will person B necessarily want the favour returned, though person A should be prepared for the request in any case.

Westerners have these relationships as well, of course, though they do not classify them. The family, the home, the office, the golf or sailing or cricket club, one's own village or neighbourhood, all contain people with whom we have relationships. Psychologists, sociologists, and historians tell us that Westerners have become less adept at recognizing and managing these relationships over time. For the vast majority, society and relationships give them their context, show them where they belong, and are used to help their personal and business ventures flourish. These are strong similarities with the Chinese system of relationships. The difference is that in China, it's impossible to get anywhere significant without good relationships, whether they are with other staff members, customers, or the local government.

These components need to be seen in a competitive environment in which they act on two levels: a strong enough relationship gains entry to the consideration set, and then the relative *guanxi* affects the probability of doing business. The bigger the risk, the stronger the *guanxi* will need to be. For example, tendering for large contracts in China is rarely the free-market auction that Westerners might normally expect. In part, the supplier may be determined by *guanxi*; only the terms of that business are determined by the tenders.

We are not alone in seeing *guanxi* as an alternative to contract law; no less a figure than Singapore's Lee Kuan Yew has made the same observation. One could argue that it is also a great deal cheaper, but the US (to take an example) and Chinese systems are not easily compared in financial terms.

Guanxi and business

For the Western manager coming to work in China, an understanding of *guanxi* is critical. It can also be a very difficult concept to understand, especially for someone coming from America, or another highly individualistic society. Academic research tells us that many Western businesspeople are bad at building and maintaining relationships. That means that in China, these managers will automatically start out with one hand tied behind their back. A good translation of *guanxi* is 'goodwill'. In that light, it is not so hard to understand. Goodwill exists everywhere. An American or British civil servant or bureaucrat will be more inclined to help someone whom he or she likes, or even went to school or university with. So it is in China, except that *guanxi* is more powerful in China than it is in Western societies.

Guanxi may be a substitute for, or reinforcement of, the institutional framework. It is this aspect of *guanxi* that most people think of, and to Western businesspeople it is often the aspect that is most apparent to them. For centuries and until recently, China has had what may be described as a 'weak institutional framework', and this fact probably accounts for the great importance of personal relationships in China. Central and local governments clearly played a key role in the economy, but there was no *coherent and consistent* body of laws and regulations. As the economy started to grow, and opportunities grew with it, entrepreneurs turned to building personal relationships with key government officials in order to further their projects, because local government officials were in a position to say which road and building could be built, which products could be sold, and even sometimes which products from outside the region (whether from China or from overseas) would be excluded, perhaps on grounds of 'safety', but in fact often in order to protect local producers. It was not just businesses that benefitted. Government departments and agencies, themselves floundering as they tried to bring about a new economic order, were grateful for these relationships too. A word in the right ear could see a vital new power plant or highway built, making the otherwise cumbersome tendering and approval processes little more than just a matter of formality.

Today the situation has changed, and the Chinese Government under Xi Jinping has adhered strongly to legal instruments to regulate the Chinese environment, rather than arbitrary and often under-the-table deals. Nevertheless, *guanxi* (or goodwill) with government and other Chinese business people, remains of primary importance for any businessperson, Western or Chinese. Observers are unanimous on this point: *guanxi* with government officials plays a much more critical role in business growth and profitability than does *guanxi* with other managers.

Guanxi *builds strong organizations*

Another point, which is often made, is that *guanxi* is the property of individuals, not organizations. Businesses do not have *guanxi*; the people within them do. The point is that unless the people within the business are prepared to use their *guanxi* on behalf of the business, nothing will happen. Therefore, the argument goes, it is necessary to build strong *guanxi* within the business as well as outside of it. Chinese businesses, except for very large ones, seldom have organizational flowcharts or diagrams showing who is responsible for what. And in those large organizations, particularly the old-fashioned state-owned enterprises (SOEs), the value of these flowcharts is questionable.

Things get done because people know, often at an unspoken, or even subconscious level, to whom to go. For example, if a purchasing order needs to be filled quickly, do not submit a memo to the head of purchasing, go instead to Ms Li the under-manager who was a classmate at university and who can be trusted to do the job as required. It might sound chaotic, and sometimes it is, but the evidence from Chinese businesses is that it works. Chinese managers, when they want something, are far more likely to pick up the phone (or send a message via WeChat) than write a memo or an email.

The role of *guanxi* in building goodwill and a strong, durable business in China cannot be overstated. Poor internal relationships can result in such problems as high staff turnover, difficulty in recruiting skilled staff, and so on. We shall discuss this further in Chapter 9.

There are more specific uses of *guanxi*, of course. Good *guanxi* with external partners, especially government, can give access to scarce resources: land, raw materials, distribution networks, markets, labour, money. Strong *guanxi* within the organization not only helps pull people together and enables leaders to function effectively but it also leads to shared knowledge and ideas. Again, it has been remarked in recent research that Chinese companies are much better at pooling ideas than are Western firms. There are clear benefits for innovation and R&D, for example. All these are strengths that a manager can use to advantage, provided she or he is willing to build *guanxi* in the first place.

Government

Since economic reform began in 1978, the government of China has consciously orchestrated legal and commercial changes so as to maximize China's economic interest, both domestically, and globally. Relaxation of rules on foreign ownership and investment, reforming state ownership, and liberalization of the economy and financial system generally are pragmatic tools. The government sees the free market as a means to its own ends, not as an ideological principle.

A good example of the role of the free market in China is the Chinese Government's action in 2020–21 to curb and moderate the Chinese real estate market. Since private ownership of property was permitted in 1997, the Chinese private and commercial real estate market has grown by leaps and bounds. Initially the super-fast growth of Chinese real estate after 2002/03 was to satisfy massive unmet demand. In 2010, about 75% of new apartments in China were bought by first-time Chinese buyers who previously had been renting their home. But as this huge household demand began to be satisfied and to moderate, developers continued building, and real estate became more an asset class for Chinese investors. Owning an apartment or two (or three) became the favourite investment vehicle of the Chinese newly rich, because (it was thought) the price of real estate would never fall. Indeed, prices continued to rise. Yields on private property fell to around 1%, a very low return on a global basis, indicating how overpriced Chinese property had become.

At last, Xi Jinping's government decided that the problem, which was obviously non-sustainable, had to be addressed. They considered that it was much better for the government to engineer a controlled property shakeout in China than for the shakeout to occur spontaneously and get out of control. They turned to a market-based solution to solve the problem. The first step was the issuing of new rules in 2020, called in China "The Three Red Lines", which limited the amount of debt that property developers could take on. The Three Red Lines are ratios of liabilities (ex-advanced proceeds) to total assets, net debt to equity, and cash to short-term debt. Step Two, implementing the rules, started early in 2021. Within six months, with massive inventories of unsold apartments, some developers, now cut off from their usual supply of bank credit, had started to suffer. At the time of writing (late-2021), none have gone bankrupt, but it is clear that the over the next year or two, the Chinese real estate sector will be substantially rearranged, and the number of developers will fall as some disappear, and others merge.

The point here is that, when faced with a huge and apparently insoluble problem, the Chinese Government turned to a market-based solution. They are able to implement it without the crash of the whole system because the government in China, not the Chinese market, is omnipotent, and about 75% of Chinese banking assets belong to Chinese banks owned by the government, making it possible for the Chinese Government to transfer money from one of its pockets to another, in a way which would be difficult or impossible in the United States or other Western economies. The Chinese Government likes to say that the market in China exists within a legal system set up and maintained by the government.

Beijing keeps a tight grip on the power to appoint, and remove, senior local officials. But this does not mean that local Chinese authorities have no freedom of action. Consequently, one of the principal rules of dealing with government in China is to recognize that several different departments at several different levels may have – or may believe they have – the right to interfere in your business. Furthermore, they may each be working to entirely different agendas. But the best starting point is always the local government, because it is there that your affairs will be monitored and where fruitful mutual understanding can be cultivated.

The paragraphs that follow, therefore, are tinged with envy rather than criticism. The PRC bureaucratic process works remarkably well, from their point of view. They invented the concept of mandarins, after all, and experienced centuries of managing the country with very few, but highly intelligent and well-trained civil servants.

Government in China has considerable powers. It can deny approval for proposed projects and can withdraw licences from existing ones. On a single day in 1996, the government of Tianjin withdrew licences for over a hundred joint ventures, for reasons ranging from disputes between partners, to lack of profitability. The central government has in recent years pushed hard for a 'small government' campaign, to trim proliferating approval and licensing requirements and to cut down on red tape and excessive discretion. How well this campaign will eventually fare has yet to be seen, while anecdotes of bureaucratic pushback have already been told around the dinner table.

The government also has great authority. As distinct from power, this means that the government in China often gets its own way without having to invoke its formal powers, by 'suggesting' that companies or individuals should pursue a certain course of action. This is very much in line with the Chinese avoidance of confrontation and preference for arriving at mutually agreed solutions. It is a form of politeness, because ultimately, the local Chinese Government's powers are extensive and they can almost always get their way. But usually, officials prefer to drop hints rather than issue edicts, especially if there is a good working relationship between local officials and the foreign business in question.

It follows that if you have good relationships with the relevant branches of government, you are more likely to get what you need, be it permission to build, develop, sell goods, set up a factory, form a joint venture, or whatever. Good relations with government can make the wheels of bureaucracy turn faster, even allowing you to 'jump the queue' and get approval more quickly than you might expect. Poor relationships or none at all, conversely, can put ventures at risk. One notorious example remains that of McDonald's in Beijing in the 1990s. Having been granted permission to establish a restaurant in a prime location on the south side of Tiananmen Square (ironically enough, almost opposite Mao's mausoleum), a few months later the company discovered the permission had been revoked and the site had been given to a Hong Kong-based developer. After three years of wrangling, McDonald's finally recovered the site. Less lucky was Starbucks, kicked out of its prime site inside the Forbidden City in Beijing amidst a rising tide of populist feeling that the presence of an American coffee bar was not appropriate in the middle of one of the landmarks of Chinese culture. Starbucks was told without ceremony to pack its bags.

Outside the PRC, Governments are also interventionist to some extent. Democracies like Taiwan have more restrictions on the powers of government and more give and take between government and business. In Singapore, Thailand, and Indonesia, on the other hand, government is every bit as omnipresent as in China.

Bureaucracy

China has a large bureaucracy, as befits a huge country which is centrally controlled in great detail, but the bureaucrats are usually well-trained, have much experience and, normally, are highly competent. Bureaucracy can intervene anywhere it wants, but China's economic benefit is a common reason for doing so. Decisions are intended to be made by consensus and the extent of lateral communication can be remarkable. Normally, the decision process begins with reports from subordinates, which are sent upwards to superiors. Decisions then come downwards from supervising authorities, after substantial consultation both up and down the hierarchy and across different functions and ministries. Individual responsibilities are not as clear as in the West but, since the goal is consensus, they do not need to be. There is much informal reporting, and personal relationships play a key role.

Every department or agency has its own area of responsibility, but frequently these areas overlap; and, since every department also jealously guards its own privileges and responsibilities (just like in the West), disputes are frequent. One Western firm trying to set up a plant in Lanzhou ultimately gave up in frustration after securing approval from Beijing, but then being persistently blocked by local government. To repeat: it is not enough to cultivate relationships with one level of government only; you need to attend to the local level of government just as much as the central or higher regional levels.

This problem used to be further compounded by the fact that bureaucrats held many different positions simultaneously, including some in the private sector. Today, largely as a result of Xi Jinping's reforms and anti-corruption drive, that has all changed. These days, it is unheard of for local officials to have more than one job. An official may certainly have many relationships with private interests, but, in today's China, he would not think of displaying multiple loyalties and interests. As in Western countries, like France, senior civil servants can be chief executives of major SOEs, then go on to positions of responsibility at government; and vice versa. Indeed, many SOE bosses tend to take a keen interest in senior government appointments; in particular, ones that carry with them authority, power, and influence.

As with civil servants the world over, taking the initiative is to be avoided. The aim is to reduce the in-tray by whatever means necessary, and react only when one has to. In fact, decisions get passed all around the organization – up, down, and sideways – but not for reasons of insecurity. Rather, the factor at work here is the Chinese dislike of confrontation. Any decision which could result in confrontation (with its possibility of loss of face) is bypassed; either it is handed on to someone else, or simply ignored. When faced with a problem, Westerners typically feel the urge to resolve it. Chinese bureaucrats do not. Indeed, forcing a Chinese person to make a decision where consensus cannot be achieved may put the latter under real personal stress. (For example, Chinese managers, especially those in state-owned firms, can be very reluctant to fire workers).

When working with government, it is useful to consider carefully the various interests involved, and reflect on how they interact and how this interaction leaves you, the supplicant. From this process it is often possible to determine a successful way of approaching the Chinese decision-makers and the people who influence them.

Beijing Air Catering Company

Beijing Air Catering Company (BACC), China's oldest foreign-funded joint venture, was set up in 1980 to provide in-flight meals for airlines flying out of Beijing International Airport. The company was founded by

Hong Kong businessman James Tak Wu and his daughter Annie who was commissioned to develop the business. It was prompted by the first flights from the USA (PanAm) following Deng Xiaoping's historic visit to the USA and memorandum of commercial cooperation.

It was a remarkably brave move for James Wu to put up US$2 million from his own pocket as a gamble without any approvals or agreements.[1] And it took Deng Xiaoping personally to give the approval only a month before the first flight. Annie Wu said later, "nothing is illegal and not everything is impossible". At the start, BACC serviced only three airlines, but a decade later this had grown to 20 clients. By then, its staff were preparing up to 12,000 meals a day on antiquated equipment with a theoretical capacity of 4,000.

In 1987, the company decided to embark on a second stage of development. The Chinese investor, the Beijing Management Department of the Civil Aviation Administration of China (CAAC), and its foreign partner, the Hong Kong Chinese Food Company, injected more capital to build a second production line which was supposed to be ready for the 11th Asian Games in Beijing in September 1990. Eighteen months after the games ended and despite more than 100 stamps of approval from various higher authorities, work had still not begun. Differences between the various government departments, including disputes over the complicated procedures required for the import of much-needed new equipment and other facilities, were the main reasons for the delay. The company was regulated not only by the Beijing Civil Aviation Administration but also by the Beijing Municipal Finance Department, Personnel Department, and several others.

Better analysis of the *guanxiwang* would have avoided many of these problems, but these were early days. The company has gone from strength to strength since then and, by 2011, Dr Annie Wu had become the Vice-Chairman or Managing Director of more than 15 joint venture air catering and services companies in the People's Republic of China.

Branches of government

At the top of the pyramid is the legislature, the National People's Congress (NPC), whose responsibilities include approval of national economic plans, state budgets, and state accounts. The NPC also makes national statutes of fundamental importance; these will be discussed in Chapter 5. The Standing Committee of the NPC interprets the Constitution and the laws, enacts national laws (when it comes to lawmaking authority, the line between the NPC and its Standing Committee is not clearly demarcated), and has the power to annul or change the decisions of lower organs.

In theory, the State Council, the executive body, which currently is chaired by Premier Li Keqiang, is subordinate to the NPC. In practice, like any executive group, and wide council, effective power rests with the State Council, which meets much more frequently than the NPC. The premier, his vice-premiers, and state councillors administer China through roughly 100 organizations under State Council supervision.

The courts, of which the highest is the Supreme People's Court, settle civil disputes, including commercial cases, and punish criminals. Chinese courts can also engage in judicial review of government Acts, though their abilities to do so are much restrained and have been underutilized by businesspeople. The notion of the separation of powers between the executive, legislative, and judiciary branches has been firmly and emphatically rejected by the Chinese leadership. The ideology here is close to one of parliamentary supremacy: the executive (the State Council) and the judiciary (the Supreme People's Court) are both created by the NPC (and its Standing Committee), and they are answerable to the NPC.

Provincial and municipal governments mirror the structure of the central government. The chain of command among government units has, as noted above, given rise to a Byzantine system of multiple reporting. For example, a major state-owned drug factory located in Shanghai might report to both the Shanghai State-owned Assets Supervision and Administration Commission (SASAC) – a unit of local government – and to the National Health and Family Planning Commission – part of central government in Beijing. Various other agencies – the local labour bureau, the local environmental bureau, and so on – would have a say in certain activities of the factory. Also important to consider in the relationship matrix are the industry associations and commissions (known as 'mothers') that sit above the immediate partners, and other authorities such as taxation departments, who are known as 'mothers-in-law'. "Too many mothers-in-law" is a frequent complaint by Chinese managers overwhelmed by bureaucracy.

However, Xi's government has reorganized and strengthened market regulation in China. In 2018, three regulatory agencies, which each covered different areas of the market, were merged into one, called the State Administration for Market Regulation (SAML). In February 2021, SAML issued an announcement stating that it would "stop monopolistic behaviour in the platform economy, and protect fair competition in the market". It followed this up in October 2021 by elevating the anti-trust department of SAML to vice-ministerial status. The Chinese Government has made it clear that no company, however large and profitable, will be allowed to dominate Chinese society in the way that Google, Amazon, and Facebook have dominated in the West.

Of course in China, government is not only active as a regulator; it is also an active player, owning and controlling hundreds of thousands of businesses. One result of the reform programme has been to relax control over individual businesses in certain sectors, either by assigning a greater measure of autonomy to their managers or by encouraging private capital to invest.

But in some sectors and regions, government has held onto, even consolidated its control. The state owns and controls enterprises which are considered fundamental to the country's operation. These include utilities (China Telecom, China Mobile, China Nuclear, and many others); banks (Bank of China, ICBC); builders of ships and aeroplanes; car companies and so on. 'Privatization' has never really existed in China; instead, in certain sectors, like autos, and especially e-commerce and social media, it is private companies started and run by Chinese entrepreneurs who have taken up the running from the state-owned sector. China's economy really is a 'mixed economy', with enormous state-owned companies dominating many traditional sectors, and often very dynamic privately owned companies (all started within the last 20 or so years) which have led the way in other fields. In some sectors like real estate, state-owned companies (for example, China Resources Land, China Overseas Land) compete head-on with privately owned developers. The same is true in the auto industry, where the Shanghai government is a powerful player via its joint ventures with Volkswagen and General Motors, as well as through its wholly owned operations which produce the Rewe (China's very successful version of Britain's Rover, acquired from its British owner and shipped to China). At the same time, Geely Auto, a wholly private Chinese company based in Hangzhou (whose parent company acquired Volvo of Sweden in 2009) occupies about 5% of the Chinese auto market, the world's largest auto market by far. Another private Chinese company, BYD is a world leader in automotive electric battery development.

Although government is less involved in running businesses, it is still very much involved in ownership; not only centrally, as in the case of the much discussed and much debated – in the discourse of 'state capitalism' – national champions: mega state-owned firms supported by government to compete globally for markets and influence, but also locally through local government-controlled firms. As for those enterprises under collective ownership, there is no clear separation between state and private ownership, with many hybrid forms in between. Change is constant and ongoing, but does always point in the same direction; the government is quite capable of backtracking and reasserting control over sectors that are regarded as strategically important for its ruling of the economy. In recent years, the Xi Jinping administration has underlined its authority in certain sectors that it considers important, either because of strategic significance (like aerospace or shipbuilding), or because it wishes to correct apparent social ills, like the private tutoring of Chinese children for the famous *gaokao* (an exam taken by all Chinese 18-year-olds to qualify for university).

Understanding the direction and purpose of Chinese regulation requires a foreigner to be in touch with Chinese officials, as well as conversant with and understanding of the aims of Chinese Government policy. Between 1980 and 2020, the government's economic policy aimed mainly at GDP growth, with first exports, then urbanization, and infrastructure building as the main channels for achieving this. As the building mania spread from Shanghai and Beijing throughout China, annual economic growth rates in excess of 10%

were seen for a time in the early part of the new 2000 millennium. Today, however, Chinese GDP growth has been replaced as the main objective by the levelling-up of society, with the development of private consumption as the main channel for achieving general prosperity, spreading out from the cities into China's countryside where, prior to 2020, many Chinese hardly saw any benefit from the earlier years of rapid growth.

Within this overarching policy goal, local governments in China have considerable discretion, and some municipal and provincial authorities can be very strong-minded and take their own approaches to business. Shanghai has a reputation for being co-operative and helpful, Guangdong may be less helpful but is more easy-going, and Beijing municipality tends to be bureaucratic and insists on the letter of the regulation being adhered to. However, there are plenty of exceptions in these three centres, and plenty of other variations in other provinces and cities. Much depends on the attitudes of local government, which can range from old-style Marxist (still to be found in parts of the west of China and Manchuria, for example), to go-ahead neo-capitalist (more common in the east in provinces like Zhejiang, near Shanghai).

The Communist Party

The best guide to the Chinese Communist Party is a book published in 2010 called *The Party: The Secret World of China's Rulers*, written by Richard McGregor, a long-time correspondent for the *Financial Times* in China, and latterly its bureau chief in Beijing. McGregor explains clearly and insightfully how the Party controls China, and itself. China's president carries the twin title of the General Secretary of the Chinese Communist Party. The ruling group is called the Politburo Standing Committee, consisting of (currently) seven men who have spent their adult lives in the Party and who all operate significant networks of influence inside the Party. These men are all immensely powerful, and usually come from the main cities of China, especially Shanghai and Beijing. They control the 25-man Politburo, and the Politburo controls the Central Committee which consists of about 370 members. The Party extends its tentacles throughout China via 31 provincial committees, 665 city committees, 2,500 county committees, 41,600 township committees and 780,000 village committees, all supported by the most extensive system of surveillance to be found anywhere in the world. Wherever you go in China, you are in range of a surveillance camera, unless you are on a mountain or well out in the fields. Hotels are always covered by internal cameras and there may also be listening devices, so conversations which are private and confidential should be made out in the open air or in a car.

Around 2010, as the economy grew, and many Chinese became wealthy, the belief emerged amongst many Chinese that the Chinese Communist Party was about to become a relic of history. The Party, always sensitive to its perception by the Chinese people, developed a strong sense of paranoia when it started intercepting and reading private conversations between Chinese citizens on Chinese social media – usually WeChat, operated by the Chinese private company Tencent. Ordinary Chinese people, unaware that their social media chats were being monitored, described the Party as lazy and corrupt. Many expressed a desire to replace the Party with something different – perhaps even a different system, which looked more to the Western tradition than to the Chinese one.

This anti-Party feeling came to a head with the murder in 2012 of an English assistant of the wife of a senior Party official, Bo Xilai. Bo was at that time Communist Party Secretary of Chongqing, with the pedigree, track record, and popular support to rival Xi Jinping for the position of China's next president. Normally, this kind of scandal would have been hushed up by the Party apparatus. But in this case, because an Englishman was murdered, foreign newspapers were able to uncover most of the lurid details, including the Englishman's poisoning in a hotel outside Chongqing for fear that he would make public the massive corruption which Bo Xilai's wife Gu Kailai had been orchestrating. Additional juicy newspaper copy was provided by another dramatic, related event: a car chase and helicopter flight by Bo Xilai's police chief Wang Lijun from the rooftop of a hotel to escape to Beijing from policemen sent by Bo Xilai to ensure his silence.

So in 2012, Bo Xilai did not become President of China, but Xi Jinping (also the son of a former senior Party official) did. Xi immediately addressed the corruption issue, by adding real teeth to the anti-corruption drive, and boosting his own position by focusing the anti-corruption police onto many senior officials within the Party. Most observers thought at the time that Xi's new anti-corruption drive would go the way of its predecessors and fizzle out after a few months, but it did not, and within a year or two, thousands of Party officials found themselves serving long jail sentences for corruption, a few even executed for particularly egregious crimes. As his rivals and enemies disappeared into prison, or were silenced in other ways, Xi's personal power increased.

Today, Xi Jinping controls the Party completely. His description as China's most powerful leader since Mao is not an exaggeration. Xi has used his powerful position to overhaul the Party structure, and reinforce the Party's grip on Chinese society. At the Party's Sixth Plenum in November 2021, a resolution was passed confirming Xi Jinping's ideas as "Marxism for the 21st Century", representing "the essence of Chinese culture and China's spirit". There were only two previous resolutions of this kind since the Party came to power: one in 1945, which anointed Mao as leader of China; and the other in 1981, which was an attempt to brush away the memory of Mao's Cultural Revolution by apologizing for "Mao's mistakes". So it can be seen that Xi Jinping has truly cemented his position at the top of the Chinese system, and it appears, at the time of writing, that he will remain in charge at the top for some time to come.

Xi faces the stern task of restructuring the Chinese economy and spreading prosperity wider. He sees his main tool for this task as the Party, controlling a system in which private enterprises, both Chinese and foreign, operate successfully and profitably in China to provide growth and new employment. Xi is not out to destroy private enterprise in China, but he is determined to make it operate lawfully and in a way which brings social as well as economic benefit to Chinese society. That is why it is critical for any foreign company entering or operating in China to develop close working relations with the local government, meaning the Chinese Communist Party.

Traditionally, the Party has an important role in the workplace, with enterprises managed by a triumvirate of the commercial manager, the senior trade union official and the senior Party official. The Party official is the top decision-maker. For state-owned firms, the presence of the Party organization is mandatory. A well-established practice in the state sector is a fusion of the two top roles – the manager role and the Party role – into one. So, the chairman of an SOE would also concurrently act as Party Secretary of his/her firm. In state-controlled companies (many of which are listed on a stock exchange and have minority stakes which are owned by public shareholders, for example, China Telecom, Beijing Enterprises, and Shanghai Industrial), in universities, and other public institutions, the Party Committee, in practice, also serves as the ultimate decision-making body, leaving the shareholders' meeting and the board of directors, the nominal decision-makers, with only a rubber-stamp role.

Why do Chinese join the Party? Some join because they believe in it and they see a Party career as a vocation; others join less out of a sense of ideological commitment than out of a desire to gain access to privileges and take advantage of the enormous networking opportunities. Party officials enjoy power and privilege, but in return, are expected to work competently and honestly, as well as be loyal. As networks go, the Party is excellent, with access to key players at every level of government and industry. Outsiders should consider these advantages as well; establishing contacts within the Party can mean opportunities to get around bureaucratic roadblocks and evolving and executing a strategy which makes sense both to China and to the foreign company. Today, the Party should be seen as an elite club, created as much by its ability to select the most talented applicants from each generation as by ideology. In 2012, I was very surprised to find out from my undergraduate class at Peking University that about half of them planned to join the Chinese Government as officials when they graduated.

The army

The army's commercial involvement has waxed and waned since its glory days of the mid-1980s when Deng encouraged the People's Liberation Army (PLA) to move into commerce, initially defence sales, to offset the 25% (one million personnel) cutback in the armed forces. The military was people heavy, cash light. Furthermore the top brass and their relatives were able to exploit their relationships with senior military buyers in other countries. Senior officers became businessmen and increasingly became involved in shady and highly profitable activities such as drug smuggling.

In July 1998, Jiang Zemin 'directed the armed forces to completely shun all their business operations'. The PLA was seen as being distracted by commercial matters and corruption from readiness. A separate source of income could decrease loyalty to the Party. The PLA's enterprises were passed over to private companies operated by former senior officers. Procurement was changed from a system in which the PLA owned its supply channels to a Western style contracting arrangement. Splitting the PLA from commerce was claimed to be mostly complete by 2000, facilitated by senior officers, with their families being rewarded by the outplaced businesses.

However, many officers were still left with business connections and opportunities to acquire wealth. In 2015, Xi Jinping turned his anti-corruption drive onto the PLA. Several senior generals and many more junior officers were convicted of corruption, including two former vice-chairmen of the Central Military Commission. The military was ordered in March 2016 to put an end within a three-year phase-out period to all of its remaining commercial services, such as military-run hospitals, and hotels open to the public. Xi Jinping's aggressive posture overseas with respect to the South China Sea, and to Taiwan, has placed a heavy demand on the military capability of the Chinese armed services to fight effectively. Huge investment in training, weapons, ships, aircraft, and military vehicles has transformed the PLA into the world's largest and one of the world's most formidable fighting units.

Commercial relationships

The opening section describing *guanxi* may have seemed intimidating but in fact, is quite normal. We all develop relations based on goodwill throughout our lives, and we all have our *guanxiwang* (a network of relationships) with key business contacts. Business associates within a network are referred to as being *zi jia ren* (one's own family). In a Confucian society, *guanxi* represents a natural blurring of the line between the professional and the personal. In China (and in the rest of Asia), business is personal.

Guanxi, or networking based on personal relationships, is a powerful social force in all Chinese cultures. People's sense of themselves, their self-perception, and their self-worth, is determined mostly by their relationships with others. It is important not to confuse *guanxi* with the 'groupist' traits noted in Japanese society. Chinese do not identify solely or even primarily with the group to which they belong; the self is, and always has been, a very important concept. The distinction is subtle, but there is a difference between the individual defining the network (USA) and the individual being defined by the network (China). The Chinese are both individualist *and* group oriented, and the relationships between group and individual are complex and deep rooted. Thus personal (and business) relationships are always formed on two levels; with the person both as an individual and as a member of a reference group.

So important is *guanxi* that some used to maintain that you could not get anything done in China without it, even simple things like buying a train ticket. That is no longer true, but in a commercial sense at least, establishing *guanxi* with partners, suppliers, and even customers is an essential prerequisite. Virtually every major success story involving foreign companies in China involves the building of a widespread network before proceeding with business. Companies like IBM China and Shanghai Volkswagen have devoted literally years to this process.

Getting on the inside has been, and remains, Asea Brown Boveri's (ABB) corporate strategy. The Swiss–Swedish power engineering giant is seeing its payoff. The company was part of the consortium for the 1,980 MW Shajiao C coal-fired power station in the Pearl River delta and provided the steam turbine and plant in the US$34.5 million Fushun power plant in China's northeastern Liaoning province. ABB's business strategy aimed for solid vertical penetration, each step increasing its understanding of, and interdependence with, the China market.

Becoming an 'insider' required ABB to:

1   Enter first as a technology seller; China most wants foreign investment and technology
2   Licence and transfer technology
3   Build market understanding and sales by opening representative offices and entering pilot joint ventures
4   Establish a network joint venture that would absorb the representative offices.

The Chinese corporate reform of 2020, effective 2025, aims to remove the need for these kinds of special tactics in China, by placing foreign companies on the same legal basis as Chinese ones. Without doubt, this reform will make a difference, but personal relationships in Chinese business will not suddenly become less important. *Guanxi* takes time to develop. Relationships, once created, are hard to break; the obligations you accept when you enter into *guanxi* are not easily avoided. Most Chinese are therefore cautious and proceed gradually step by step. The first steps in relationship building, however small, are critical: as one Chinese friend says, "a satisfied beginning is equal to half the success".

On the whole, Westerners have tended to be suspicious of *guanxi*. We like to think that in our societies, everything is done openly and fairly and everyone has access to the same opportunities and the same information. Indeed, we tend to regard instances where people do favours for friends in business as bordering on corruption, if not actually stepping over the line. The equation of *guanxi* with corruption is common. In China, state employees earn relatively little and can exert a great deal of power over private concerns. Small salaries but large fringe benefits (such as housing) encourage them to stay in their posts but to earn cash on the side.

But it is important to be clear that engaging in bribery (or grease payments, or whatever the name it goes under) is not only illegal in China but not sustainable, and is not true *guanxi*. Many foreign companies have discovered that in China, it is possible to create solid personal relationships with local government officials, customers, suppliers, and Chinese partners without any money passing under the table.

Conclusions

Government, the law, and *guanxi* all interweave and are difficult to separate. No one 'connection', however good, is adequate. In cultivating multiple connections, we have to remind ourselves that they are reciprocal: favours received are credits against future favours expected. Be cautious about the favours you accept.

To the Chinese and others in the Pacific region, cultivating and using relationships is second nature, a natural part of the environment and doing business. Western business culture is different to the Chinese or Asian business culture. Trying to apply Western business culture in China is usually a path to failure. Approach Chinese society with humility. Be ready to appreciate and learn, by watching, listening, and participating, and build your networks carefully and patiently.

Note

1 Address to the 10th HK Forum by Dr Annie Wu, Managing Director, Hongkong Beijing Air Catering Ltd (March 2011).

Bibliography

Bucknall, K. (2002) *Chinese Business Etiquette and Culture*, Raleigh, NC: Boson Books.

5   Business and the law

Contributed by Chao Xi, Professor and Outstanding Fellow of the
Faculty of Law at the Chinese University of Hong Kong, China

> Over the past quarter century, the PRC has been engaged in the most
> concerted program of legal construction in world history.
> (William Alford, testimony before the US Congressional-Executive
> Commission on the People's Republic of China, 2002).[1]

Fifty-five years ago, at the height of the Cultural Revolution, the *People's
Daily*,[2] the mouthpiece of the Chinese Communist Party, published an edito-
rial tellingly entitled "In Praise of Lawlessness", denouncing law as the pro-
tector of bourgeois social order. In that decade of political turmoil, laws were
replaced by Party policies and ideologies and, sometimes, by Mao's words.
Courts were sidelined, and lawyers were outlawed. China has since emerged
as a global economic power but the impression that it has hopelessly been
trapped in a state of 'lawlessness' seems to have remained with many
Westerners, still influenced by what they have seen and heard in the media
about the Cultural Revolution or rampant copyright piracy.

This impression clearly is a myth, one among many myths about the modern legal system in the Middle Kingdom. As Steven Dickinson rightly cau-
tions in the November 2007 issue of *Business Week*,[3] these myths can lead
businesspeople to make costly mistakes when doing business in China. The
hard truth is: the Chinese business and commercial law regime has been
evolving and it has developed a level of sophistication and maturity. To put it
bluntly, it would be naïve to assume that Western businesses can count com-
fortably on *guanxi* alone to navigate the sometimes stunningly complex web
of laws and regulations that apply to them. Choosing to ignore and disregard
these legal rules will cost them dearly.

In this chapter, I cast the limelight on certain key aspects of the Chinese
legal and institutional infrastructure that distinguish it from the all-familiar
legal systems in the West. The question in mind is always how these features
might bear on business formation and operation in China. I begin by looking at lawmaking. National and local lawmakers have in front of them ambitious legislative agendas. In a normal year, the National People's Congress
and its Standing Committee, China's top legislative body, makes and amends
dozens of national statutes; local legislators annually produce local regulations and rules in the rank of hundreds. This lawmaking activism is

DOI: 10.4324/9781003241164-6

transforming the Chinese legal system in favour of modernity, if not Westernization. The downside of it is that it also leads to conflicts between pieces of legislation, creating difficulties for Western (and Chinese) business-people seeking to determine which particular conflicting law applies to them. The answer is that, unfortunately, even Chinese judges do not always have a ready answer. This is a message gleaned from a high-profile court case, as we will highlight below. In theory, when two laws conflict, the superior law prevails. But the inferior law could remain valid and still affect investors even though it does not, in theory, bind them.

Confucianism has a strong preference for the resolution of disputes through mediation, with litigation being the last resort. Like its East Asian neighbour countries (Japan and South Korea), the Chinese society is not immune from an explosion of litigation in recent years. In 2021, Chinese courts accepted and handled a gigantic body of cases (over 33 million). The court has emerged as a primary forum for resolving commercial disputes. Chinese courts are not best known, however, for their independence, impartiality, and neutrality; tales of judicial bias (and corruption) are exchanged at the dinner table. Foreign investors should understand the alternatives. They can use the court system, which might seem more familiar but is susceptible to potential problems (for both sides, of course); or they can go down the more traditional (in Chinese eyes) route of mediation which, although may seem more unfamiliar, probably offers the better chance of a soft landing; alternatively, they can try arbitration which itself is still on thin ice when it comes to enforcement of the arbitral awards. This chapter discusses these options.

With this evolutionary process in mind, this chapter looks at the following:

• Lawmaking and the legislative process
• Courts and judges – who are they and how are they appointed?
• Lawyers and the rise of the legal profession
• Contracts and contract law
• Arbitration and mediation as ways of resolving disputes
• Intellectual property.

Lawmaking

One would be surprised at the great number of legislative bodies that have been granted formal lawmaking authority; they exist in the order of hundreds in China and in a hierarchy of four levels. The National People's Congress (NPC) is China's highest legislative body and is situated at the top of the hierarchy. The NPC and its Standing Committee are vested with the power to enact, amend, and interpret the Constitution (yes, China does have a Constitution!) and national laws. The State Council, China's Cabinet, is the next highest authority in lawmaking, and it makes the so-called 'administrative regulations' that also apply nationally but with a lower legislative status than national laws (and certainly the Constitution). The third level in the hierarchy consists of the people's congresses of the 23 provinces, five autonomous regions, and four municipalities directly under central government, as well as close to 300 major cities (local legislatures), and their standing committees. The so-called 'local regulations' with jurisdiction are confined to their respective administrative boundaries. At the bottom of the hierarchy are the departments, ministries, and commissions of the State Council, which make 'ministerial rules' that apply nationally, as well as the governments of provinces and major cities, which make 'local administrative rules' which only apply locally.

For readers who are already lost in this complex, formal legislative hierarchy, be prepared for a shock: many of the local Chinese governmental bodies that grant various licences to businesses and regulate their operation – for example, departments of provincial and city governments – are simply outside of the legislative hierarchy as described in the preceding paragraph, and thus do not have any formal lawmaking authority. They do, however, issue rules, and they do so often. These rules are referred to as 'normative documents' which are, in theory, not legally binding, and Chinese courts are not supposed to enforce them. That these rules do not have a formal place in China's formal legislative system does not, however, mean that they do not matter to businesses, and that they can be discarded as something of irrelevance. To be blunt, never assume that they do not affect the operation of businesses. Investors may well run into trouble with a government agency if they choose to disregard the non-legally binding rules it makes. Thus investors are advised to, at least, show a measure of deference to them.

Those Chinese national and local legislatures with the formal authority to enact law, which exist in the rank of hundreds, have in recent times created a huge body of legislation, covering virtually every area of business and personal life in this civilization which historically showed a strong apathy with respect to formal legal order. By the end of 2011, the NPC and its Standing Committee had made 200 national laws and decisions on law, the State Council had made 706 administrative regulations, while 31 provinces, autonomous regions, and municipalities under central government had made over 8,600 regulations and rules.[4] The body of national and local legislation has continued to expand since. In 2021, close to 2,000 pieces of legislation were enacted. Remember that as recently as 1979, when China reopened itself to the global economic order, there was virtually no national legislation in the country. Creating a legal system with a measure of sophistication within such a short spell of time is nothing short of a miracle. Thus, Professor William Alford at the Harvard Law School once told the US Senate that "the PRC has been engaged in the most concerted program of legal construction in world history".

The Chinese legislative system is, however, seen by critics as a victim of its success; many of these newly made laws are not always consistent and coherent.[5] This problem needs first to be understood in light of a key feature of

Chinese lawmaking: a high level of generality and abstractness. Like EU Directives, national laws enacted by the NPC and its Standing Committee are characteristically general, broadly drafted, and sometimes vague and ambiguous. Lacking legislative competence and capacity might well be a contributing factor; it also might well be a legislative strategy though – to accommodate the, sometimes stunning, discrepancies in regional social and economic conditions. The one-size-fits-all approach simply does not work for an economy in transition; as the argument goes, a good degree of flexibility is a virtue in lawmaking.

Thus, before any general, abstract statutory provisions can be properly enforced, they often need to be supplemented by more specific regulations and rules that adapt the statements of general principle in the national laws to suit local conditions. This business of legislative adaptation is the ball game for local legislatures. It can, and it does, give the local authorities the ability to interpret and implement laws in a way that best advances local interests – sometimes to the extent of contradicting the laws themselves. If local authorities don't like new laws handed down from on high, they might well find ways to twist them to suit their own agendas. Examples of contradiction and inconsistency in law are abundant. For example, the *New York Times* on 28 November 2005 reported a high-profile case (the "Seed Case") in which the local court found that a provincial seed regulation conflicted with the national Seed Law.[6]

The central authorities are not unaware of this problem. They have made various attempts to resolve inconsistencies between different pieces of legislation – with the 2000 Legislation Law (which underwent a major overhaul in 2015) being a milestone – but with limited success. The Seed Case highlights the need for further reforms. In this case, the local court held that the provincial seed regulation was 'spontaneously invalid' because it contradicted the national Seed Law. This decision, however, almost cost the responsible judge her position when the local legislature condemned her for overstepping the court's authority. Under Chinese law, judges do not have the power to review the legality and, where appropriate, declare provincial regulations invalid; such power rests with the Standing Committee of the NPC (NPCSC). It was not until recently that the NPCSC started to lay down formal procedures (many feel these are excessively onerous), and build up institutional capacity to review inconsistent legislation. The NPCSC had in recent years identified thousands of regulations and rules to be in conflict with national legislation, but only a small percentage of these had been annulled or amended. Lacking the power to judicially review legislation, Chinese courts have worked out their own solution, one that is characteristically pragmatic: they apply the superior law and refrain from touching the inferior law that conflicts with it. This solution is problematic for investors, as the inferior law remains intact and can continue to bear on businesses until they are amended.

Inaccessibility to laws is another issue that has concerned foreign investors. This concern has to a large extent been alleviated with respect to trade-related laws. As part of China's WTO accession protocol, China has committed to make public all trade-related laws, regulations and measures, and enforce only those laws that have actually been published. Most trade-related laws and regulations are now published in the *China Foreign Trade and Economic Cooperation Gazette*. Some have been translated into English and are available at www.fdi.gov.cn. Anecdotal evidence suggests, however, that there still exist some 'internal' regulations, whose contents and even whose existence may not be divulged to foreigners.

Overall it is perhaps unsurprising that so many laws conflict with each other and that sometimes laws, once enacted, need to be changed; this happens in the West as well. In Britain and elsewhere, however, there are established procedures for doing these things. In China, hasty lawmaking by inexperienced lawmakers sometimes leads to problems, and mechanisms and institutions that have been put in place have yet to offer effective solutions.[7]

Courts and judges

Chinese judges serve at one of the four levels of courts in China: the Supreme People's Court (SPC) at the central level, the Higher People's Courts at the provincial level, and the Intermediate People's Courts and the Basic People's Courts at the local level.

In many common law jurisdictions, judges are chosen from lawyers who have had distinguished careers as private practitioners. By contrast, Chinese judges are, like their German and French colleagues, almost invariably career civil servants who expect to rise through the ranks by diligent effort in their job. The overall level of competence of the Chinese judiciary was once startlingly low. Until 1995 – when China enacted its first law on judges – there were virtually no requirements or qualifications to be a judge. Judges were often drawn from the ranks of military officers who had received little legal education and tended to be more loyal to the state. In 2001, China amended the law to impose higher standards for judges. Now, newly appointed judges must be in possession of at least a bachelor's degree, plus at least five years of experience in law. In addition, they must pass a unified national legal qualification examination (with a pass rate as low as 10% in some years). Recently, the percentage of judges with a bachelor's degree rose from 6.9% in 1995 to a comfortable 90% plus across China. The percentage is generally higher in the court divisions that handle commercial disputes and in economically more developed regions. Training for sitting judges is also moving up China's legal reform agenda. All judges are required to undergo regular training, and many have done so in leading law schools in the West.

Public access to Chinese court decisions was traditionally limited and patchy, and varied greatly both across the country and at different levels of court. So, for a long period of time, the Chinese courts were enveloped in tales, myths, and stereotypes. The Chinese judiciary and its processes had long been seen by litigants, the general public, and even learned observers as something of a 'black box'. China Judgments Online (CJO; wenshu.court. gov.cn), a recent SPC-orchestrated initiative, promises to make improvements on transparency. The full-text open-access database makes a large volume of Chinese court judgments and rulings (over 130 million by February 2022) freely accessible online. But CJO does not intend to present a full picture; court cases are uploaded selectively and it has been suggested that only around 60% of the Chinese court judgments rendered have eventually made their way to the CJO database.[8]

While the Chinese authorities are encouraging the development of more professional and competent judges, the notion of 'Western-style' judicial independence has been firmly and emphatically rejected. The Chinese judiciary is not intended to be an independent branch of government. Judicial independence, though recognized by the PRC Constitution, is limited, both in law and in practice. Three particular sources of external influence could bear on the court's decision-making. Constitutionally, courts are responsible to the people's congresses (legislature) that create them. Politically, and more importantly, courts are subject to the influence and control of the Party. Courts are also financially dependent on local governments for funding, though recent reforms have helped to reduce this reliance. In commercial cases, undue influence of these sources can be overwhelming, in particular, when key local interests are at stake. Courts may be pressured into making a decision that unfairly favours the local parties.

Lawyers

As the Chinese legal system matures, law is playing an increasingly important role in the planning and execution of business transactions. As a result, for almost every aspect of their business ranging from contracting to day-to-day operations to dispute resolution, foreign investors will need professional legal services on an ongoing basis. And this is so even if their *guanxi* with the authorities is strong; local governments themselves now turn, from time to time, to lawyers for help. Some 30 years ago, it might have been difficult to find a Chinese lawyer who could communicate in English at a professional level. This is no longer a problem; indeed the problem is the other way around. Many younger-generation Chinese lawyers are fluent in English and, annoyingly, almost every Chinese lawyer who speaks English claims expertise in foreign investment issues. Then how to find a good lawyer who can deliver results in a manner that foreign investors rightfully expect?

Many investors find it more comfortable to work with representative offices opened by international law firms in China, because these offices generally have a deeper understanding of foreign clients' needs and interests than many other peer Chinese law firms do. By 2020, some 300 such offices had been authorized to operate in China, and there is a concentration of their presence in Beijing and Shanghai. Professional services rendered by these offices are not inexpensive, though many believe they offer value for money. Some offices are willing to lower their fees for new clients, hoping to generate repeat business. Foreign investors who are handed a (large) legal bill by those offices for their advice on PRC law may be surprised to know that, under Chinese law, these foreign law firms are actually prohibited from providing legal opinions on PRC law. Yet, people on the ground report that many foreign offices do not precisely follow the law in this respect. They routinely provide clients with advice on Chinese law behind the veil of a disclaimer, which might read:

> Please note that we are a foreign law firm registered with the Ministry of Justice of the People's Republic of China. Under current Chinese regulations, we are allowed to provide information concerning the effects of the Chinese legal environment, but we are not authorized to practice Chinese law or to render legal opinions in respect of Chinese law.

It was rumoured at some point in 2006 that the Chinese authorities were going to crack down on some foreign offices because of their unauthorized practice of Chinese law. The feared crackdown has not as yet happened.

There are a handful of top-tier Chinese domestic firms (commonly known as 'Red Circle' firms) that have been able to compete head-to-head with foreign law offices for lucrative foreign investment business. Their profound local knowledge, combined with their closer ties with Chinese regulatory authorities, tend to give them a competitive edge. Sometimes they are able to deliver results in a way that is envied by their foreign competitors. Senior lawyers in these firms typically have extensive experience in serving foreign clients, and they tend to know their foreign clients well enough. The rates of these lawyers, however, may not be significantly lower than their counterparts in the leading foreign law offices operating in China. More recently, liberalization of the PRC legal profession has enabled leading domestic firms to internationalize and partner with peer international firms. A prime example is the merger of King & Wood (a leading PRC firm), Mallesons (a leading Australian firm), and SJ Berwin (a leading UK firm) to form King & Wood Mallesons. How well these 'joint venture' firms will fare in the cut-throat competition with their domestic and international rivals remains everyone's guess. Some commercial publications, such as Legal 500's *Asia Pacific Legal 500*, and Chambers & Partners' *Chambers Asia* provide some useful guidance on leading firms and lawyers, both foreign and domestic, who practise in various areas of law in China.

Top law firms and high-flying lawyers come at a cost, sometimes very significant. If a deal is smaller in size or less sophisticated in nature, then it can be more cost effective to use smaller but boutique local firms. Some regional law firms have developed extensive connections with local regulatory authorities and can obtain the necessary approval or licence in a matter of days, rather than weeks or months. Many of these firms are now associated, formally or informally, with foreign firms that do not yet have a physical presence (via a representative office) in China. Foreign investors can check with the lawyers they use in their home countries if they have any associated Chinese local firms to which they can be referred. They could also consult international networks of law firms – for example, Advoc (www.advoc.org) and Lawyers Associated Worldwide (www.lawyersworldwide.com) – for information.

Investors from the Commonwealth jurisdictions will be interested to know that there is no formal divide between barristers and solicitors. Lawyers are licensed to engage in both litigation and non-litigation business. The English 'loser pays costs' system that makes the losing party in the litigation pay some or all of the winning party's legal expenses does not exist in China. Chinese courts generally leave each side responsible for its own lawyers' fees, regardless of who wins. Contingency fee arrangements have operated in China for many years. Chinese lawyers charge clients on a 'speculative' basis in a growing variety of cases, ranging from industrial injury compensation to recovery of non-performing bank loans. The range of the contingency fee percentage is reportedly from 10–40% of the recovery, though a State Council regulation promulgated in 2006 set a cap of 30%, and in certain areas has banned the use of no-win-no-pay.[9]

Contracts

Contracts have a different place in Chinese negotiations. In the West, it is not unknown to begin with draft contracts and use them as working documents until agreement is reached. China is becoming acquainted with Western ways, but historically such a move would have seemed like bad faith. Other countries in the region, with longer exposure to the West, tend to be more attuned to the needs of Western businesses.

Contracts should be drafted in Chinese as well as the language of the foreign investor, ensuring of course that they are identical in all material respects. Some 'China hands' recommend having important documents translated twice by independent translators, and then comparing the two versions. Back-translation is also recommended: translate an English document into Chinese, then ask a second translator to translate from Chinese back into English and look for discrepancies. Checking translations is vital to ensure that the wording of the contract is unambiguous, unless ambiguity is what both parties have intended. Anecdotally, one European firm found itself committed to a technology transfer deal whereby the Chinese partner was not obliged to pay any royalties until they were capable of producing a 'first-class product'. Needless to say, they never did so; but they did manage to produce and sell profitably a great deal of 'second-class products' without paying a penny to the technology supplier.

Under Chinese law, contracts that must be approved by Chinese government authorities in order to take effect do not become legally binding upon signature, but only when the necessary approval is secured (this is standard procedure in the West too). Central government ministries and subordinate provincial or municipal agencies are responsible for issuing approvals. The level of approval depends on the amount of investment involved and the nature of the project. China's new investment law regime has embraced the notion of 'negative list' – a regulatory arrangement that eliminates, for many industries and sectors, much of the need for foreign investors to seek governmental approval in order to set up businesses.

Having the business set up is only the beginning of a long process. Separate applications must be made to the tax authorities, foreign exchange authorities, customs administration, and perhaps more importantly, the sector regulators. Furthermore, the consent and active support of local authorities must be obtained for a host of matters under local jurisdiction such as assuring the supply of utilities, materials and labour, the plans and costs for the construction of buildings, and compliance with environmental regulations. Consultants advise that, when possible, these approvals and commitments should, ideally, have been ensured before signing the contract; failing that, make the contract conditional on their satisfactory resolution.

Arbitration and mediation

Mediation and arbitration are not the same thing. Mediation, seen in the Chinese tradition as good and desirable, is the process of facilitating agreement between two parties. Arbitration, seen as a poorer solution, is the process of finding some fair compromise by a third party (typically, a panel of arbitrators). Most Westerners do not notice the difference, even though this is an important distinction in China. Not surprisingly, there are many mediators in China (some 16 million in 2020), but far fewer arbitrators. The courts and tribunals encourage mediation between the parties even after litigation proceedings have commenced. As arbitration is so ingrained in Western business thinking, however, the Chinese are learning to accommodate it.

China has used mediation for centuries, and its methods stem from the teachings of Confucius. Essentially, mediation seeks to resolve disputes in a way acceptable to all parties, without loss of face; it is primarily a method for defusing or dispelling confrontations. Much mediation concerns family and social issues, not commercial, and is also informal. The Chinese are encouraged to solve their disputes on their own initiative through mediation committees or mediation groups in their neighbourhood or workplace. Mediators are chosen within the neighbourhood, and no formal training is required to qualify. Recently there was also a significantly increased emphasis on using mediation in judicial proceedings. The SPC went as far as instructing local courts to mediate civil and commercial lawsuits whenever possible. Some 60% of first-instance civil cases were reported to have been solved by mediation in China. This SPC-orchestrated revival of mediation in judicial proceedings has started to fade more recently. Judges are regaining their reputation as professional adjudicators, rather than mediators.

Arbitration is much more formal. Where both parties to a dispute are Chinese entities, arbitration must take place within China with one of the established arbitration commissions. Where one of the parties is foreign, a foreign venue may be selected. Sweden, for reasons going back to the eighteenth century, is a preferred venue for arbitration involving joint venture disputes in China. The dispute between PepsiCo Investment (China) and the Chinese partner of its Sichuan joint venture was solved in a Stockholm arbitration in 2005.[10] Arbitration in the high-profile Danone–Wahaha dispute over the fate of their Chinese joint venture also took place in Stockholm before a settlement was announced in September 2009.[11] Singapore, London, and Hong Kong are now keen competitors with Stockholm for the settlement of disputes by arbitration.

It is important to bear in mind, however, that this choice of an overseas forum for arbitration will be denied where both parties to the arbitration are, in a legalistic sense, Chinese. Foreign invested enterprises set up under Chinese law (including wholly foreign-owned enterprises, equity joint ventures, and cooperative joint ventures) are all deemed to be Chinese enterprises (not foreign), even though from an economic point of view they are foreign funded. Thus, as the Wind Farms Arbitration case demonstrates, the Chinese subsidiary of a foreign firm is generally treated under Chinese law as a Chinese enterprise, with no recourse to international arbitration in the event that its relationships with its Chinese partner in a joint venture go sour.

Wind Farms Arbitration[12]

Just because the two parties to a commercial contract in China agree that they would have recourse to international arbitration in the event of a dispute between them, that may not necessarily happen.

China is well aware of the need to shift electricity generation from coal to renewables. In 2007, China's electricity generation was 83% coal, 15% hydro, 1.3% nuclear, and only 0.27% wind[13] but the share of wind is rapidly increasing.

China's installed wind capacity will grow from 115.6 GW in 2014 to a whopping 347.2 GW by 2025. China's growth will take place alongside a global stabilization towards the end of the forecast period, with annual installations peaking at 56.8 GW in 2022. Interestingly, unlike other wind power giants like the UK, China's wind capacity will be dominated by onshore wind, which is expected to account for over 96% of all installations, or around 334.7 GW — that leaves just 12.4 GW for offshore wind.[14]

China installed nearly half of the 63 gigawatts of wind power added globally in 2015.... and now accounts for about a third of the world's installed wind power capacity. That is almost twice the figure for the US (17 per cent) and three times that of Germany (10 per cent), the biggest by capacity, according to the council's data.[15]

One way and another, this would seem to have been a great time to be involved in Chinese wind power but not all has been harmony.

"In 2006 the largest wind power plant in China was built in Jiangsu province ...a demonstration model in China"[16] with 108 megawatts wind power. The plant was constructed by a joint venture, Jiangsu Wanyuan Company which had a purchase agreement with LM Tianjin Co., a wholly owned foreign enterprise held by LM Denmark Co., the Danish-owned world's largest wind turbine manufacturer, to purchase their turbines.

The dispute resolution clause of their agreement set out that:

- The agreement shall be governed by the **United Nations Convention on Contracts for the International Sale of Goods** (Vienna, 11 April 1980).
- If the dispute cannot be resolved through friendly negotiation, then the dispute shall be submitted to the International Chamber of Commerce ("ICC") for arbitration in Beijing.

Jiangsu Wanyuan then also resold and installed the wind turbines bought from LM Tianjin to other buyers in China. Though it is not stated in the court proceedings, this may well have been why the two parties fell out: the Danish subsidiary would not have been pleased by being undercut by its own customer. Be that as it may, the Jiangsu Higher People's Court and then the Supreme People's Court decided that LM Tianjin could not have recourse to international arbitration, even in Beijing, because both parties to the contract were, technically, Chinese.[17]

The SPC has three criteria for international arbitration to be acceptable, where:

- One party or both parties are foreign nationals, stateless persons, or foreign legal persons
- Or the subject matter of dispute is located in a foreign country
- Or the issues occurred in a foreign country.

Foreign investment enterprises, contractual and equity joint venture companies, and wholly owned foreign enterprises incorporated in China with foreign investment are all 'domestic' entities under PRC law.

An exception to the above principle appears to relate to wholly foreign-owned enterprises incorporated in China's Free Trade Zones. A Shanghai court in a judgment handed down in 2015 showed willingness to give effect to the choice of Singapore as the seat of arbitration by two Shanghai Free Trade Zone incorporated wholly foreign-owned enterprises.[18] It is not yet empirically known to what extent this approach has been embraced by other Chinese courts.

Intellectual property

As is well known, intellectual property has been a large legal minefield in commercial international relations with China, and is probably one of the most difficult legal issues to resolve. According to the World Customs Organization, 75% of counterfeit goods seized worldwide between 2008 and 2010 came from China. A 2013 study by the Commission on the Theft of American Intellectual Property estimated that the annual cost to the US economy of global intellectual property rights theft at $300 billion, of which losses China accounted for 50% to 80%. For years, China has been on the "priority watch list" published by the United States Trade Representative, which notes that intellectual property protection and enforcement has remained a significant challenge.

Part of the problem is that there was no sustained tradition of protecting patents or copyright in imperial China. This does *not* mean, as some journalists have written, that the Chinese do not see anything wrong with piracy. Piracy is wrong, and it is illegal in China. China's leadership has publicly acknowledged the critical role that the protection for intellectual property rights (IPR) plays in spurring innovation domestically and moving its economy up the value chain. However, enforcing anti-piracy laws is taxing the powers of the legal and enforcement system to the limit. Online IPR infringements are only adding to China's IPR enforcement under-capacity.

To be fair, China's legal and institutional framework of IPR protection has been improving. China has fine-tuned its Patent Law, Trademark Law, and Copyright Law regularly, and has periodically issued new IPR regulations and rules. Nationwide IPR campaigns have been rolled out; capacity building has been high on the national government's agenda to combat IPR infringement. Many Chinese courts, including the SPC, have long set up a specialized division to hear intellectual property-related cases. Four specialized intellectual property courts have recently been set up in Beijing, Shanghai, Guangzhou, and Hainan Free Trade Port to develop a central pool of expertise and to improve efficiency of IPR enforcement. But even with these new laws and institutions, foreign companies do not feel entirely at ease from IPR infringements.

Starbucks

Starbucks Corporation (Starbucks Co.) registered its 'Starbucks' trademarks in 1996 in China, and registered in 1999 the transliteration of Starbucks in Chinese characters – 'Xing Ba Ke' (in Chinese, *'xing'* means star, and *'ba ke'* sounds like bucks). When Starbucks Co. decided to expand its business in Shanghai in 2000, it found that a Shanghai local company set up in 2000 – Shanghai Xing Ba Ke Coffee Shop Ltd

(Shanghai Xing Ba Ke) – had already started using a variation of the green Starbucks logo and the name Xing Ba Ke.

Starbucks Co. brought an action in December 2003 against Shanghai Xing Ba Ke. Shanghai No. 2 Intermediation People's Court decided in December 2005 in favour of Starbucks Co., ruling that Starbucks and its Chinese name Xing Ba Ke are "well-known marks" and thus deserve special protection under Chinese law. Shanghai Xing Ba Ke was ordered to pay Starbucks Co. compensation of 500,000 yuan, and was prohibited from using Xing Ba Ke marks. After the ruling, Shanghai Xing Ba Ke appealed. Shanghai Higher People's Court in January 2007 upheld the first-instance decision.

Well-known trademarks are protected by law in China, even if they are not registered or the trademark owner registers the mark late. However, Chinese law gives the court the discretion to determine whether or not a mark is well known. Despite Starbucks' victory in the court, there is uncertainty involved. Pfizer has lost its legal battle to register the Chinese transliteration of 'Viagra', because a Guangzhou local company had already registered it. More recently, a Chinese court reportedly ruled that a businessman in Wuhan could legally sell products bearing the transliteration of 'Louis Vuitton' in Chinese characters, since the lawful owner of the LV brand had not registered the brand's Chinese name in China. (See note 5)

A few simple precautions can make it easier to locate violators and obtain compliance:

1   Prepare an intellectual property inventory
2   Appoint an intellectual property manager responsible for keeping the inventory current and scouting the China market for infringements
3   Register everything as quickly possible *in both English and Chinese in China*, in order to avoid the prohibitively high costs of litigation, both in terms of fees and time (consider the Starbucks case), as well as uncertainties (consider Pfizer's misfortune)
4   Conduct regular market surveys to determine if trademarks, patents, or copyrights are being violated
5   Go to court even if redress is not seriously expected, because the authorities will not take the matter seriously until the matter reaches the courts (and attracts media attention).

The problem of intellectual property infringement is by no means unique to China, and it can be argued that China is doing more than some jurisdictions to deal with it. Taiwan is also home to many software and music pirates (strangely, the US government gets far less excited about these than it does about those in mainland China), and Indonesia, Malaysia, and Thailand all have their pirate kings. And never mentioned, of course, is the scale of routine, everyday software piracy that goes on in many homes and offices in the West.

Conclusions

To sum up, the legal system in China is developing a greater measure of complexity and sophistication, and this has implications for businesspeople. On the one hand, there is more legal protection for businesses, including Western businesses, now than probably at any time in China's history. At the same time, going to law is a complex and risky option, not least because the legal system is still in a state of evolution and flux.

Thirty years ago, few businesses operating in China would have seen the need to hire a Chinese lawyer, even if they could find one; priority was given to forming the right *guanxi* and connections. Now, hiring a lawyer to check contracts and advise on national and local business laws and regulations makes sense, even if not essential. We think that, save for major and complex investment projects, local Chinese law firms probably offer better value, having more local knowledge and better *guanxi* with government. That said, China is still a long way from having a Western legal system where the court is a primary vehicle for resolving disputes. Arbitration and mediation remain important. If or when a dispute surfaces, choose the route most likely to give satisfaction in China, not the one that worked best back in the home country.

And remember: important though the law is, it is no substitute for *guanxi*. The two systems, legal framework and relationships, operate in parallel, often in tandem.

An ethical interlude

Two main consumer rights are universal: the right not to buy again and the right to inform others about a product. Repurchase rates and word of mouth are powerful marketing forces which may apply in China with *relatively* more importance, in the absence of other rights which Westerners take for granted. This section pauses to reflect on the general question of 'rights' and the dark side of *guanxi*, namely corruption.

The section is arranged as follows:

- **Development**. Centuries ago, both Eastern and Western societies were more concerned with responsibilities than rights. Here we mean rights of all kinds, human as well as political and economic. The assertion of rights has grown faster in the West than in China. This, like democracy, has both advantages and disadvantages. We see no *higher authority* grounds for asserting one orthodoxy over another, but we do see *evolutionary* benefits in going with the flow. Each set of ethics simply reflects the way that culture polices its people. As global cultures tend towards fusion, we are evolving toward a universal view of rights and ethics. But it is not so simple, as we are seeing both globalization and localization happening at the same time. The Balkans provide an example.

- **Contract law**. Business practices in the West are backed up by contract law and in China by *guanxi*. Legal processes carried to excess are as corrupt as *guanxi* carried to excess, but the corruption lies in the excess, not in the product itself. Determining where healthy business practices degenerate into corruption depends on the culture concerned. Some Chinese practices would be corrupt in the USA but, conversely, some US practices would be corrupt in China. The issue turns on whether they reduce the public good in that context, not whether they have intrinsic merit. This is, of course, the relativist position.

- **If marketers act responsibly, do rights take care of themselves?** We conclude with pragmatic advice, offered without warranty.

The development of rights and responsibilities

The need for harmony between rights and responsibilities has long been noted in East and West but they are not a zero-sum game. Having fewer rights does not imply having more or fewer responsibilities; the concepts are linked but independent. From the earliest times, the individual's place in the community has been described by responsibilities, for example, Confucius. The idea of rights is more recent; in the West it mostly hails from the Age of Enlightenment 300 years ago. You will not find much, if anything, about rights in the Christian Bible. The New Testament drills home the need to be responsible to God, and then your neighbour. The Old Testament is even more obligation heavy.

Probably Descartes, with his focus on identity, helped develop the idea that, if others have responsibility to me, then that gives me some rights, or at least expectations. If the husband should be faithful to his wife, then the wife may expect faithfulness from the husband. 'Rights', in the sense of human or consumer entitlement, were given eighteenth-century support as a matter of fairness. Given a choice between having rights or no rights, I would rather have rights. And, given that, why should I have them if others do not? There was a recognition of reciprocity. Slaves had no, or not many, rights and it was not until recently that the human race had a problem with that. 'Rights' etymologically derive from the word 'straight', like the Greek 'ortho' in orthodox. It is reasonable to recognize that others have similar rights to those one expects for oneself.

What is important here is that rights grew from responsibilities and the demands for rights have been increasing. How far should that go? The increase of one does not necessarily imply a decrease of the other. However, if everyone demands their rights and no one exercises their responsibilities, society will fall apart. Eastern commentators like Singapore's Lee Kuan Yew have pointed to the moral degradation of the West, meaning just that: responsibilities to others are buried by demands for one's own rights. Human, and consumer, rights are important but may not have much value unless others exercise their responsibilities. The world has seen ever more small countries demand, as a democratic right, to have full independence. At the same time, the EU, a vociferous supporter of universal human rights, creates a new treaty for itself without allowing its citizens a vote on the matter (because, of course, they would lose the vote). And Americans lock prisoners up in Guantanamo Bay for years on end, with little if any regard for their human rights. The Chinese have some justification for cynicism.

Second, for whatever reasons, the creation of rights from responsibilities happened far more slowly in China than in the West. That may be because, as we suggested in the last chapter, settled communities could manage well enough with reciprocal responsibilities and had no need of rights or contract law. Wang Gungwu, former Vice Chancellor of Hong Kong University, once remarked that, 'The ancient Chinese only knew of duties but had no notion of rights'.[19] Whatever may be the position in the PRC, it is clear that overseas Chinese have latterly adopted the notion of rights with enthusiasm.

Third, whilst the concept of rights and responsibilities is universal, the particular selection of what they are varies from culture to culture and from era to era. They are evolving. Today Britain attributes rights to animals too. As computers become more intelligent, we can expect computer rights at some point in the future. We see no evidence of any of this being God-given: rights and responsibilities are what different societies decide them to be.

While the Western media harp on continually about human, or civil, rights, these are only part of a continuum of rights, including economic rights. The introduction of the free market in the PRC has undoubtedly had a dramatic effect on the latter and some commentators suggest that PRC consumers are far more interested in economic than civil rights. We are now witnessing globalization forcing cultures to accommodate each other's standards for rights and responsibilities. That does not make any one set either correct or universal, as some of our American friends seem to believe. Indeed the Iraq invasion of 2003 has encouraged the view that America thinks that universal human rights are whatever America says they are.

The reality is that a shrinking globe is forcing the world to share their cultural evolution. The imposition of ethical standards by one culture on another is ethical fascism, in the original sense of 'fascism'. On the other hand, as we are going to have to live together, it would reduce conflict and misunderstanding if we allowed our standards to co-evolve. This in turn would require each culture to respect the de facto ethics of the other, at least in the sense of seeking to understand their philosophic and historic roots. Asserting one's own standards as universal is both arrogant and unhelpful. It used to be called colonialism.

Western linear thinkers are puzzled by the Chinese ability to hold on to a mass of apparently contrary philosophies at the same time – ancestor cult,

Daoism, Confucianism, Legalism, Buddhism, Christianity, and Communism to name but a few. The Westerner tends to *replace* one set of beliefs with the next, whereas the Easterner tends to *add* them. This may be due to the Daoist tradition itself.

Be that as it may, in Confucianism, the individual is defined by his relationships with others, whereas in the West our relationships are defined by our self-identity. This overstates the distinction in order to make the point. The virtuous person only acquires rights to the extent to which he gives them to others: do as you would be done by. Descartes' *cogito, ergo sum* (I think, therefore I am) owes nothing to anyone else. As we noted in the last chapter, the Chinese did not even have a word for 'rights' until recently: 'they borrowed from Japan a term, *chuan-li*, manufactured for translating Western political thought about a century ago'.[20]

Contract law versus guanxi

The divergent cultures of the law in the US and *guanxi* in China may have arisen from the essential difference between cowboy and farmer communities. *Guanxi*, personal connections, implies reciprocal altruism. There is just a responsibility when a favour is accepted that one day, when it is needed, the favour will be returned. But this implies that the two parties can expect to be in the same community for long enough for that to happen. For many centuries, the vast majority of Chinese citizens lived all their lives in their home villages. The shift to the cities is very recent. Conversely, America was formed by immigrants constantly on the move and there was little point in expecting favours from people who would not be there next week.

Contract law was never a big deal in Europe until the nineteenth century, when citizens began to move about. A man's word was his bond and if he failed to honour it, society shunned him. Although speculation, we believe that a shift to contract law takes place where the reciprocity has to be clearly stated and is enforceable.

Contrary to some Westerners' beliefs, *guanxi* cannot be purchased. In that sense it is priceless, and this explains why in China one builds friendship before seeking to do business, whereas in the US the order is reversed. In the West we feel vaguely uncomfortable doing business with friends, whereas in China, one would be uncomfortable if they were *not* friends.

So passing money in red envelopes may or may not be corrupt, but it is not *guanxi*. If you define doing business with friends as corrupt, then the 'corruption' arises from your definition. Others may regard *not* doing business with friends as unethical because it offends the expectations of that society. Who is to say which is right?

Thus it is a question of context: ethical Chinese practices may be corrupt in the US and – now this is controversial – ethical US practices may be corrupt in China. Where *guanxi* is the norm, behaving in a non-*guanxi* way will degrade (corrupt) business. The importation of some Western business practices into China today is doing just that. The 1999 Disney negotiations between Shanghai and Hong Kong, while probably fair competition in a US context, can be seen as corrupt in China.

In the largely settled, rural communities that made up China until very recently, relationships between individuals and between families were very long, and *guanxi*, with endless chains of gift giving, is the very foundation of their relationships. The main reason, in our view, for the importance of improving legal processes in China has less to do with importing Western business practices than with finding new enforcement rules where people are moving in huge numbers from one part of the country to another.

Corruption is, of course, a major issue in China. Since economic reform, it has become one of the biggest problems facing the Chinese economy and has deeply distressed many ordinary Chinese. It played no small part in the protests of 1989. It has also led to a growing number of officials receiving a bullet in the back of the head from the official executioner. The Chinese are fearful of it for the same reason that Germans fear inflation: they remember the damage it did in their past.

But this merely reinforces the point that *guanxi* and corruption are *not* the same thing, any more than drink is the same as drunkenness. One can enjoy the one and still avoid the other. One Chinese term for corruption, *zou hou-men*, or 'going through the back door' can be applied to relatively innocuous practices such as the giving of a *hongbao*,[21] a red envelope containing a small amount of money. But in context it certainly is not. Gift giving is a long and honourable tradition in most parts of the world.

Christmas presents between businesspeople are less prevalent in the UK than they used to be, but that probably has more to do with accountants than morality. Accountants plead morality just as the UK chancellor claims to be improving the nation's health when he raises duties on alcohol, cigarettes, and petrol.

The line between corrupt and harmless practices is not easy to draw. The US Foreign Corrupt Practices Act specifically excludes 'grease payments' and tipping, that is, money given to encourage officials to do what they should do anyway. Some governments regard those as necessary salary adjuncts, that is, they save money for the taxpayer. Corruption, that is, bribery, involves paying someone to do what he should not do.

But it is not as simple as that either. A British Chief Financial Officer of a pharmaceutical multinational in China was recently surprised to receive an envelope from the taxman with a substantial amount of cash. He was told it was a thank-you for handing over the PAYE collections from the payroll so promptly – clearly an unusual event. He decided it would be wrong to rock the boat and credited the money in the company's books. He was not personally corrupt and it is not immediately obvious that the taxman was. But was he wise? What happens when the taxman needs a favour? This is not *guanxi*, which cannot be bought, but it may be starting a chain that should not be followed.

Many businesspeople think that corruption is an acceptable and necessary part of doing business in China. Or at least getting started. It is all very well for IBM and Johnson & Johnson (or Xian Janssen) to act high and mighty, but the newcomer without brand equity has to go through the back door if he cannot get through the front.

Bribery is expensive, tends rapidly to get more so, damages reputations, and leads to pseudo-*guanxi* with the wrong people. There is also the risk of substantial legal penalties in China and at home. Yet it is difficult to be too whiter-than-white about it. The entire alcoholic drinks distribution infrastructure in the US is founded on illegal and corrupt (by any standards) relationships built during prohibition. And it has stood for over 60 years.

If marketers exercise their responsibilities, will consumer rights take care of themselves?

This chapter has represented the idea that rights are a recent, not wholly desirable, outgrowth from responsibilities. This is a step back from the fashionable notion that rights are a universal human entitlement. Indeed, there is some inconsistency in the secular age that has rejected God and higher authority claiming such rights. By whom are these rights given?

A more consistent idea, which can be drawn from biology, is that social groups do better with reciprocal altruism, that is, rights balanced with responsibilities. So they are not God-given but just part of a useful strategy for beneficial development. Rights, in short, are only as moral as the responsibilities that underpin them. We should worry more about responsibilities than rights: if marketers behave responsibly, consumer rights will take care of themselves. Furthermore, in China it is not enough to do the right things; they have to be done in the right way (*li*). Bombing the Chinese embassy in Belgrade during the Kosovo conflict was clearly the wrong thing, and the American and British problems thereafter were compounded by a failure to observe the correct form. A quick and apparently insincere apology made things worse. Genuine contrition required a proper investigation and explanation. Thus marketers should not only act responsibly but do so according to the conventions of the local market.

It would appear that the Chinese have a very hazy view of both sides of this marketing coin relative to established foreign markets. Consumers are quite happy buying goods known to be counterfeit, on the grounds that they are similar but cheaper. They do not expect any consumer protection and, so far, show little sign of wanting it. Retailers develop amnesia when faulty goods are returned. As marketing develops, so will both rights and responsibilities because reliable products and strong branding are in the commercial interests of both sides. Consumers should behave responsibly in their own long-term interest because merchants will respect them more and not, for example, dismiss complaints because the motives are suspect.

The idea that we should focus more on marketer responsibilities than on consumer rights is perhaps more Chinese than American. Yet this is supported in the West by the declining profile given to consumerism since the 1970s. *Which?* magazine, the journal of the UK Consumers' Association, is struggling to keep afloat. One cause is probably the greater dominance of brands. With so much investment in these assets, their owners *have* to act responsibly and the need to protect consumer rights thereby diminishes.

Few China market entrants will be concerned with the theoretical and long-term implications of branding. They want to know whether to pay off Mr Li. All official advice will be to avoid doing so but ours is more complex. Whether everyone else is doing so is relevant but everyone else may not own up. Bribery (paying people to do what they should not do) is definitely a bad idea. Not only is it illegal; it damages the reputation of firms that do it. Grease payments are the problem.

Grease payments fall into two categories: tips and service payments where the amounts are minor compared to possible costs, and extortion. It has long been the custom, for example, to leave RMB100 notes in envelopes under the plates of senior people invited for lunch and a business presentation. The money is ostensibly to pay for travel expenses. Clearly that $10 or so is not going to make much difference to anyone. The practice is being replaced by small gifts like ties and pens and only the most petty-minded would regard it as unethical.

Extortion, where quite a large sum is involved before something happens (unloading cargo for example), is another matter. Here it is tempting to regard the payer as the victim and the payee as corrupt but it is a brave, and probably foolish, foreigner who blows the whistle.

International businesspeople have long got around the difficulty by hiring consultants at rather larger fees than they might otherwise expect so that they can take care of these matters. This 'monkey's paw' approach is less noble in China than West Africa because of the negative effect it can have on long-term *guanxi*. This really is the issue. If the business is too small or too under-funded to survive without the grease payment, *and* the longer-term effects are not damaging to true *guanxi*, then it is an option we could not deny – especially if it is standard practice. On the other hand, there is little point in surviving if *guanxi* is harmed. Going out of business will just take a little longer and probably be more painful and expensive. Another solution needs to be found.

Finally, foreign companies can, and should, help themselves through their trade associations. If an industry is being collectively held to ransom, then it is up to the industry *collectively* to do something about it. Differing national cultures may complicate matters. Americans worry that collective action is anti-competitive. Other countries are sometimes puzzled why the Anglo-Saxons make so much fuss about ethics. Until quite recently, bribes (and we are talking bribes, not grease payments) were legitimate tax deductions in France and Germany. As a collective US/French/UK example, the drinks industry in China found itself paying escalating bribery to bartenders.[22] They all agreed to stop doing it. There is always a bit of cheating and disinformation on these occasions but, by and large, the ban held.

In this interlude, we have reviewed the philosophy of rights and ethics and taken a relativist position. In other words, they reflect society norms and not some external absolutes. At the same time, as the world shrinks, they are co-evolving to a common, or more similar, future. After touching on consumer rights and marketer responsibilities, we moved to some pragmatic advice on bribery, extortion, and grease payments. We have sought to be responsible but it is offered with no warranty: do not call us, call your lawyers.

Notes

1 https://www.cecc.gov/sites/chinacommission.house.gov/files/documents/hearings/2002/CECC%20Hearing%20Testimony%20-%20William%20Alford%20-%202.7.02.pdf.
2 *People's Daily* [Renmin Ribao], 31 January 1967.
3 https://www.cecc.gov/sites/chinacommission.house.gov/files/documents/hearings/2002/CECC%20Hearing%20Testimony%20-%20William%20Alford%20-%202.7.02.pdf.
4 To put the figures in context, the UK enacts about 100 new laws each year, and around 3,000 statutory instruments or pieces of secondary legislation. About 300 of these are laws, or regulations, which affect business. Comparisons are difficult because lawmaking structures and terminology differ. The EU, which is perhaps a better comparison than the UK, approves about 100 directives per annum (requiring member states to pass equivalent laws) and 2,000 'Regulations' which do not need to be duplicated by member states but 97.5% are not laws; they are just Administrative Orders.
5 An example is China's notoriously complex medical negligence law. See Chao Xi and Lixin Yang, "Medical Liability Laws in China: The Tale of Two Regimes" (2011) 19 *Tort Law Review* 65
6 Jim Yardley, "A Judge Tests China's Courts, Making History" *New York Times* (28 November 2005), available at https://www.nytimes.com/2005/11/28/world/asia/a-judge-tests-chinas-courts-making-history.html
7 One such mechanism is rulemaking by Chinese local courts. See Chao Xi, "Local Courts as Legislators? Judicial Lawmaking by Sub-National Courts in China" (2012) 33 *Statute Law Review* 39.
8 See Björn Ahl, Lidong Cai and Chao Xi, "Data-Driven Approaches to Studying Chinese Judicial Practice: Opportunities, Challenges, and Issues" (2019) vol. 19 *The China Review* 1.
9 Lawyers' fees are regulated in China. See Michael Palmer and Chao Xi, "The People's Republic of China" in Christopher Hodges, Stefan Vogenauer and Magdalena Tulibacka (eds), *The Costs and Funding of Civil Litigation: A Comparative Perspective* (Oxford: Hart, 2010) 261.
10 Russell Flannery, "Pepsi's Chinese Torture" *Forbes* (22 December 2003), available at https://www.forbes.com/forbes/2003/1222/086sidebar.html?sh=5b11f52f6a78.
11 Reuters Staff, "Wahaha seeks China arbitration in row with Danone" *Reuters* (14 June 2007) available at https://www.reuters.com/article/china-danone-idUSSHA13541020070613.
12 Arthur Dong, "China Supreme People's Court Holds That a Dispute Must Meet 'Foreign-Related' Requirement for Arbitration at Foreign Arbitration Forums", available at https://www.chinalawvision.com/2013/11/arbitration-and-litigation/china-supreme-peoples-court-holds-that-a-dispute-must-meet-foreignrelated-requirement-for-arbitration-at-foreign-arbitration-forums/
13 *China Electricity Power Newspaper*, 1 November 2007.
14 *GlobalData* reported 22 September 2015, http://cleantechnica.com/2015/09/22/chinas-wind-energy-capacity-triple-2020-globaldata/
15 *Global Wind Statistics* 2015, published 10 February 2016, http://www.gwec.net/wp-content/uploads/vip/GWEC-PRstats-2015_LR.pdf

16 Shi peng fei, 13 January 2008 "The progress of wind power industry report in each Chinese province" quoted in *Wind Power In China*, Yun Zhoun and Quanfeng Wang, June 2009, Master's Thesis in Energy Systems, University of Gävle.
17 "China Supreme People's Court Holds That a Dispute Must Meet "Foreign-Related" Requirement for Arbitration at Foreign Arbitration Forums," Arthur Dong (dongxiao@anjielaw.com), 22 November 2013.
18 Siemens International Trade Co. Ltd. v Shanghai Golden Landmark Co. Ltd. (2013), available at https://cicc.court.gov.cn/html/1/219/199/204/766.html.
19 M. Boylan (ed.) *Gewirth: Critical Essays on Action, Rationality, and Community* Rowman & Littlefield Publishers (1998) p.152.
20 C. Hansen (1996) "Chinese philosophy and human rights: An Application of Comparative Ethics" in G.K. (eds) *Ethics in Business and Society. Studies in Economic Ethics and Philosophy*. Springer, Berlin, Heidelberg. https://doi.org/10.1007/978-3-642-61442-2_7.
21 These are traditionally given out by more senior people at the Chinese New Year, by uncles to nephews, by bosses to subordinates, and so on.
22 Corkage is a cash amount paid for every branded cork or bottle top returned by the retailer to the brand's local distributor.

Bibliography

Ahl, Björn, Lidong Cai and Chao Xi, "Data-Driven Approaches to Studying Chinese Judicial Practice: Opportunities, Challenges, and Issues" (2019) 19 *The China Review* 1.

Boylan, M. (ed.) (1998) *Gewirth: Critical Essays on Action, Rationality, and Community*, Rowman & Littlefield Publishers, p.152.

Flannery, Russell, "Pepsi's Chinese Torture" *Forbes* (22 December 2003), available at https://www.forbes.com/forbes/2003/1222/086sidebar.html?sh=5b11f52f6a78

Hansen, C. (1996) "Chinese Philosophy and Human Rights: An Application of Comparative Ethics" in G.K. Becker (eds), *Ethics in Business and Society. Studies in Economic Ethics and Philosophy* (Berlin, Heidelberg: Springer). https://doi.org/10.1007/978-3-642-61442-2_7

Palmer, Michael and Chao Xi, "The People's Republic of China" in Christopher Hodges, Stefan Vogenauer and Magdalena Tulibacka (eds), *The Costs and Funding of Civil Litigation: A Comparative Perspective* (Oxford: Hart, 2010) 261.

Reuters Staff, "Wahaha Seeks China Arbitration in Row with Danone," *Reuters* (14 June 2007) available at https://www.reuters.com/article/china-danone-idUSSHA13541020070613

Siemens International Trade Co. Ltd. v Shanghai Golden Landmark Co. Ltd. (2013). available at https://cicc.court.gov.cn/html/1/219/199/204/766.html

Xi, Chao, "Local Courts as Legislators? Judicial Lawmaking by Sub-national Courts in China" (2012) 33 *Statute Law Review* 39.

Xi, Chao and Lixin Yang, "Medical Liability Laws in China: The Tale of Two Regimes" (2011) 19 *Tort Law Review* 65.

Yardley, Jim, "A Judge Tests China's Courts, Making History," *New York Times* (28 November 2005), available at https://www.nytimes.com/2005/11/28/world/asia/a-judge-tests-chinas-courts-making-history.html

6 Creating harmony

Establishing businesses in China

The Way (*Dao*) gives birth to the one.
One gives birth to two.
Two gives birth to three.
And three gives birth to the myriad things.
The myriad things bear yin and embrace yang.
By combining these forces, harmony is created.

(Laozi)

Strategic approaches by foreign companies to the challenge of operating in China have changed considerably since 1990. Thirty years ago, China was the Wild West for most companies from Europe and the United States. Then, it was still a relatively small market, albeit with possible large potential. Many foreign companies were happy just to have their products sold in China, usually by a third party, like the Hong Kong-based British trading companies Swires or Jardine Matheson. Locally based distributors, acting for Coca Cola, or for the famous Bordeaux-based claret Chateau Palmer, for example, were able to turn their local Chinese contacts and market knowledge into fat margins and profits, while their suppliers based several thousand miles away were happy with the incremental revenue which their 'toe in the Chinese market' gave to them.

Of course, China had been effectively closed to foreign business during Mao's Cultural Revolution and its aftermath. But in 1979, the first glimmer of opening to the outside world appeared, with a new Chinese law which permitted a foreign company to invest in China via a joint equity holding with a Chinese partner in a joint venture. As a few foreign companies started cautiously to experiment with the very backward, but potentially huge Chinese market, the Chinese Government expanded its legal framework to include wholly foreign-owned enterprises in 1986, and then in 1988, the co-operative joint venture, which increased flexibility, by providing the possibility of either partner (Chinese or foreign) contributing its equity in some form other than currency (for example, a factory site or machinery), and permitted the distribution of profits in a different ratio from that of capital contribution.

DOI: 10.4324/9781003241164-7

The economic growth which followed these relaxations persuaded many multinationals to take a closer look at the country, although some sectors of the Chinese economy, like financial services, remained entirely closed to foreign participation, while most others were still open only to joint ventures between the foreign company and a Chinese partner. This was the case when General Motors and Ford both decided, in the early 1990s, that they had to participate in China. The battle to become the partner of Shanghai Auto was won in 1995 by GM. (Some years later, Ford partnered, not very successfully, with a Chongqing-based motorcycle company called Chang'An). Since car production started at the GM joint venture in 1997, the GM-Shanghai Auto project has provided GM with the revenue and profits to redevelop and rebrand its auto franchise in its traditional market, the United States. In 2019 GM sold 2.9 million vehicles through its joint ventures in China, more than the 2.4 million which it sold in the United States.

In November 1999, after an internal battle in which the would be isolationists were defeated by the expansionists led by Chinese PM Zhu Ronji, China agreed terms with the United States under which it would join the World Trade Organization, thereby bringing its economy within the scope of a global organization with widely agreed rules and regulations. Since then, the growing evidence of the large benefits brought to the Chinese economy by foreign capital, technology, and know-how has persuaded China to continue to open up many previously closed sectors, in most cases to 100% foreign ownership.

On 1 January 2020, a new Chinese law governing foreign investment was promulgated, which changed the investing landscape for foreign companies in China. The three formats previously governing foreign investment into China, of equity joint venture, co-operative joint venture, and wholly foreign-owned enterprise were all abolished. They were replaced with one corporate entity which, from 2025, will apply equally to foreign- and Chinese-owned companies in China. From 2020, no new equity or co-operative joint venture or WFOE may be established in China, while the many thousands of existing corporate structures of this kind have until 2025 to adjust their operations to the new law, because after 2025, they will not be able to operate in the previous corporate format.

As will be seen below, the purpose of this new law was to make investing in China less arbitrary and more certain, and to remove the considerable scope enjoyed by local Chinese Governments to interfere in foreign-owned enterprises in China, often to favour local companies at the expense of the foreign competitor, or to force foreign companies to import new technology as a condition of operating in China. This change has removed conflicts which had previously existed between joint venture or WFOE law and Chinese corporate law. The previous requirement for new investors in China to be individually approved by the Chinese Government has disappeared, to be replaced by two 'Lists': a 'Negative List' and an 'Encouraged List'.

Prior to the investment law taking effect on 1 January 2020, foreign investors, who had been operating in China for decades, had faced certain hurdles on business establishment and investment treatment, compared to their Chinese counterparts, and had been restricted from investing in particular sectors unless in a joint venture with a Chinese party. Moreover, foreign investors had needed to navigate through the three Chinese laws governing foreign investment in China, which imposed specific requirements on corporate formation, foreign ownership ratios, corporate governance, and operational management. In addition, insufficient protection of intellectual property rights and trade secrets, mandatory technology transfer, and lack of participation in the legislative consultation process had been significant concerns for many foreign investors.

The new foreign investment law has been designed to take steps to address such concerns. Comprised of 49 articles, it focuses on foreign investment promotion, protection, and administration and imposes legal liabilities on both foreign investors and Chinese regulators who violate Chinese laws.

The most significant highlights of the 2020 foreign investment law are summarized as follows:

Investment Promotion: to further promote foreign investment in China, the law stipulates that foreign investors must be treated equally with domestic companies regarding access to government funds, land supply, tax exemptions, licensing, project applications, and so on. Foreign-invested companies may comment on new legislation and administrative rules concerning foreign investment. Only published documents may form the basis for the exercise of administrative authority. Foreign investors may enjoy preferential policies in certain sectors and regions as designated by the Chinese authorities; they may participate in government procurement through fair competition; and they must not be discriminated against in such procurement processes with respect to their manufactured products and the services they provide. In China, the law specifically allows foreign-invested enterprises to raise funds through public offerings of debt and equity securities. Clearly, these new provisions are aimed at encouraging more foreign investment into China.

Investment Protection: The law clarifies that foreign investors' capital contributions, profit, capital gains, income from asset disposals, royalties from intellectual property rights, lawfully obtained compensation or indemnity amounts, and proceeds from liquidation may be freely remitted in or out of China, in renminbi, or in foreign currency, with no limit on size, or frequency of remittances. A swift collaborative protection mechanism to facilitate the settlement of disputes over intellectual property, and the protection of the IP rights of foreign investors is provided for. Government officials are prohibited from forcing foreign investors to transfer their technology. The law requires authorities to take effective measures to protect the trade secrets of foreign investors that they have learned while performing their duties. Local governments are compelled to comply with policy directives affecting foreign investors and must reasonably compensate foreign investors if agreements have to be changed due to national or social public interest reasons.

Investment Administration: Foreign-invested companies in China are now subject to the China Company Law and Partnership Law, which contains different rules on corporate governance, voting, share transfers, profit sharing, and so forth. Existing joint ventures or wholly foreign-owned enterprises have until 2025 to convert to the appropriate corporate form and update their articles of association and shareholders' agreement to comply with the new rules. There is a requirement for a national security review of certain foreign investments in sensitive industries and sectors.

Legal Liabilities: If foreign investors invest in prohibited industries or fail to comply with investment access restrictions, they are required to divest and/or rectify their non-compliance and may face other legal sanctions. Government authorities and personnel could face legal liability for breaching the foreign investment law. The law allows for countermeasures to be imposed in China in response to prohibitive or restrictive rules against China established by other countries.

The Negative List and Encouraged Industries Catalogue prohibits and restricts foreign investment in certain sectors and provides incentives for foreign investment in other sectors. To further open up the Chinese market, the 2019 Negative List removed restrictions in certain sectors. For example, a joint venture with a Chinese partner was no longer required in oil and gas exploration. In 2021, certain financial sectors (securities, futures, and life insurance) became fully open. Goldman Sachs took advantage of this change to convert its joint venture Gao Hua Securities into a 100% foreign-owned company. At the same time, the Encouraged Industries Catalogue was expanded, so as to attract more foreign investment in high-end and intelligent manufacturing, advanced service industries, pharmaceutical and agricultural industries, advanced technology, new materials, and other promising sectors.

A sub-catalogue lists those sectors outside eastern China where foreign investments are encouraged: agriculture and goods manufacturing in Yunnan, for example, or automotive, and high-end manufacturing in Sichuan. The benefits enjoyed by foreign investors in the 'Encouraged' sectors include customs duty exemptions on imported equipment for self-use, and a preferential 15% income tax rate for foreign-invested enterprises in certain sectors and industries.

A 'special case' arose in the 1990s for dealing with foreign investment into sectors in China that, technically, were open only to Chinese citizens, like internet-based businesses, or so-called 'tech' companies (China does not allow foreigners to invest directly in, or control its telecoms or internet companies). This was called the variable-interest entity (VIE), an offshore company (based in the Cayman Islands or similar) controlled by senior officers within the onshore Chinese company (for instance, Alibaba, and its founder

Jack Ma), having a legal claim over the profits from the onshore company. When these offshore VIEs are listed, say on NASDAQ, investors who buy their shares gain a legal right to participate in the profits of the onshore Chinese company. The share price of the offshore, listed VIE responds to its profit share and entitlement to dividend payouts from the onshore Chinese company. Alibaba, for example, listed shares in its VIE in September 2014 at $68 per share, raising $21.8 billion, which made it the largest initial public offering in United States history (larger than Google, Facebook, and Twitter combined). Note that foreign investors, in this 'special' case, did not invest directly in the Chinese company, but in an offshore vehicle – the VIE – which is legally entitled to profits from the onshore company. The legality of this device within China has been questioned, but it has brought billions of dollars of foreign investment into Chinese 'tech' companies, and the Chinese authorities have (so far) allowed it to continue, probably in the knowledge that they can use the threat of outlawing VIEs in order to exert control over companies like Alibaba, Tencent, and many other multi-billion Chinese companies which use VIEs.

It might seem unbelievable to some readers that huge private Chinese companies like Alibaba and Tencent attract foreign investment by such apparently dubious means, but the Chinese, above all, are practical. Alibaba, Tencent, and the other Chinese 'tech' companies provide important and popular services in China. At the time of writing (late-2021), it has not seemed appropriate to the Chinese regulators to move against VIEs. The foreign investment law of 2020 aims at regularizing the mass of largely arbitrary rules which until then governed foreign investment in China. Making the VIE illegal would be consistent with this process of regularization, but so far the Chinese Government has not wished to upset the operations of these companies, or the powerful interests which benefit from them.

As the Chinese economy has grown to become the world's second largest, Chinese Government priorities have shifted. Thirty years ago, it was all about maximizing inflows of foreign capital, creating employment, and export promotion. Today, as can be seen from the Encouraged Industries Catalogue the emphasis is on creating incentives for technology-rich foreign enterprises to settle in China and share their products and know-how. Naturally, developing exports and creating well-paid jobs are still important, but they are overshadowed today by China's drive for greater economic self-sufficiency.

The creation of a level playing field, at least in legal terms, between Chinese and foreign companies operating in the Chinese market helps foreign companies because it removes many of the previous barriers to operation in China, many of which are shadowy and arbitrary. Before 2020, it was quite easy for local Chinese companies to influence decisions in their favour over government purchasing, even if the foreign product was cheaper or better. Now, it's much harder. Nevertheless, in almost all market segments in China, there are serious Chinese competitors. For example, in China's automotive market (the world's largest), in September 2021 Chinese-made cars occupied a share of 42% of vehicles sold, with ten Chinese brands out of the top 20 brands sold.

Previously, the basic decision for foreign companies operating in China was: shall we find a Chinese partner or shall we go it alone? As the China market opened up in the 1990s and 2000s, going it alone, unhampered by a Chinese partner, seemed the obvious route to a speedy success. Many foreign multinationals travelled along that route. But joint ventures proved surprisingly durable, because working closely with a good Chinese partner brought many advantages, such as understanding market trends, negotiating with the Government, and attracting good Chinese staff.

Although the equity and co-operative joint venture vehicles have been removed by the new foreign investment law, this decision still remains, because it is still possible to establish a Chinese company, constituted according to Chinese company law, as a joint project between two or more companies, whether they are Chinese, or non-Chinese. Therefore, the history since the 1980s of joint ventures in China between foreign and Chinese partners remains relevant today.

Looking at this history, we can see that some joint ventures have been very successful, while others have been the opposite. Both Volkswagen and Heineken entered China in 1983. The Dutch global beer company Heineken experimented with various joint ventures and wholly foreign-owned enterprises, before finally deciding in 2017 on a partnership, via a share-swap, and licensing agreement, with one of its major China competitors, CR Beer, which produces one of the leading beer premium brands in China (Xuehua or Snow). Heineken spent several decades trying to find the correct formula to turn its well-known global brand into a leading premium beer in China. Part of Heineken's problem may have been the high costs associated with Heineken's state-of-the-art breweries which it established in Shanghai, Jiangsu, and other parts of China. The high amortization cost of installed equipment made the price-point for Heineken's beer uncompetitive relative to local brands. But the main reason was that it could not find a partner with whom it could stand up to strong local brands like Tsingtao, Snow, and Yanjing, plus the brand of American brewer Anheuser-Busch, whose Budweiser brand has captured a large Chinese market share.

At the other end of the scale, Volkswagen's 1983 car joint ventures in Shanghai and northern city Changchun produced by 2020 a 20% market share in the world's largest and one of the most competitive car markets – a larger market share than Honda (nr. 2) and Toyota (nr. 3) combined. Volkswagen's China business in 2020 provided about half of VW's global net profits.

The real question is: What is the best kind of venture for this particular business at this particular time? Multinationals like IBM have used a mix of going it alone and partnering with Chinese firms, depending on what their purpose is for a specific project, and also where they are operating within the country. IBM China was established as a wholly foreign-owned enterprise in 1992, only after IBM had been operating in China for more than ten years and had built up an impressive portfolio of contacts including a former Chinese vice-premier. Jiahua IBM China functions in every respect as a

Chinese company; it pays taxes to Beijing, hires Chinese employees directly, and trades in local currency. But even now, after many years of China experience, for big projects, IBM China prefers to collaborate with Chinese partners. Why? Because the Chinese Government is the most important buyer for large IBM projects, and IBM knows it can negotiate the Chinese political arena much better if it proceeds hand in hand with a Chinese partner.

Chinese consultants point to the risks involved in establishing a business in China, especially for the first-time entrant. Joint ventures, they argue, provide more benefits than just profit. A good partner can help a Western company learn very quickly about the market and business environment and can provide access to resources, labour, key officials, markets, distribution channels, and the like. There are many barriers to success for a foreign company in China, some of which are invisible: for example, the correct price-point (as Heineken discovered), the best store location, and the perception of Chinese suppliers and customers towards your company and its products. A good Chinese partner can be very valuable in understanding these critical factors.

But, there is no doubt that local collaborations can be difficult and risky. A common (but not inevitable) outcome is for the partner with more skin in the game to buy out the other. It is preferable for the rules which govern that outcome to be agreed at the beginning. In the worst outcomes (see the Berry Brothers case in this chapter) everyone loses. In the West, surveys have suggested that most joint ventures fail within the first eighteen months. And if this is the rate of failure among companies within the same or very similar Western cultures, how much more difficult must the problem be when one firm is Western and the other is Chinese?

Mark Edwards, Diageo's general manager in China, told me that, while Diageo look for clarity in making their joint venture arrangements, the attitude of the Chinese partners tends to be "We have a good feeling. Let's get together, and we'll work it out as we go along". He also told me that, when negotiating with a Chinese partner, the real bargaining is not in the meeting, it's in the dinner afterwards. Perhaps surprisingly, the joint venture failure rate is about the same in China as in the West. Some companies enter the China market blindfolded and set up unsuitable collaborations based largely on ignorance, which then quickly collapse sometimes before the ink is dry on the contract. Others, aware of the cultural differences and the risks, take more care than they might in the West and negotiate ventures that last. The key success factors for business collaborations in China are much the same as anywhere else: a good fit between the partners; the establishment of trust and understanding between them; and commitment to the notion that the venture is there to make money for all the parties involved, not just one or the other. Assuming good faith on both sides, equity is important: if both sides think the balance between risk, contribution, and rewards is fair, it should endure.

The history of business in China suggests that collaborations have always been a standard format. Certainly the *huaqiao* (or overseas) Chinese companies of East Asia have used collaboration as an important strategic principle.

The joint venture is a business vehicle well suited to the Chinese way of doing business which stresses networks and collaboration. Unlike the West, where all business alliances have to be seen as temporary, Chinese collaborations, based on deep personal relationships extending to the family, can last for generations. In *huaqiao* firms, joint business ventures often lead to personal ties between family-run firms, such as intermarriage between families. Large *huaqiao* firms in Singapore, Malaysia, and the Philippines are frequently linked in this fashion.

Some Western companies see collaboration with a Chinese partner as a way of learning more about China. They become a vehicle as much for exploration of the new market and its potential opportunities as for profit-making. This is a productive way to look at joint ventures.

Turning to practical problems, expectation is one of the most common stumbling blocks. The goal sets of the three relevant parties – Western and Chinese businesses, and the Chinese authorities – are not likely to be the same. The goals of the Chinese partner may include gaining access to newer and higher-level technology and using the kudos of partnering with a foreign company, especially a well-known one, to boost its own company reputation in China. The Western company will wish to learn how to do business in China, with the Chinese partner acting as teacher and guide. And local government will certainly want to increase its tax revenues and employment, as well as introduce modern, competitive technology into its district. Recent research on Western investment in Chinese collaborations has concluded that unsuccessful joint ventures have been characterized by a lack of investment in key areas, especially in the critical area of human resources. Asking for a majority stake in a venture and then failing to back it fully is a recipe for failure.

Despite rapid technological advances in China, some in the West still treat China as a backward country in which second-rate or less than state-of-the-art products and technology can be dumped. In China, however, people are very much conscious of their status as the world's second largest economy. Unsurprisingly, they demand to be treated with respect. They are quick to spot when they are being fobbed off with something that is second rate. Demands for leading-edge technology at second-hand prices (being a poor country entitles them to that too, or so it is sometimes claimed) leads to lively negotiations.

A business collaboration needs complementarity: the two partners both have to want something that the joint venture can give them, be it profits, knowledge, technology, access to scarce resources, or some combination of all of the above. Because of the distance and time involved, to say nothing of the capital commitments, there has to be a strong bond of trust. Good communications between the parties are essential. Chinese firms and institutions often take a long time to set up a joint venture. The venture itself may not be complicated, but they will not move forward until they thoroughly know their prospective partners and their motives and attitudes. Identifying the core issues is key, so that in the negotiation process, there is absolute clarity on what can be relinquished and what has to be retained. There is no special magic to doing business successfully in China, but the four Cs of clarity, courtesy, communication, and common sense will go a long way.

Joint ventures are often seen as risky, but a good one will reduce risk. Shared responsibility, the bringing in of more expertise, including local market knowledge, *guanxi* with other firms, government, and customers are all potential benefits.

It is commonly believed that Chinese collaborations will only succeed if the Western partner takes a majority stake and has control. Consultants often treat this as a necessary condition when negotiating on behalf of clients. Several studies have suggested that foreign-company majority joint ventures are more likely to be profitable than 50/50s or minorities. The key phrase here is 'more likely'. American lawyer Dan Harris argues that obsession with majority stakeholding misses the point. Most Chinese firms do not recognize that owning the majority of equity gives the right to control the company. Harris says that, in China, the key levers of control are the power to appoint both the China joint venture's legal representative and the general manager of the joint venture, and control of the company seal, or 'chop'. If the Chinese partner has control over even two out of these three, says Harris, then effectively that partner controls the Chinese company, no matter what the equity stake.

On the other hand, minority holdings in Chinese companies can, and do, work. The most important thing is to get the right fit between Chinese and Western partners, allowing both to reach all or most of their goals for establishing the venture in the first place. A study by BCG (2016) of joint ventures in the automobile components industry suggests the best projects are those that tailor to local conditions and adapt to fit the needs of both partners, and also where a strong relationship between partners exists outside the framework of the company. Slavish adherence to principles of how a joint venture ought ideally to be established can get in the way.

As for 100% foreign-owned companies in China: most market entry is a matter of progressive commitment. As we show later, firms do not like to gamble, so the key factor is balancing and containing risk. There is a high risk of going it alone and making a large investment in a market where a firm has no developed relationships or contacts, there are high levels of regulation, poor infrastructure, and rapid economic change, growth, and uncertainty. However, for companies with the right experience and resources, going it alone, without a Chinese partner, can work: good examples are 3M and Procter & Gamble.

Much of the point in going it alone in China is making a fresh start and not getting tangled up in existing webs. Most 100%-owned foreign investments in China are greenfield operations, but some have resulted from buying out existing Chinese partners or taking over going concerns.

Up until 2020, WFOEs accounted for about three-fifths of foreign investment in China, with JVs, licensing, and equity stakes in Chinese firms making up the remainder. Going it alone provides 100% control over the firm's assets and how they are used, especially intellectual property. But two caveats must be noted. First, as we said at the beginning of this section, no company in China is an island; government is always there, and relationships with government are vitally important, much more so than in a collaboration, where some of the local relationship building can be left up to the trusted Chinese partner. Second, without sound local knowledge and experience, the foreign owners of a 100% foreign-owned Chinese company are entirely reliant on their local managers and staff. If these are capable, motivated, and trustworthy, all should be well. However, if they lack any one of these three things, the business will struggle; just as it would anywhere. Good local knowledge, however, will enable the owners to spot problems, understand their sources, and fix them more easily.

Identifying and negotiating with Chinese partners

This section covers:

- The go-between
- What type of partner
- The time horizon
- Negotiating.

The go-between

One of the key aspects of relationship building is the role of the *hongniang* (go-between, or literally, maidservant). The *hongniang* has a long and honourable history in Chinese society. Go-betweens are used for functions as diverse as village matchmakers and mediators who help settle legal cases. A go-between is a perfectly natural way to put a business deal together and for the go-between to be a part of that deal and take a percentage from it. The Chinese Government has welcomed foreign consulting firms who come in to act in a *hongniang* role. I operated a company in the 1990s in China which introduced many European companies to China, and advised them on establishing their business there, including joint ventures. Today, major accounting and law firms are able to carry out this role, and there are also numerous special-purpose consultancies with good representation in China and strong track records. Companies looking for such assistance can find advice in Britain from the China-Britain Business Council, and in Europe and the United States from the European and American Chambers of Commerce in China. Such intermediaries usually have considerable experience, and may also be able to provide strategic advice on the sector concerned, its major local players, and opportunities for finding a local partner.

The growth and development of China and the increasing sophistication of its businesses and managers may suggest that the day of the *hongniang* is drawing to a close. I suspect the reverse is true. In the old days, the foreigner was likely to be compelled to do business with just one company or agency.

Now there may be thousands. Cyberneticists tell us that the most successful and flexible systems are also the most complex because they have so many different parts to enable responses to different situations. As China's economy has grown and become more competitive and flexible, it has also become more complex. The role of the go-between, who can deal simultaneously with younger brothers (potential partners) and mothers-in-law (government officials), may well be essential to maintaining harmony within the business family.

What type of partner?

When it comes to choosing a business partner, the Daoist way would be to look for complementarity rather than similarity. IBM went into business with a railway company to deliver its computers. A US East Coast flight simulator company went into business with a Chinese provincial tobacco monopoly. Both succeeded. On the other hand, Diageo's spirits company had no success from a collaboration with a Chinese spirits business. No doubt other factors were at play, but the point remains.

The Economist Intelligence Unit (EIU) (1995) defined three types of partner and, by and large, their classification still holds good:

- *The 'nuts and bolts partner'.* This partner's primary function from your point of view is to help solve problems of access to land, resources, labour, government, distribution, or other factors. The usual quid pro quo is technology transfer or skills training. The EIU notes that these tend to be set up with a short-term focus, and problems can arise once the immediate problems have been solved. Nevertheless, this can be a partner for a first-time entrant.
- *The 'well-endowed godfather'.* These are more powerful partners, and the EIU identifies them primarily as government authorities, such as the (now dissolved) Ministry of Posts and Telecommunications, or the China National Automotive Industrial Corporation. Now that government agencies themselves have been prohibited by the Chinese central authorities from officially engaging in businesses, GONGOs (government-organized non-governmental organizations) affiliated to them do – though typically in more nuanced ways. While somewhat slow and bureaucratic, these partners are also very powerful and have access to resources. Their primary contributions are during the start-up phase, and as powerful 'godfathers' who can help sort out problems down the road. They normally take minority stakes and have little direct involvement in day-to-day management. One of Heineken's unsuccessful joint ventures was with the State-owned Assets Supervision and Administration Corporation (SASAC), the Chinese holding company for the Chinese Government's interests in a wide range of state-owned companies, many of them very large like PetroChina, Sinopec, and China Mobile. Although SASAC certainly has enormous power in China, it's not immediately

obvious that it would exercise its considerable clout to benefit a collaboration with Heineken. And that is what turned out to be the case.

- *The 'four hands on the wheel partner'*. This is a more strategic partnership in which the Chinese partner is interested not just in technology transfer, but also in building its own strategic position. In my opinion this is the best kind of Chinese partner to have, because there is a much better chance of each partner's longer-term interests coinciding with the other. The EIU cited the example of the strategic partnership between Rohm and Haas and Beijing Eastern Chemical Works, which expanded together to set up operations across China. Instead of setting up lots of small JVs to get national coverage, the single JV has expanded and set up sub-ventures. Not surprisingly, this type of partnership is believed to have a higher chance of survival. Shanghai Auto had an obvious interest in using its partner Volkswagen to carve out a strong position for itself in China's emerging vehicle market, and that is what happened. The successful Chinese brand Roewe belongs 100% to Shanghai Auto, which acquired it as Rover from the British owner, modified it, and rolled it out itself across the country. In 2021, Roewe sold about 420,000 cars in China.

Six key factors to consider when choosing a partner in China

1 *Partner goals*. The closeness of each partner's strategic vision to the other is the most important point to consider because, all else being equal, it is the determinant of the collaboration's success or failure. What do the partners want? Are they 'nuts and bolts' partners, or might there be true strategic vision in their thinking?

2 *Technical expertise*. What skills does the prospective partner have? Can the Western firm provide the missing skills, and at what cost? Often, the technology, or know-how brought by the foreign partner will be a vital reason for the Chinese partner's co-operation. The treatment and protection of intellectual property and know-how is a very important element in the relationship.

3 *Facilities*. What facilities (production, distribution, etc.) does the prospective partner have or have access to? Almost certainly these will need to be upgraded, or a new facility constructed at substantial cost.

4 *Location*. Is the Chinese partner geographically well placed to exploit market opportunities? This is particularly important given the physical problems associated with distribution in China. Setting up an operation in Guangzhou (southern China) to market in

Sichuan (western China) or in Shaanxi (north-western China) may not be practical for reasons of cost, regional power politics, and local branding.
5   *Relationships*. How good is the Chinese partner's *guanxi* with other firms in the supply chain, customers, and government?
6   *Reputation*. Does the Chinese partner have a good reputation with local government, as well as with other foreign firms or local Chinese firms? Are its owners and senior managers considered trustworthy? Often a visit to the local government, followed by a frank discussion, is the best way to answer this question.

The time horizon

Relatively speaking, Chinese companies care for long-term relationships and interest. It can be a considerable shock to realize that Chinese companies may be thinking in decades, not years. Investment in China should be regarded by multinationals as a medium- to long-term payback. Shanghai Volkswagen, established in 1985, repatriated profits for the first time in 1993. Coming to terms over the duration of the vision is important.

Negotiating

Much is made of the difficulties of negotiation in China. They can be long and frustrating, and there are plenty of tales of negotiations dragging on for months or even years. Some are amazed when all is concluded within a few weeks, but the home office should be prepared for the long haul. Negotiations mostly run into trouble in China for the same reason that they run into trouble everywhere else. The days when negotiations were bedevilled by political issues and cultural misunderstanding are largely over. The Chinese now understand the Western game, although the reverse is less true. While Western negotiators spend a large part of their time trying to figure out what their opposite numbers are thinking, Chinese negotiators seldom worry about what the Westerners are doing. They focus and refuse to deviate from what they believe to be the best outcome, whereas Westerners are sometimes too quick to conciliate in the mistaken belief that they will give offence on cultural grounds.

   Chinese negotiating techniques can take some getting used to. A typical ruse is to conceal the identity of the most senior player. Westerners, on the other hand, typically exhibit the pecking order all too clearly. When Wall's (Unilever's ice cream business) was negotiating a fire safety certificate for their new plant in Beijing, they worked very hard to satisfy the smart man in the suit only to find that the badly dressed, tramp-like figure sitting quietly at the end was in charge. (The owner of a Yorkshire brewery used to play the same game with unsuspecting sales reps. He would stand with a broom in the yard and accept tips for looking after their cars. Then reception would call him to the meeting and he would dish out the same level of respect he had received in the yard).

A more typical manoeuvre is to keep the boss entirely out of sight. This slows things down quite a bit as regular reports are made and the Westerners are prevented from seeing any body language. This sort of behaviour is becoming increasingly rare, particularly when dealing with larger firms. How quickly one gets to see the boss can also be indicative of how much the company wants to deal with you.

Language, as discussed earlier in the book, is an important issue. A rising generation of younger, internationally educated Chinese executives speak English, though with varying degrees of fluency, though fluency is not necessarily an indicator of fundamental understanding. However, as Chinese businesses become more confident and assertive, there are stories of Chinese executives exercising that assertiveness by demanding that negotiations are conducted in Mandarin, even though they themselves might have good English: my country, my rules. Many Westerners are horrified by this and think it the height of rudeness; on the other hand, how rude is it to show up in another country and expect to do business without speaking their language? The Chinese, like the French, are perfectly entitled to expect other people to speak their language in their own country. Negotiators should either speak good Mandarin or have equally good interpreters with them. Some good Chinese speakers actually prefer to use interpreters who can bring much to the party, in particular, local knowledge. Good negotiation requires top class listening skills and two can often listen better than one. I have conducted several negotiations in Chinese, using interpreters. It's a little like driving a car in heavy gloves – one loses some touch and feel, but it can work perfectly well, and has done on thousands of occasions. It's a good idea to ask for the day's discussions to be summarized at the end, in both languages, preferably in writing. Then both sides are clear on what they have discussed and agreed. That is very important.

What does not change is the Daoist advice to see the problem and potential solutions from both points of view. Defending a position politely, firmly, and consistently may seem boring, but it will impress those who are comparing their notes with those of several hours, days, or months ago. Creative new arguments may free the logjam, but they may also provide a whole new area for exploration and reconciliation – especially if the language is complex or subtle. The negotiation becomes easier if the Chinese side can understand the logic of your overall position. Otherwise, a refusal to, say, introduce certain new technology, or to extend the collaboration beyond a certain date, can seem unreasonable and illogical, and offence may be caused to the other side, which in turn undermines the prospects for a successful outcome.

Negotiations in China are at once both formal and personal. Due recognition must be given to protocol, procedure, and precedence. Informal small talk before and after each negotiating session is expected; and rushing is rude.

If talks are going along well, they may be accompanied by drinks, dinners, and even banquets. Gifts may also be exchanged.

Earlier, I mentioned Western attitudes to Chinese negotiators. There are two poor extremes: (a) the bull in the China shop approach, where the Western negotiators go in hard, lay down their demands and stick to them, and (b) the softly-softly approach, where the Western party gives way too quickly (motivated by too-strong cultural sensitivities, post-colonial guilt, or whatever) and thus appears weak. Deference to your potential partners is one thing, giving away the store is another. Firmness and politeness need to go hand in hand. It's essential to decide before starting what your must-haves are, and how easily you are prepared to give up your nice-to-haves. If progress cannot be made without giving up a must-have, then make it clear that a particular point or demand is a deal-breaker. Walking away from a negotiation may be necessary. If it is, do so politely, because in China your reputation will go before you.

Five key points for negotiators in China

1 Collaborations, even when all partners appear willing, can take up to two years to negotiate. The new foreign investment law has simplified the licensing and approval process by removing the need for the Ministry of Foreign Trade (MOFERT) to approve each foreign investment. The Negative List, referred to earlier, now performs this role, and if a company's proposed activity does not appear on the Negative List, then it can go ahead without approval.

2 In my experience, it is never a good idea to show irritation or anger in negotiations in China. Always be polite, even when stating unpalatable facts or opinions. A sense of humour is a valuable tool, because most Chinese love a good joke, especially about the Japanese. Don't make jokes which reflect badly on China or the Chinese.

3 Silence is considered a valuable negotiating tool.

4 Words and gestures may have hidden meanings, especially in the early stages, and many devices are used to test sincerity and commitment.

5 The time component, or pace, of negotiation is actively managed. For example, they will be conscious of when the foreigners have to leave and of the pressure from the home/head office to reach a deal. Part of the reason for lengthy negotiations is that it gives time for both sides to get to know each other better. It is also a mark of respect not to rush a negotiation which may make it seem unimportant.

Research and a tight definition of strategy and goals are an essential part of preparation for doing business in China. All the warnings about negotiating in China can add to the usual fever of speculation until the Western team get spooked by a dinner cancellation which is no more than they said it was. Holding on to a clear agenda, being unfazed by any side issues, and displaying a calm and friendly demeanour works wonders.

Berry Bros. in China

Berry Bros. & Rudd (BBR) is probably the most prestigious wine merchant in the world. It still trades from 3 St James's Street, London, where it was established in 1698. It is still family owned and has been supplying the Royal Family since the reign of King George III. Until the mid-twentieth century the top end of the wine trade, traditionally burgundy, claret, and port, was dominated by the British market, but that then transferred to the USA, and now China has become a major player.

Berry Bros. & Rudd first established themselves on the ground in China with the Hong Kong Wine Club, modelled on the UK equivalent, in 1997. In the following year Chinaplus Wines Limited was set up as the BBR distributor to develop their wine business in Hong Kong, Macau, and PRC. Chinaplus Wines is a subsidiary of Chinaplus International Limited, founded in 1995 by Hong Kong entrepreneur Mui Kok-Ki.

In December 2012, the partnership fell apart. The facts are hard to determine. It seems likely that BBR decided that the Chinese market was so important they wished to tackle it themselves. It appears they paid too little attention to the fact that it was Mui, through his connections, who opened up the PRC for them, and that sacking Chinaplus would mean considerable loss of face for him and, if it came to a fight, Mui had considerably more resources than BBR.

The BBR accounts to 31 March 2013 showed a £7.3M, revised to £7.7M pre-tax loss, of which £4M was due to, possibly irrecoverable, debts BBR believes it is owed by Chinaplus Wines. The overall pre-tax losses for the following two years were £5.7M and £11.4M (£2.4M and £5.7M for Hong Kong), respectively. Quite a big hit for a company with 319 employees.

The trouble between the partners began in 2008 when the financial crisis in the USA and Europe, and its knock-on effects on the wine trade, coincided with Hong Kong's decision to remove duty on wines creating a wine flood which the local industry, or at least the Chinaplus/BBR joint venture, appeared unable to handle.

Investment in wine for storage by the vendor became all the rage amongst the affluent in Hong Kong. The trouble seems to have been that the JV, and/or BBR back in the UK, simply could not manage this flood of business. Customers' first growths were short delivered or not delivered at all. Correspondence went unanswered and, it was alleged, BBR refused to allow customers to check their own stock.

Making the choice

Each strategic option carries its own levels of risk and reward. The usual evolution is to use organizational learning in such a way that risk is reduced at the same time as commitment is increased. In the Chinese context, *guanxi* is part of that, because it is the traditional way to manage and reduce risk. Thus firms like IBM began with agency arrangements, then JVs, then a WFOE, and now a mix of joint ventures and wholly foreign companies to cope with their R&D, production, and distribution interests.

In making the choice, it is worth analyzing risk more closely into investment, presence, and control risk components.

Investment risk is clearly the risk of losing invested money, plus the time and effort, often considerable, which also has been invested.

Presence risk refers to the rewards that may accrue from a lack of physical presence in China, or the penalties that may be associated with absence. Being there may hurt, but *not* being there may hurt more. As noted in earlier chapters, the Chinese, especially the Chinese Government, value commitment from Western firms and tend to reward it eventually. Companies that show they are prepared to 'stick with' China (IBM and Volkswagen are two prominent examples) tend to have higher levels of success when negotiating new ventures and securing permission to expand. Investment in China is obviously a way of demonstrating commitment. Agency relationships may give brands some profile in the Chinese market, but their lack of commitment could tell against future expansion. Presence risk has to be assessed against the firm's own future plans for China and the region. It may be that a loss-making initial investment may assist in unlocking further, more profitable investments.

Control risk refers to the ability of the firm to control its operations and products in the Chinese market. Operations which are 100% owned obviously offer far higher levels of control risk than agency relationships because so many more things can go wrong, and each from a higher base. In collaborations, the risk varies, as different partners will agree to different levels of control. However, the worst-case scenario is one where the foreigner has to, de facto, pick up all the risk without having enough managerial control to spot and prevent the leakages. This, in essence, is why companies wish to go it alone. However, in China, every company has a partner – the Chinese Government. There is no such thing as complete control.

Risk management is an important exercise, but the reader is referred back to Chapter 4 and the role of *guanxi*. In China, *guanxi* plays an important role in minimizing risk because relationships are both based on trust and can build further trust. The starting point for a risk assessment in China, then, should be the level of *guanxi* that has been built up over time with potential partners. The type of venture comes second.

On a medium- or long-term view, the Chinese picture should be attractive for many foreign companies. If one has to be there one day, now is cheaper than later. The only good time to do it is when the firm can afford it, and when the opportunity arises. *Guanxi* will gradually take care of risk if it is properly and patiently managed.

Xian Janssen (Johnson & Johnson) launched their joint venture in October 1985, when this was the only way to enter that sector in China. It went into production in May 1991. Those five and a half years spanned the Tiananmen incident and the amount of naysaying in the home office can only be imagined. Today it is a huge success with market leadership and competitors trailing far behind. We can count the cost, but it is still too soon to count the profits.

Bibliography

Boisot, M. (ed.) (1994) *East-West Business Collaboration*, London: Routledge.

Boston Consulting Group (2016), "How to successfully manage joint ventures in China", *BCG Perspectives*, 1 March 2016, www.bcgperspectives.com/content/articles/corporate-development-finance-successflly-manage-joint-ventures-china/

EIU (1995) *Moving China Ventures Out of the Red and into the Black*, London: Economist Intelligence Unit.

Fang, T. (1998) *Chinese Business Negotiating Style*, Thousand Oaks, CA: Sage.

Pye, L. (1992) *Chinese Negotiating Style: Commercial Approaches and Cultural Principles*, Westport, CT and London: Quorum Books.

Tang, J. and A. Ward (2002) *The Changing Face of Chinese Management*, London: Routledge.

Verstappen, S. H. (2008) *Chinese Business Etiquette*, Berkeley, CA: Stone Bridge Press.

7   Reaching the Chinese consumer

The plan of Heaven is more certain than the plans of men.

(Chinese proverb)

More than 50% of Chinese shopping was conducted online in 2021. (The proportion in 2020 was 44.8%). Britain is the most active e-commerce country in Europe, but still lags behind China substantially, as does South Korea, at 29% in 2020. Chinese e-commerce grew by 28% in 2020, and by around 21% in 2021.

But in 2011, the e-commerce share of total retail sales in China and the US were about the same: around 5%. In 2021, China recorded about US$2 trillion more than the United States in online sales (although in 2020, the US led China in overall retail sales, US$5.5 trillion to $5.1 trillion).

What happened?

First, Alibaba. The ubiquitous, revolutionary easy-to-use e-commerce platform gave Chinese consumers and SMEs access to everything they needed or could imagine. Successful e-commerce platforms like Alibaba, Pinduoduo, Jingdong (JD), and Meituan have driven Chinese e-commerce. Second, Alibaba and Tencent introduced new kinds of payment systems (Alipay and WeChat Pay), which were far ahead of their Western competitors and based on smartphones. Third, Chinese e-commerce bypassed state-owned-enterprise-style customer treatment and choice in Chinese stores. Fourth, a huge Chinese immigrant population living in the cities provided efficient, low-cost delivery. Finally, the under-35 Chinese generation rely entirely on their mobile phone for news, chats, banking, entertainment, and shopping.

Any company, foreign or Chinese, without a strong online e-commerce strategy in China is a non-starter. The share of Chinese sales from e-commerce for the cosmetics companies Lauder (from the United States) and L'Oréal (from France) reached 40% in 2020.

Any foreign company which is hoping to sell its products to Chinese consumers or households must start with the fact of the deep penetration of

DOI: 10.4324/9781003241164-8

e-commerce into China. As Instagram has affected the decision-making of young Western consumers by enabling product comparisons and the passing of product information, so too with Chinese social media.

Italian fashion brands have enjoyed enormous success in China because they created their own communities of Chinese fans and interacted with them on the main Chinese social networks Weibo and WeChat. Prada's China microblog had reached more than 200,000 followers by October 2020. Bottega Veneta conducted its 2021 New Year campaign on Douban, a Chinese cultural online platform. Another Italian brand, Yoox launched its own online store to test how the Chinese market would react to its luxury goods. Yoox provided precise product information, good photos and videos, and a smooth efficient payment and delivery process. It was a huge hit amongst China's flourishing middle class.

We therefore start this chapter on marketing in China by describing the evolution and current structure of the Chinese internet, and then outline the Chinese consumer market, especially the emergence of the Chinese Generation Z and its interaction with online shopping.

Between 2015 and 2020, internet penetration in China's urban areas rose from 66% to 80%, and in rural areas, from 32% to 56% (China Internet Watch, 2021, China Retail and e-Commerce). China is by far the world's biggest user of the internet, because so many of its enormous population are internet users, mobile penetration amongst younger Chinese is so high, and because so many useful and interesting applications exist on the Chinese internet. China is way ahead of most other countries, including Great Britain and the United States, in using the mobile internet to conduct personal relationships, entertainment, and business.

China is even further ahead when it comes to using the internet for transactions between companies (B2B). Most Chinese people, especially younger ones, have become accustomed to living a big part of their life online, and Chinese corporates have followed this trend. Internet interactions play a much bigger part in Chinese society than they do in Western societies.

Why is this so? Part of the reason is that in the 1990s, when the internet migrated from specialized military and academic use to civil society, Chinese distribution and retailing were primitive and highly localized. At that time there were no national distribution systems in China. In the early 1990s, the American household product company Procter & Gamble had to establish a joint venture with the Chinese army to distribute their products from their base in south China to Shanghai and Beijing. At that time, anything, even an army truck, was better than nothing.

The other reason was that China produced a generation of talented entrepreneurs, most of them from humble roots, with the intelligence to see the opportunities which the internet could (in theory) provide, and the hunger to undergo the risks, failures, and setbacks that are inevitably the entrepreneur's lot. Their ideas met a Chinese population hungry to improve their lives, without legacy systems or entrenched buying habits to forget. These young leaders created groups of like-minded young Chinese people, sprinkled here and there with foreign expatriates. These formed the core of what were to become the huge, enormously influential Chinese private corporations of today, which provide every kind of service to the Chinese population online. (While living in Beijing, I even became involved with such an organization at the start-up stage, between 1999 and 2002, writing its business plan, helping it to raise funding, and promoting its services. My knowledge of China's internet ecosystem is therefore based partly on my personal experience in those early days).

The consequence today of the combination of these two factors – a lack of legacy systems, and an abundance of smart, hungry Chinese entrepreneurs – plus huge unmet needs, is that China boasts the richest e-commerce ecosystem in the world, complete with online videos, shopping comparisons, virtual stores, online payment, and everything imaginable which can make online shopping attractive, interesting, and efficient.

The handful of young Chinese entrepreneurs in the late 1990s were inspired by the success of the first internet-based companies in America, like Amazon, and eBay. Their efforts were greatly assisted by the booming capital markets created by America's easy-money policy in 1998 and 1999, which culminated in the so-called 'dotcom boom'. This made it relatively easy for entrepreneurs in China to raise capital from investment banks and private sources. Several important Chinese internet-based companies were born at this time, including Tencent, Alibaba, and Baidu, companies which today have grown enormously to become (in Tencent and Alibaba's case) among the world's largest companies. Each of these important Chinese internet pioneers started out with a different focus. Tencent concentrated initially on business-to-consumer (B2C) applications, including a mobile-based instant messaging service, called QQ, and internet-based games, which had become very popular in South Korea in the 1990s. Alibaba started initially by constructing an internet gateway for non-Chinese sourcing companies around the world to investigate and buy online from Chinese factories. Baidu focused on becoming China's answer to Google, providing a Chinese online search engine called Youku.

Although the dotcom boom turned to bust in 2000 and 2001, some of these Chinese internet pioneers were able to survive the harsh economic climate that followed, in a still very undeveloped China, by attracting substantial cash investments from overseas companies (in Alibaba's case, Softbank of Japan, and in Tencent's, Naspers of South Africa). Within a few years, they supplemented these early investments by selling their shares on the public capital markets, either in Hong Kong (Tencent) or the NASDAQ in the United States (Alibaba, Baidu). Alibaba, founded in 1999, did not make a profit until 2010, but was able to keep going over a decade of losses thanks to the self-belief and charisma of its founder Jack Ma, which inspired venture capitalists and stock market investors to back him with their cash. Rapid mobile phone adoption, fast-increasing incomes, the evolution of Chinese bank cards to be used for online payments, and enormous increases in mobile speed and capacity (2G, 3G, then 4G, now 5G) were the key factors that eventually enabled the build-up of online revenues in Chinese internet-based businesses.

By 2006 Chinese internet penetration was growing fast. The emergence of Apple's first smartphone in 2007, quickly copied by Samsung, and then by Chinese manufacturers like Huawei and Xiaomi, acted as a huge stimulus to Chinese consumer-based internet applications, like online payment and banking services, music, video, and games. The early Chinese movers, already on their way to becoming the giants of the industry, began to use their capital and industry standing to extend their strategies into other applications. China's huge population encouraged many of these new applications to be consumer based. Alibaba developed an online shopping mall called Taobao, which allowed Chinese consumers to shop online, and with it, an online pay function linked to the consumer's bank card, called Alipay. As millions (then billions, and trillions) of renminbi started to move across Alipay, Alibaba evolved a banking service which offered higher rates of interest than Chinese commercial banks on cash deposits. Alibaba also developed a hosting service called TMall, which gave Chinese companies a shop window on an increasingly used platform to make their sales pitch and display their products to Chinese consumers. Today, Alibaba's B2B and B2C site TMall hosts more than 500,000 different companies (many non-Chinese), selling all kinds of products and services to Chinese consumers.

In 2010, Tencent migrated its highly successful messaging service QQ into WeChat, which has since become a universal messaging mobile-based app in China. Tencent also developed an online payment function (WeChat Pay) to rival Alipay. At the same time Tencent built on its leadership in online games, adding virtual reality and turning the games into addictive activities which (as of mid-2021) continue to generate the largest single component of Tencent's huge revenue.

Meanwhile, a mass of other internet-based companies, inspired by the early Chinese pioneers and the growth of applications in other countries, were emerging in China. Initially, these focused on ways of streamlining everyday activities which needed information, or a connection with an agent or middleman, like ordering taxis, comparing and booking restaurants, and arranging air travel and holidays. Online payment was still a novelty, and most people preferred to complete their purchase offline, using cash over the counter, or a bank card. After 2010, as systems improved, online payment gradually became commonplace, and as familiarity grew, consumer habits evolved. By 2015, as mobile speeds grew with 4G, and as the Chinese consumer switched fully to online product search and payment, a huge ecosystem of online shopping websites or 'apps' started to evolve. Tencent, Alibaba, Baidu, and Sohu, the four pioneers who had managed to stay in business during the bleak years between the disappearance of the dotcom boom in 2000 and the beginning of China's online consumer society around 2010 were able to leverage their large balance sheets to invest in many of these cash-hungry start-ups. They were joined by more traditional sources of early stage capital, including the Japanese venture capitalist Softbank which backed

Alibaba in 2000 (and which still owns 26% of the company). Today, for example, Tencent owns 18% of e-commerce company JD.com (a direct competitor of Alibaba's Taobao), 17% of Pinduoduo, which gives consumers direct access to rural food producers, and 20% of Meituan Dianping which enables meal ordering and delivery, and 44% of the Chinese short video market, through its minority ownership of three companies: Kuaishou (26%), Bilibili (10%) and Weishi (8%). By 2020, Tencent had made investments in 800 companies, of which around 100 have reached a market capitalization of more than US$1 billion, some of which are based outside China.

I have described in outline the evolution of China's internet-based economy because it is essential for foreign companies doing business in China to comprehend that in China, the internet is ubiquitous and used much more extensively, and for a much wider range of daily activities, than in most other societies, and is ahead of all Western economies in this sense. In 2020, the overall global share taken by internet-based retail sales was 18%. In China, about 800 million people do their shopping online (about 80% of the internet user base), and the share of online shopping in China is over 50%.

Here is an example of how a 30-year-old Chinese person uses online apps, already available and downloaded on his/her mobile phone, through his or her workday:

Table 7.1 Typical usage of apps

7 a.m.	Wakes, checks messages
7.45	Orders and pays for a taxi to travel to the office
8.30	Buys breakfast at a store, using an online pay app
9 a.m.	Starts work, checks work messages online
10	Uses a work break to chat with friends online
12 noon	Buys lunch using an online delivery service
12.45	Shops online, using Taobao, or JD.com
5 p.m.	Browses news online
6	Buys groceries online
8	Watches TV, listens to music, plays games, chats with friends – all online

Today, the Chinese internet ecosystem is the world's largest, and still developing fast.

A complex set of relationships exists between hundreds of tiny and not-so-tiny Chinese start-ups, and a few much larger companies who act as central nodes in the Chinese e-commerce network. The large nodes are early starters (like Tencent and Alibaba) who were able to reach critical mass early in the 2000s, and raise substantial funding in order to create their own internet ecosystems. Literally hundreds of different websites, apps, or service providers are clustered around the principal nodes, most of them owned or part-owned by the main players, and providing a service related in some way to their node's principal business. The nodes provide capital and, in return, they partner with the new companies to integrate their ideas and technology with their own existing markets and user bases. Tencent's early focus on messaging, and its ubiquitous messaging app WeChat gives it an advantage over Alibaba in introducing new services and technologies to its massive B2C user base. Alibaba's strength in e-commerce, via its Chinese consumer website Taobao and its shop-window service TMall give it the edge over Tencent in online shopping and online B2B services.

The ecosystem nodes are focused on Chinese internet companies Tencent, Alibaba, Baidu, JD (e-commerce), and Qihoo 360 (internet security); on hardware manufacturers Lenovo and TCL (computers) and Xiaomi (smart-phones); and on investment company Fosun, which combines its many interests in Chinese internet companies with 'content', extending to ownership of Wolverhampton Wanderers Football Club in Great Britain, among many other consumer and leisure-focused investments. Alibaba and Tencent are the largest 'nodes' in the Chinese tech network.

Popular business model elements adopted by Chinese start-ups include cost innovation; speed in execution, scale-up, and cloning; opportunity facilitation (rather than service provision); ecosystem-driven innovation; customer-centricity (even at the expense of core competence focus); mechanisms for minimizing the need for trust; analytics-driven models; external capacity exploitation; and large niche specialization.

One of the larger nodes in the network, Xiaomi, provides a good example of the innovative approach of Chinese private companies to business development, an approach which is closely integrated with internet applications. Xiaomi has evolved over the last decade from a manufacturer of affordable smartphones into a consumer electronics brand known for its array of products spanning smart wearables, appliances, and mobility devices. Although Xiaomi is a hardware manufacturer, it defines itself as an internet company. It charges almost no margins on its mobile phones; and its TVs, which use the same panels as those in higher end models, sell for significantly lower prices than their competitors. In order to move fast and minimize the financial risk associated with failure of any one product, the company taps into China's vast manufacturing ecosystem, taking a minority share in selected OEMs (original equipment manufacturers). Chosen products then undergo several design iterations and smart features are added to plug the devices (like robot vacuum cleaners) into the company's online platform.

China's business environment is changing rapidly. Engagement with start-ups brings new ideas and relationships which enable existing companies to cope with rapid change in the business environment, both from a sales and innovation perspective, and to leverage external technologies and business models.

It is argued that the tech 'crackdown' which started in China toward the end of 2020 has as its primary motivation the desire by the Chinese Government to damage China's private sector for ideological reasons, and swing the balance back toward the Chinese state. In fact, we perceive the new regulations much more constructively, essentially as a catch-up by China to the developed world, to regulate an industry which previously was completely unfettered. The termination of online lending and borrowing (so-called peer-to peer –P2P) and online tutoring are designed to protect Chinese society, rather than impoverish Chinese entrepreneurs (although the new regulations did crash the stock prices of some high-flying NASDAQ-listed Chinese 'tech' companies, like TAL US and Yirendai). Recent new rules have introduced greater control of content, some of which although undoubtedly designed to protect the position of the Chinese Government, are also directed at increasing security through data control and better balancing the relationship between the large platforms on the one hand, and users on the other. In short, we don't believe that new regulations in China over internet platforms are aimed at destroying entrepreneurship and the private sector, and we don't believe they will have this effect.

How has the Chinese consumer responded to this new, virtual world of shopping? There is an important split in consumer habits, by age. Most people in the age range 35–45, and everyone under the age of 35, who grew up into adulthood accompanied by internet-based services, rely on their mobile phone to search for products, compare them and their prices, buy them, and arrange for their delivery. Conversely, most Chinese people over 50, who developed their shopping habits in a pre-internet age, still stick to their old habits, and prefer to go to a store to see products before they buy them.

Thus, one way of segmenting the Chinese consumer is by age: under 35, 35–50, and over 50. An important target shopper is the 30 to 35-year-old Chinese woman, because she shops for her family, and tells her husband and her parents what to buy. Increasingly, she uses her mobile phone to shop, while another, younger target group, Generation Z, totally depend on their smartphone.

Any foreign company selling consumer products or services in China has to have an online strategy. If the Chinese age-group under 40 is a target, then the marketing strategy needs to be focused online, perhaps with offline support – TV-based for advertising and in-store for promotion and sales. This may seem a tall order for a foreign company that knows little about China and contains few, if any Chinese speakers or citizens.

The best way around this problem is to call on expert advice. Companies have been established in the last year or two specifically to help foreign companies to sell their products in the Chinese market using online strategies. These strategies focus on establishing a shop window on a popular Chinese shopping platform like TMall, where the product range can be displayed, then supporting it by using popular Chinese websites and chat platforms like Weibo, WeChat, JD and VIPShop, and using key words (or Chinese characters) to draw online shoppers to the product and the company's website. Such keywords are found by frequent online searches which identify the dozen or so characters or expressions which draw online shoppers in China. The online strategy is usually supplemented by offline activities focused on key spending times in the Chinese calendar, of which the so-called 'singles' day of 11.11 and Chinese New Year are the most important, out of about a dozen. Offline activities could include sponsored days out: for instance, hiking days for an outerwear company.

One of the principal characteristics of the Chinese consumer is a lack of trust. This is the result of being bombarded by advertising messages of all kinds, 24/7, and by the unscrupulous behaviour of some of China's consumer product companies, in an imperfectly regulated Chinese shopping environment. Too much information online, offline, and on TV has led to consumer disloyalty; a reluctance to connect emotionally, to change from surfing into a deeper examination of a product or a reluctance to stick with a known product in the face of attractive alternatives. The Chinese consumer searches for authentic ways he or she can connect with products. Chinese opinion leaders and celebrities therefore play a more important role in Chinese advertising than they do in America or Europe. Providing authenticity is an important way of breaking down the relatively high barriers to communication in China between brand and consumer. Streamed videos are another popular way in China of building the relationship between the product and the buyer or user.

Chinese nationalism, stoked by Xi Jinping's strong utterances on "making China great again", has become a feature of Chinese consumer behaviour in recent years. Foreign companies, which 20 years ago found it easy to persuade Chinese consumers of a better product, even at a higher price than locals, no longer have it all their own way. In fact, outside of segments like medicine (where Chinese buyers may believe that a foreign company's research and development is better than the Chinese competition), there's nothing to choose today in the Chinese market between foreign and Chinese products, and the nationalist element may even promote a Chinese brand over its foreign counterpart.

If this all sounds difficult, it is. China, now neck and neck with the United States for the position of the world's largest consumer market, is a highly competitive marketplace. But the opportunities and the rewards for getting it right are significant.

The story of Shein

Shein is a Chinese fast fashion company which started in 2008, and in 2021 grabbed top market share in the United States, beating former segment leaders Zara, H&M, Forever 21, and Fashion Nova.

For those not aware, fast fashion is a style aimed at young women developed by Inditex (which owns Zara), and H&M, for weekly or fortnightly changes of look. Clothes are cheap enough to change frequently. Shein (former name Sheinside) has succeeded by using the online-based strategy in the US that it learned in the Chinese fashion market.

Shein's consumers are young women who spend much of their days on their mobile phones. The company uses analytics software to trawl through media. Shein makes a large number of sales via mobile apps rather than by conventional websites, and has borrowed ideas from the world of gaming, such as countdown clocks and games with discounts as prizes, to boost engagement and spending. Before shoppers check out, Shein's app entices them to continue adding to the basket with the lure of gifts and express delivery if they hit a certain spending threshold. Although such practices are common among fast fashion retailers, Rouge, a website and branding agency, found that Shein included more prompts to users to spend more money or disclose personal data than any other fast fashion company.

Dimitrios Tsivrikos, a consumer psychologist at University College, London, says that Shein has turned shopping into a form of online entertainment. "Social media has been a very effective promotional outlet for Shein, especially with the rise of TikTok." (*Financial Times*, 10 December 2021 "Shein: the Chinese company storming the world of fast fashion"). Established fast fashion companies have relied heavily on Instagram, but Shein produces short videos on TikTok, a Chinese streaming app which has attracted global interest. In early 2021, Shein's app downloads in the US were second only to those of Apple.

Low prices (only Primark's prices are lower than Shein's), good use of artificial intelligence, growing dominance in mobile apps, a well-organized supply chain, weekly changes in product, and heavy use of streamed videos featuring 'influencers' who advertise Shein clothes – these are the keys to Shein's stunning success in the United States. Do they sound familiar? To anyone operating in the Chinese market, they should.

In China, product/customer segmentation is essential, and can lead to real success with the right application of creative thinking. Kentucky Fried Chicken – whose appeal is universal in the US – targeted children in China. In 1987, they were the first Western fast food chain in China, a 60%-owned JV and not without their problems. Although the original product was not to conventional Chinese tastes, they knew the 'little emperors' would be indulged. This strategy has worked: KFC remains (anecdotally) the number one venue in China for children's birthday parties. By 2013, they had 4,563 outlets, the most of any chain in China, arguably the strongest brand and about up to 50 different product permutations including 'Dragon Twister', a wrap with fried chicken, cucumber, spring onions, and duck sauce like Peking duck. Much advertising in China for other products focuses on children for one-child family reasons; following the herd may or may not be a good strategy.

Guerrilla strategy (and Mao Tse Tung is a good guide here) dictates reining in one's territorial ambitions and selecting the smallest, most favourable ground (market) one can hold. Never mind where the brand 'should' be;

where can it win? Westerners tend to act conventionally and start in one of the big four centres (Shanghai, Beijing, Guangzhou, or Shenzhen), which are easily accessible, rather than the hinterland where competition may be weaker. Once you get on the ground, you can overlay the geographic strengths of each competitor on a map of China before choosing.

Leading marketing companies, having analyzed their own company's capabilities in its competitive environment and empathized with the end users (consumers) and E+3C (Environment, Consumers, Competitors, own Company), write the brand's 'positioning' down in a short statement. By 'brand', we mean the product being marketed, whatever the sector, including the product and its packaging. Reputation is just as important in industrial marketing as branding is for the consumer. A positioning statement is effective when it is focused and sacrifices all the easy compromises. It should identify the immediate customer and end user and pick out the single reason why it is (a) different and (b) better from their point of view, relevant to the most threatening key competitor. Not a woolly 'everyone' but the firm you would most like to take business from and least like to lose it to. A few other key strategies may need inclusion, but a positioning statement should not exceed one page, no matter how big the brand or market (China).

Products, branding, and packaging

A *Harvard Business Review* article from 1994 describes *guo qing*, which means 'Chinese characteristics' (or perhaps more accurately 'Chinese circumstances' or the "special situation in China"), and advises that foreign companies need to adapt to it in order to reach Chinese consumers. There is, of course, a broader debate about localization and globalization more generally, and each has its proponents. IKEA has the standard international approach of opening a market with their usual range of products and only adapting when they have to. In the US, IKEA took many years before the eventual adaptations suited Americans and the stores began to make money. History repeated itself. In 1999, Chinese visitors thronged into the new IKEA stores in Beijing and Shanghai, but few bought. The furniture seemed too expensive. IKEA has since managed to establish itself in the market, and has three of its five largest stores worldwide in China. Our point that adaptation needs to be based on what is necessary in reality, not theory, is borne out by the extraordinary way that Chinese customers began to use the beds and sofas in IKEA stores for kicking off their shoes and sleeping or even finding parents for their future children. By 2015 the problem had become so widespread that, while testing beds and sofas for comfort was still allowed, removing shoes to do so was not. There are other stories of Chinese parents visiting IKEA stores in order to see how a Western living room is laid out, and taking the idea home with them to put into practice for themselves. Other Chinese visited IKEA because they liked the Swedish food on offer in the canteen.

One good example of how creative adaptation can create a market in China seemingly out of nothing comes from the diamond merchants De Beers, who already had a successful track record in adapting their product to the Japanese and other East Asian markets before going into China. On the face of it, diamonds do not easily lend themselves to adaptation. But what De Beers set out to adapt was not the product, but people's *perceptions* of it. In the West, diamonds are marketed with heavy connotations of romance, not just engagement rings but gifts on wedding anniversaries and the like. The assumption is that men buy diamonds for their wives, partners, and girlfriends. But the Asian notion of romance, just like the Asian notion of law, is different from that of the West. In the Tiger economies, De Beers started marketing diamonds directly to women themselves. The attractiveness of the stone itself, not the romance surrounding it, became the key feature, and women were encouraged to buy diamonds to make themselves feel good and more desirable.

In China, yet another approach was taken. Many young Chinese are decidedly materialistic, so the East Asian approach might have worked, but De Beers decided there was another way to position diamonds: as a symbol of an enduring relationship. Harmony, rather than love, was chosen as the key connotation, and ads featured husbands giving wives rings on their wedding days and then flashed forward to show subsequent years of happy and prosperous marriage. In fact, Western-style weddings have become big business in parts of China, with couples getting married in formal gear and white wedding dresses in the morning – sometimes even in a Christian church – before going on to a traditional Chinese banquet in the evening. Adaptation takes place on both sides.

Some new products introduced from the West may well have problems of perception in China. Marketers introducing unfamiliar products might do well to consider using methods such as personal demonstrations and sampling. Mary Kay Cosmetics and Avon used these methods when introducing their health and beauty lines in Guangzhou and Shanghai, though they have since had regulatory problems. Colgate, Rémy Martin, and Tang Orange all used this method, as did Coca-Cola.

For consumer goods, therefore, a small sampling and/or demonstration promotion in a key entry market should be standard practice until it is shown to be unnecessary; that is, when more sophisticated techniques prove more productive. For products like automobiles and farm machinery, a showroom is necessary. Before 1949, major international automobile companies all had showrooms in China, employing salespeople to persuade potential buyers to have a close look and take a drive. Now, cars and farm machinery are being displayed once again in showrooms. In the early 1990s, these showrooms were usually the offices of the agents who imported the products, and they tended to lump many different products together. This has changed, certainly as far as the luxury car market is concerned, and some companies have experimented with setting up networks of dealers specializing in their own cars. (The Chinese Government has an ambivalent attitude to the car. Auto production was at first encouraged and then discouraged, but popular complaint over the lack of cars to buy forced the relaxation of production restrictions. As a result, air pollution and traffic jams worsened).

The importance of branding and packaging cannot be overstated. Packaging is one of the ways in which economic reform has changed some aspects of Chinese culture. The universal big bag (*midai*) for carrying home the rice has been replaced by packaged rice as supermarkets take over. The brightly coloured shopping bag carrying the retailer's brand has also become commonplace. Packaging's key role is communication; it is the carrier of the brand name and symbol. This is where 'Chinesing' has to start. Specialist consultants are available to explain how Western brand names and packaging will be seen, said, and understood – in all the major Chinese languages.

Tang Orange, which is advertised as a 'fresh-squeezed-orange taste instant drink', has the Chinese name *Guo Zhen* (fruit treasure). The mark and the package are both very appealing: the latter carries the wording "Selected by NASA for U.S. Space Flights", and the advertising strapline is, "the drink in space time". The Changsha Refrigerator Factory, which uses Italian technology in its manufacturing, adopted the brand name 'Zhongyi', which means both 'Sino-Italian' and 'satisfactory' or 'to one's liking'. Sometimes successful brand names can be construed from Chinese words which sound like the company's Western brand name; thus Gillette used the Chinese name *Jili*, which means 'lucky'.

Numbers are also important: for example, eight is lucky and nine is everlasting. Animals have symbolic significance: the tortoise stands for longevity, while fish mean wealth. Colours also have strong significance. The scarlet, imperial yellow, and gold are now a cliché; you will see them most commonly on Chinese goods that are destined primarily for sale to the West. White is the funeral colour and seen as unlucky.

Unsurprisingly, in a culture where symbols are so powerful, brands need to develop a unique iconic symbol. Research in the West indicates that non-letter logos (for example, those for Apple or Shell) communicate more effectively than words or Roman letters (BP or IBM). In Chinese culture, non-letter symbols can be even more powerful. Rémy Martin's centaur ('man-horse') has positive associations and has much to do with that brandy's dominant market share.

The quality of consumer goods has improved markedly over the past few years; even where quality is still not as high as for Western goods, the price differential more than compensates for this. Chinese marketers have been getting better at reinforcing their brands too, and can offer the additional appeal to Chinese cultural values. In Beijing, the modern shopping district of Wangfujing may have all the big foreign names, but go south and west of Tiananmen Square and you will find that Chinese shops selling Chinese branded goods are booming. The restoration of the centuries-old pharmaceuticals brand Tong Ren Tang, in its elegant flagship store off the market street of Dazhalan, is a symbol of the resurgence of Chinese brands. In the nineteenth century, Tong Ren Tang had a nationwide presence; today, as it opens or reopens stores all over China, it is achieving this again. Other old brands like the roast duck restaurant Quanjude have re-emerged.

The reassurance of a famous brand, whatever the price, is still very important to Chinese consumers, but that brand need not be foreign to be successful. Consider too that many consumers quite happily buy counterfeit brands. They are not fooled; but they believe that, if the counterfeiters have gone to so much trouble, the quality is probably a reasonable match for much less money. Experience with rip-offs will reinstate the importance of genuine brands, in time, but without much help from the law.

Brands will probably be *more* important in China than internationally in the long term, but which brands will end up winning out long term is still, in part, to be decided. The positions of foreign brands like Volkswagen (which occupies about 20% of China's car market), and European cosmetic and luxury product companies like L'Oréal, Hermes, and Ferragamo seem assured, but there is plenty of room for others in a huge, rapidly changing Chinese market. Our reasons concern overseas Chinese behaviour, *guanxi*, and the associated lack of consumer rights enforcement. Overseas Chinese consumers, who have been buying in sophisticated free markets for some time, still exhibit high levels of loyalty to brands. In an uncertain world, consumer-brand relationships should prove enduring once they settle down. Brands will remain more expensive than local unbranded, or private labels (which are actually retailer brands), or counterfeits, but they are also reassurance and reduce risk. Economic factors play a part and the long-term strength of brands needs a sufficiently large middle class willing to pay this marginal extra cost for these benefits. The Chinese middle class has achieved this position.

Brands convey status and achievement; their possession signals one's place within one's social group and community. The associative aspects of Chinese culture are significant. Individuality matters, but so too, in China, does the need to belong to a certain group. As people leave villages for the cities, they need to express a new urban, on-the-move identity for themselves. Hong Kong is a good example. Once a brand has the reputation of being powerful and 'good', people will wish to be associated with it.

Certainly, branding is not limited to foreign products, and Chinese companies have developed strong brands. The importance of branding has not been lost on Chinese companies. Many more strong Chinese brands will emerge.

Product issues

- Start with the packaging. What does it communicate not just in meaning but in price, quality, and other associations? How does the brand name sound; indeed is it sayable in all the main Chinese languages?
- As anywhere, forget the intentions and the rest of the world. How would/does the *Chinese* consumer use this product? What problem

does it solve for them? How could it do that better, for example, a smaller pack size? What is the primary competitive advantage from their point of view?

- Consider using demonstrations and personal selling when introducing new products, not only as a good way of introducing the product, but as a crucial market research to check on the two points above.
- Especially consider sampling on a wider scale. It is expensive but it does get the product into the hands of the end user.
- Then, more importantly, follow up to see who repurchased using their own money. This is possibly the most important metric in any brand launch.
- Finally, consider the long-term brand–consumer *guanxi*. What needs to be done to reinforce that, build confidence, and reduce risk to the consumer?

Pricing

I have already referred to the need for sensitive pricing between imported and local products. Consumer readiness to pay import prices for locally manufactured goods has largely evaporated along with economic growth. The skimming route is certainly an option. McDonald's successfully entered at a premium of four to five times the costs of eating out, but their novelty factor has evaporated long ago, and that is now impossible. Every generation of marketers believes that earlier times were easier and that 'today the pressure on domestic prices is strongly downward'.

The reality is that pricing has always been critical, but the premiums and discounts that customers will accept do change. Careful judgement is needed; once the brand's novelty value wears off, or once other high-profile competitors enter the market, prices need to come down to support continued brand growth. McDonald's did just this, by gradually reducing its premium, and the brand has grown well. Kentucky Fried Chicken, however, tried to hold on to its margin for too long following entry to Hong Kong in the mid-1970s. The business dried up; at the same time there were disruptions at a higher level as the parent company in the US was bought and sold a couple of times. Consequently, it was not until the early 1990s that KFC re-entered the market, on a small scale and well behind many of its fast food rivals. Today KFC is still leading in fast food chains in China.

No one should imagine that price is not an issue for Chinese consumers: the reverse is true. Studies in Hong Kong and Singapore show that they tend to be much more canny and discriminating shoppers than the average person in the West. But for most brands, price has a display as well as an economic role and that needs to be factored in.

Pricing issues

- Consider two entry strategy options: skimming and shooting straight for the target. 'Skimming' is entering the market at a high price and then letting price find its natural level as the usership broadens. If no one else intervenes, this can be the more profitable route, but it can alienate potential users. More often it can be killed by a bolder entrant straight shooter with a competitive price and, thereby, volume sales. However, if you enter too low, the main risk with this option is that it may be tough to get back up.
- Be 'premium' by Chinese, not international, standards. Competing on price with Chinese competitors is very hard, if not impossible.
- Pricing should be determined by the brand's strategic positioning and consumer empathy.
- If sales fail to show up, or evaporate, you will be told that price is to blame. Do not panic; that is the easy rationalization by inexperienced marketers. Look again.

Promotion and advertising

Advertising

Advertising in China seems to be more strongly correlated with sales than in, say, Britain, but that does not mean that it is more effective. Perhaps Chinese businesses are just quicker to hand cash to their agencies when sales are rising and to take it away when they are falling. Most Chinese advertisers and their agencies have very little idea of what advertising does for them, which is refreshingly honest.

Partly as a result, a large cultural gap exists between Western clients and their multinational advertising agencies on the one side and their Chinese counterparts on the other. The Chinese view is that their ad agents, who may have little expertise beyond media buying, do not deserve much remuneration and that attitude rules out the multinationals. Conversely, the multinationals expect more expertise on the part of their clients. Chinese clients admire the quality of the foreign agencies' work (though the gap is rapidly closing, and in terms of television advertising may well have closed) but do not want to pay the bills.

Given the importance of brands, advertising should play an important role in terms of both brand awareness and reinforcement. Some Western advertising campaigns have proved even more effective in Asia than in the West; Michael Jordan became a household name among children in Singapore. But advertising in East Asia does have its pitfalls for the unwary, and most of them concern culture. Simple problems with translation are of course responsible for many of these – almost everyone has probably had a laugh by now at the expense of Coca-Cola, whose slogan 'Coke adds life' was translated in Taiwan as 'Coke will bring back your ancestors from the grave'. The transmission of cultural values is often more difficult. Many 'sexist' ads on television and in newspapers are simply not acceptable in the Chinese cultures of East Asia, where relatively high moral standards prevail. This is particularly true of China, but less so of the Hong Kong SAR; ads on Star TV broadcast into the PRC are noticeably more risqué than those on China Central TV. Ads that show children rebelling against their parents are also unlikely to be well received. Finally, the problem is compounded by cultural diversity in those countries with indigenous as well as Chinese and/or Indian immigrant communities.

Is creative (emotional) advertising in China more effective than product videos (rational)?

Tim Broadbent was arguably the world's leading authority of his day on advertising effectiveness (as was his father, Simon, who more or less invented the subject). Tim died young in 2015 after six years as Global Effectiveness Director for Ogilvy & Mather, working mainly in China but finally in Singapore. O&M were good at winning 'creative' awards for original advertising and 'effectiveness' awards for ads that seemed to generate sales. But were the ads the same, in other words, is creativity just a competitive game between agencies or is it really the business?

After two years' confrontation with this issue in China, Broadbent wrote a seminal paper[1] which, inter alia, exposed three widely held views as myths:

> Myth one: some argue for product demo campaigns, because they believe Asian consumers are less advertising literate than those in the West. Not so. Asians see 55% more TV commercials a week than Westerners. For example, the average UK consumer sees 293 commercials a week, while Chinese consumers see 600 a week, and Indonesians see 1,000. Rather than being less advertising literate, Asians are obviously more advertising literate.
>
> Myth two: some say that Asians are less creative or respond to creativity in a different way. This view appears to be based on old academic psychological studies which have now been discredited, for example, because of language bias in American-created tests, or tests that did not compare like with like. More recent studies have shown no difference in the way Chinese, Japanese, and Americans respond to creative stimuli – if anything, the Chinese seem to appreciate novelty more than most.

Myth three: Some still believe that TV is the best medium for conveying basic product information, necessary in developing markets. That may have been true in America in the 1950s, but times have moved on. Nowadays, consumers mainly use the TV for entertainment and get brand information from other sources too, particularly digital. TV campaigns are mostly processed at low attention levels, which makes it a strong medium for emotive campaigns, while the internet is mainly used at high attention levels.

In short, creative advertising is likely to be even more effective in China than it is in the West.

Attitudes to advertising can be paradoxical. Advertising, in China as elsewhere, is disliked as undermining national culture, lowering standards, increasing demand for the 'wrong' things, and intruding into the landscape and/or media. Foreign advertising can be particularly offensive when it oversteps the bounds of cultural sensibilities, awakening not-so-deeply buried Chinese memories of foreign domination. On the other hand, advertising makes economic sense and consumers enjoy advertising and find it useful.

Until the arrival of digital devices, television was the main vehicle for advertising and is still important. All the provinces, autonomous regions, and municipalities and a great many large and medium-sized cities have their own television stations penetrating every corner of the country, though most have limited reach. The most powerful station is China Central Television (CCTV). It has many channels devoted to news and current affairs, sport, family, and games shows and has national reach; there is also an English-language channel, CCTV International (CCTV 4). Nationally, there are also five educational channels (CETV), one news network (China Xinhua News Network Corporation – CNC), fourteen cable networks (including MTV, HBO and ESPN) and nine digital.

Media costs in China are volatile and unrelated to prices in other world markets. Furthermore, they are sometimes not what they seem. It is not just a matter of the usual haggling but sometimes digging to determine who has inserted himself into the sales chain without making an offsetting saving for the client.

The high levels of Chinese media inflation are propped up by relatively strong demand for advertising:

The main consumer product categories underpinning China's advertising market make it less susceptible than some other countries to future economic downturns. More than half of all spend is generated from just four product categories: pharmaceuticals (including Chinese tonics), toiletries, retail, and beverages. Ad spend in China on mass consumer, daily use products is much higher as a proportion of total spend than in most other countries.

Guanxi brand–consumer principles may apply. If one can afford it, advertising early, before the product is available, can pay off even though the short-term financials are unattractive. Normally, in Europe and in North America, advertising should follow distribution. In China, a number of Japanese brands, such as Sony, were advertised for some years before coming onto the market. With hindsight, this was a smart investment, especially as advertising rates were a great deal cheaper then.

A good idea of the kinds of advertising currently used on Chinese television can be gained from watching CCTV or other main channels. Spot the differences between East and West. Most ads for Western brands are produced in China but against international strategies. Much of the Chinese advertising is imitative. Lager is promoted by clean-cut young Chinese men in a Western-style bar, while Chinese spirits use images of the Great Wall, people dancing in ethnic costume, and elderly men proclaiming how the product has helped them to reach a wise old age.

We do not take up space with advertising regulations which, following the WTO, are being brought more into line with the rest of the world. The guidelines in the box below are not intended to be taken too rigidly. In advertising, rules – but not government regulations – were made to be broken.

Some advertising dos and don'ts

- Be careful with comparative advertising and exaggeration; most of the problems with the censorship board have been in this area.
- Translate outwards and then back when approving advertising copy. Have an independent translation of the translation made to see if the original matches.
- Where direct response is being used, understand the communication and distribution problems for the responder. Be convenient for the buyer.
- Don't assume your agency knows and applies the regulations. Get yourself a good lawyer. Check on local regulations too before starting to shoot.
- Don't say your brand is *the* leader (especially if it is).
- Don't use models whose appeal is based on sex. Of course Chinese companies do, but from a foreign advertiser it is all too easy to portray this as exploitation.
- Use emotional advertising and do not believe the media costs you are offered.

Place, channels, and distribution

Poor infrastructure and distribution have discouraged more than one investor. Billions have been invested in infrastructure over the last ten years, but need always outstrips capacity. There are ways around the problem, but they often require some creativity. The Australian beer company Foster's, when expanding its interests in China, set up a whole network of joint ventures, first with producers in a number of regional centres, and second with the Hong Kong conglomerate Wheelock, which has experience in transport and distribution in China. By establishing many regional centres rather than a few large breweries, Foster's has cut down on the distance its goods needed to be shipped; and where shipping is required, Wheelock's expertise and contacts help cut down the problems. Sadly, things did not work out for them. In June 2006, Foster's sold its remaining brewer (Shanghai) to Suntory, having sold the Tianjin and Guangzhou businesses in 1999. As earlier commented in the context of the early entry of Dutch brewer Heineken to China in 1983, the Chinese beer market has proved a difficult one for foreign beer companies to penetrate successfully, in the face of stiff competition and well-entrenched local Chinese producers who understand Chinese beer tastes and pricing-points better than foreign beer companies.

Mary Kay Cosmetics in Shanghai used party plan selling to reach its potential customers, who were mostly young working women. As most people in Shanghai have fairly limited residential space, Mary Kay established its own premises and made meeting rooms available to its sales agents, who could invite potential customers to parties on the premises (where, of course, they could be exposed to other forms of point-of-sale promotion). They, and Amway and Avon, were surprised to be included in the 1998 ban on pyramid selling. After 50% losses, they renegotiated themselves into a new regulation which required, inter alia, that their salespeople pass an exam administered by the local authorities. By 2005, Mary Kay claimed to have around 350,000 agents and China was fast outstripping the US to become their largest market. Apparently, they had been profitable since 2001.

Retailing has had a chequered history. The first retail joint venture was established in Shenzhen in 1991, and since then retail JVs have proliferated. Manufacturers are allowed their own stores or rent counters in department stores in the cities, ostensibly as 'windows' to get market information. The realization is dawning, however, that retailing should be left to specialist retailers. As a result, retail quality is rapidly improving. A walk through Beijing or Shanghai shows the smartening up of department stores with traditional Chinese goods but, more importantly for the future, Chinese versions of international goods made to improving standards. The prices of imported goods leave plenty of space. Department stores remain a major force in retailing. As noted above, however, their strength is waning as consumers, as in the UK, turn to chain stores and online stores such as Taobao. 'Sincere', part of the Hong Kong department store chain, closed after only two years. Many department stores are themselves building an online presence.

Before the traumatic events in the early twentieth century (see Chapter 2), China, even more than England, was a nation of shopkeepers. Under Maoism, small enterprises were largely swallowed up by the state. After reform, the *huaqiao* from Singapore, Thailand, Malaysia, and elsewhere moved into distribution and trade, often via family members still living in China. Wangfujing, a street in Beijing, was one of the first areas to be opened up to JV retailers and was largely developed by Hong Kong money; it could be a shopping street anywhere in East Asia. Dazhalan, on the other hand, is in a historic quarter of the city and was developed using local money, and remains more distinctively north Chinese. Shanghai has also thrown open its doors to foreign retailers, including Isetan, Sogo, and Yaohan of Japan and Taiwan's Sunrise, along with a variety of Shanghai and Hong Kong-based operations.

The strategy of the Hong Kong real estate companies, in particular, has primarily been to build large-scale commercial buildings for rental to international chain store groups. However, some real estate companies have also sought to include retailing in their permitted scope of business. Where they do not, they simply set up subsidiary companies to engage in retailing directly. Kerry Everbright and Cheung Kong have both used this strategy with success.

There is also a significant European and American retailing presence. Some companies, such as those in clothing and fast food, lend themselves to franchising, as discussed in the last chapter. Metro (Germany), Makro (Netherlands) and Carrefour (France) have made strong China plays. The British are represented by B&Q (Kingfisher), and Tesco which bought 50% of Hymall in 2004 as a JV with Ting Hsin International of Taiwan. Hymall then had 25 stores.

With hindsight it seems Tesco launched relatively late in 2004, after competitors had taken the prime sites. Furthermore the Clubcard which had proved such a winner, building loyalty in the UK, failed in China because Chinese consumers prefer to shop around using a variety of store cards. No doubt there were other factors, but the hard truth was that Tesco's 2004 launch never got off the ground and was followed by years of heavy losses until, in 2013, Tesco gave up and merged their 131 stores with the 2,986 stores of state-owned China Resources Enterprise (CRE) under the Vanguard brand, leaving Tesco with a 20% stake. This strategy was similar to that followed by Heineken, who after trying unsuccessfully to go it alone, merged their China business with China Resources Beer.

Distribution issues

- Although distribution has been greatly liberalized in the last few years and state-owned firms no longer play a major part, both sales channels remain underdeveloped.

- Chinese infrastructure has improved enormously, and the east and most of the centre of China is now world class.
- Waste no time before working out paper solutions for your particular products in the territories you intend to cover. You may need, for example, a separate business with a different governance structure as well as approvals from authorities which may take a long time to arrive.
- Try to find local or foreign companies that have already set up successful distribution networks similar to what you need.
- Consider getting a nucleus of the future sales team to start calling key customers before you have products to sell. Train them in providing technical advice.

The physical problems of distribution may still be caused by an inadequate infrastructure, although Alibaba, Tencent and other Chinese online retailers have revolutionized Chinese distribution by harnessing the army of immigrant workers who exist in every Chinese city. As fast as China's road network has grown over the past two decades, the number of vehicles has grown even faster; companies shipping by road will face increased costs and uncertain delivery times and outcomes. The rail network, largely geared to China's defence against foreign invasion, is inadequate to the task of shipping goods. Water transport is usually efficient, and accounts for about 20% of all freight, but it is slow and does not reach all areas. Air freight tends to be quicker but is much more expensive. Manufacturers can also still expect to face problems in road travel and transport of goods across borders as a result of inter-provincial rivalries. Some provinces in the past have erected barriers at their borders, preventing or charging high fees for certain goods such as rice or cotton. Most of these have disappeared but some problems remain.

Conclusions

- Online shopping has become the dominant form of interaction between Chinese consumers (especially the under-35s) and companies selling consumer products.
- A Chinese online presence, with pictures and videos, is essential for any foreign company operating in China, especially companies who sell consumer products. Spend the time and the money, whatever it takes, to build a really impressive and well-functioning online sales platform.
- Of the four Ps, the product really does matter most, and repeat purchases are the best indicator of that.
- To gain trial, first impressions (packaging, demonstrations, sampling) are crucial. Use the internet to launch your product and gain first impressions.

- Once through that gate, the goal is to build a long-term consumer-brand relationship. For consumer goods, that is the role of advertising. Use Chinese social media to build your customer relationships. In business to business, industrial, and services, the customer-facing salespeople play a more important role. Industrial businesses may not see themselves as branded, but that is what they are: their reputation makes the difference between profit and not making it through the door.
- Pricing must be seen, within the context of the brand–consumer relationship and competition, as 'fair' – a term that in China, covers Hermes handbags selling for several hundred dollars each, to sneakers priced at $50.
- The way a firm goes about its marketing strategy should be the same for all sectors: concentration on a small enough target to gain enough focus and leverage to win. Too many marketers try to do too much with too little. Define the product positioning in a crisp, half-page statement; that way everyone should be able to understand and be motivated by it.
- Finally, the marketer has to think it all the way through and see it all the way through to the Chinese end user's point of view.

Note

1 T. Broadbent (2011) "Asian advertising: Asia's creativity gap", *Admap*, July/August, 2011.

Bibliography

Crabbe, M. (2014) *Myth-Busting China's Numbers: Understanding and Using China's Statistics*, Basingstoke: Palgrave-MacMillan.

8 The marketing process

This chapter continues the discussion of marketing in China, first by examining consumer research and then discussing the integration of market information and the marketing process. There is a tendency, in thinking or writing about business in China, to note *guanxi* as some sort of local peculiarity, and then get back to business as usual. But *guanxi* – indeed, the whole range of Chinese conscious and unconscious sentiment, perception and belief – is intrinsic to successful business in China. Here are some suggestions how.

Market research in the PRC

Published sources

An enormous Chinese system centred in Beijing collects and analyses information for central planning purposes. This information used to be difficult to access because it was scattered among various agencies (including commissions, ministries, national corporations, and industry councils), and the 'right' person to approach within any particular agency might be unidentifiable. Today, however, much useful regional and national data covering all aspects of life in China is collected and published in the China Statistical Review, which comes out a few months after the end of each year, and provides a wealth of information on previous years, including that just passed. These data are invaluable in providing a framework about the market as a whole, and a host of details like income levels by age and region, and so on. It is better to use this kind of data in China to paint a picture rather than to give precise information. A serious effort to position and develop a particular product in China requires a focused approach.

Bespoke research

There are many companies in China who perform market research. I prefer research companies who are small enough to be able to focus on a client's requirements, while being large enough to accommodate national research for large multinationals. One of the best is Shanghai-based China Market Research Group (CMR), established fifteen years ago by a Canadian principal

DOI: 10.4324/9781003241164-9

(of course, there are many others as well). China Market Research has performed successful investigations for foreign companies into many different kinds of consumer product in China, including one excellent study into a Chinese consumer product for a Mexican company which I was advising. The CMR team consists of a large group of Chinese professionals, from all over China (because Shanghai operates in the same way in China as New York does in the US, London in the UK, or Paris in France: as a melting pot for talent drawn from far and wide). The Chinese team is co-ordinated and directed by American and Canadian professionals. It has a lot of experience in using focus groups, one-to-one interviews and printed and online data to understand a particular market and user segment, and project their future evolution.

There is obviously a cost to Chinese market research, which will vary according to the size and complexity of the work which is being demanded. An investigation based just on local information (say, just in Shanghai) will cost much less than that based on information sourced multi-regionally or nationally. The important question is: Is the cost worth it? The answer is "yes". For any kind of Chinese consumer good or service (and for most kinds of industrial good or service), success will depend in part on successfully identifying the market, the target buyer, the buying triggers and the competition – even perhaps before some of the target consumers have identified themselves as potential product users – and good consumer research can achieve this result.

This kind of market investigation and analysis should be performed by intelligent, trained Chinese analysts, who can understand and anticipate questions and answers in focus groups and interviews, while obviously being embedded, through their upbringing and early education, in Chinese ways of thinking. Fortunately – unlike twenty or more years ago – there is today a ready supply of Western-trained 30-something Chinese graduates living in cities like Shanghai who want to do this kind of work, and can do it quickly and accurately. In the better market research companies (like CMR), an experienced research director manages a group of Chinese professionals efficiently, with the result that a research study emerges which identifies the key factors affecting the product (performance, price, colour, taste, size, etc.), analyses the target market, the barriers and opportunities, and the competition, and summarizes an effective way forward. To obtain the best results, and to ensure that the research findings match exactly to the product and the company's aspirations, it is important that the company for whom the research is being done stays closely in contact throughout the discovery and analytical research process.

Other successful market research companies in China are Daxue Consulting, also based in Shanghai, and the Survey Research Group (SRG), which was probably the first major external agency to establish itself in China in 1984. In the 1990s it merged with AC Nielsen and today alongside its mainstream bespoke research, it offers off-the-shelf studies covering beer, shampoos, air fresheners, and furniture. The new importance of digital marketing in China has produced a wave of newer market research companies, but some of the longer-established ones, like CMR, have also fully familiarized themselves with the Chinese digital world.

Large multinational clients tend to feel more comfortable with global marketing services. These big companies expect standardized modern marketing services, not least to facilitate country comparisons and also, being big, they prefer to put their faith in statistics rather than intuition. But we prefer smaller China-based market research companies, with substantial experience, but which are large enough to conduct sophisticated, large market surveys for multinational clients.

Various local factors can generate unreliability in Chinese market research. First, there is the nature of Chinese consumer psychology, which is obviously different to American or French consumer psychology. The Chinese obsession with politeness and not causing offence to others, including strangers, may mean that the Chinese responses to apparently straightforward questions in an interview or focus group can be at best equivocal, at worst wrong. It is important therefore for Chinese people (not Americans or Europeans) to construct and review individual survey questions in order to judge whether certain questions are likely to elicit the expected or desired responses, and also to review completed surveys and questionnaires to confirm their validity.

Second, there are strong regional differences in China. As noted earlier, China consists of, basically, as many markets as you would like it to. The good news is that this makes it easier to position market entry: one can make mistakes in market entry in one place, learn the lessons, and start with a fresh sheet somewhere else. The bad news is that every new market in another region of China may need a fresh start. Chapter 2 discussed some of the regional variations that can affect the nature of markets and consumers. Let us consider just one: language. When conducting surveys in Guangzhou or Fujian, should you do so in Mandarin, on the grounds that you have already learned and used Mandarin in Beijing and Shanghai? Or should you adapt to the local language? Most people will speak Mandarin, but they may be less willing to express themselves fully and honestly than they would in their local tongue. Closer is better: we strongly suggest that the data gatherers operate in the appropriate local vernacular. Written questionnaires, of course, make this easier.

The third problem is that of the layers of processing that the data may pass through. Each layer could apply some subtle spin. Given the difficulty of understanding such an enormous market, one should always check who is collecting the original data and how many hands/interpretations it then goes through. This is a good reason to employ a relatively small market analysis company.

Market researchers are rationalists, and so are consumers *when they are reporting their behaviour*. Yet much of the time, consumer behaviour is *not* rational. Applying Western logic to Chinese consumer behaviour is especially dangerous. Yet that is exactly what a firm applying Western market research methodology in China is likely to do. If the report is not littered with contradictions, it has been oversimplified.

In consequence, the marketer cannot simply commission the research and then accept the report. The research process has to be checked all the way through to the ultimate respondents, both when commissioning and during the process. This can be done by way of weekly or fortnightly review sessions, in which the research director explains by way of a set of slides the work that has been done so far, what it points to, and the future work planned. This gives the commissioner of the research the opportunity to understand better what has been learned to date, and if necessary, redirect the ongoing and future research effort to fit better with the company's objectives.

The option of commissioning two identical surveys and comparing the answers is no solution for the following reasons:

- It doubles the costs
- The second firm may find the same mismatch of questions and answers that the first encountered
- How will the differences be explained?

Today, huge advances in Chinese education and improvements in the understanding of different sectors of the economy makes it quite easy to find a highly reliable market research company in China.

Statistical information on China can be unreliable, but even if we could be sure that the information was accurate, what would it tell us? Quite often, one only needs to know that the number is big enough: 1% of a billion people is still a lot of people. It is easy to find a group of consumers: for most firms, getting into two or three of China's big cities or provinces gives them enough *potential* customers to last them for many years. The advice from consultants in China is not to worry about the numbers: a company with a good product will find plenty of customers, or the customers will find them, provided that the fundamentals of promotion and distribution are in place. Many see the big issues as getting the product and distribution strategies right, and that means knowing what it is that Chinese consumers want, where they go to buy it, and how they make their buying decisions. The focus, increasingly, is less on total numbers and more on motivation, that is, qualitative research.

Golden Hall sausages

The Jin Man Tang (Golden Hall) sausage company is based in Zhanjiang, about 230 miles south-west of Guangzhou in the far south-western corner of Guangdong. In 1898 the French acquired a 100-year lease of the port, but returned it to China in 1946. Maybe French cuisine influenced the distinctive, less fatty sausages of the area.

In 1994 Golden Hall was the dominant brand in Zhanjiang, but had no sales at all in the much larger market of Guangzhou, which was dominated by two other brands, The Emperor and Kung Ki Leng. The company contacted an advertising agency, the Sun and Moon Spreading Co., to advise it on how to break into the Guangzhou market.

The sausage market is highly seasonal. Like many traditional foods, consumption is ruled by the calendar rather than the weather. It begins with the Zhongqiujie (Moon Festival) in late September or early October and ends with the Qingmingjie (Clear Brightness Festival) in April. Sausages are made of 100% pork plus flavourings. A sausage may be a meal in its own right or may be chopped up into other dishes. As with other meat products, sausages are not cheap.

Golden Hall sausages were shorter and thinner than The Emperor sausages, which had over half the current market share and a lower fat content. It was believed that a 'lean appeal' might be successful with consumers. However, there were also production problems; Golden Hall sausages were not always fresh when sold, and there were quality problems such as variable levels of fat.

Competing with The Emperor would be difficult, as the rival company was a big spender on advertising, and Golden Hall could not hope to spend on the same level in the early days. Clearly some other tactics were going to be needed for the launch and the promotional period immediately following. The primary objective for Golden Hall was to build up some *guanhai* (Yue for *guanxi*) in the Guangzhou market.

Sadly, the launch did not work. Neither client nor agency really had the expertise, the resources nor, most important of all, good luck. The company retreated to Zhanjiang. Mr Fang acquired the business in 1999 and it was still continuing in a modest way (18 staff members) to make Zhanjiang-style sausages in 2016.

Brand leadership in Zhanjiang had been taken over by Jinquan (Golden Spring) whose current factory was built in 1982, although the company claims their sausage formulation originated from the Guangxu period of the Qing dynasty.

This case has a number of morals but chief among them is the failure in the marketing process leading to a Guangzhou launch with too many unknowns. How would the alien sausage be accepted? Distribution in new territory? The relationship with a new ad agency? What would the advertising be likely to achieve? At what level should prices be set? In short, the marketing should have been tested.

Qualitative research

In the previous chapter I addressed the need for Western companies to become less reliant on Chinese partners for marketing, and to know more about what is taking place on the ground. This is true, but there is one important exception agreed on by almost everyone, which is that qualitative research into what makes consumers tick in China *must* be carried out by Chinese moderators. Never mind the language barriers; some say there is no way that most Chinese will open up to foreigners in their homes or in the workplace in the same way that they would to their fellow Chinese. That is hardly surprising; how many of us would open up and speak as freely to a Chinese market researcher as we would to a fellow Briton, American, etc.? But some advice goes so far as to suggest that even the presence of a foreigner during the interview process can taint the proceedings. There are ways around this, of course; sitting behind a two-way mirror in focus group sessions, or (less satisfactory) listening to tape recordings can give that all-important whiff of gun smoke. And there are likely to be different reactions to foreigners for different products too; interviews concerning luxury products are less likely to be tainted than those for lower-priced consumer goods.

This being China, the opposite can also be true. It depends on the product category, how self-confident and used to foreigners the respondents are, and how skilled the foreigner is in merging into the wallpaper. The early part of any focus group is unnatural and needs to be discarded anyway. Typically the respondents forget about the microphone and the two-way mirror once they get going.

Bearing in mind the purpose of qualitative research, namely, to get close to end users, it may be worth risking distortion from having too few respondents, but being involved, rather than turn the problem over to the professional researcher to do more efficiently. The choice may depend on the researcher's empathy with client and respondents.

When setting up focus groups, be aware that Chinese are probably more visually and less aurally focused than Americans, and probably than Westerners in general. Given the subtleties of spoken Chinese, this second result is not intuitively obvious, even though the two-dimensional visual nature of Chinese written characters relative to the (topologically) one-dimensional Roman script makes the first suggestion predictable. The consequence is that Chinese consumers should *see* names and other marketing stimuli more than they should *hear* them. In other words, research, and focus groups in particular, should provide more visual stimuli than they might in the West.

Thus, the process of converting the raw gathered data into the neat folders presented to management carries the severe risk that the insights will be lost. No psychologist hired to run a focus group has the experience of the brand that the marketer should have. There is a good chance that the moderator will miss the significance of what was said. Another option is to have a second moderator behind the screen to give an independent interpretation. No moderator can notice everything.

In particular, research should endeavour to bring cultural values, the usage occasion, and the product *together* as realistically as possible. The less hypothetical or artificial the research situation for the consumer, the more reliable it will be. The Chinese consumer's response to a particular service or product is conditioned by his/her own conscious and subconscious set of beliefs and impressions. Needless to say (and as discussed at length earlier in this book) many of these beliefs and impressions are totally different to those in the West, and will even differ by region within China. It is essential to cater for these very different perceptions in the questionnaires, focus groups, and analyses that are carried out.

Other information

In principle, many other sources of information are available, including in-house staff, especially the field staff, customers, trade associations, journalists, and competitors. Even if there were time to track all these down, one would have to know what one does not know and what is important. And one would need much more openness than one can expect in China.

Essentially, we are talking about reducing all the flotsam floating around marketing decision-making to the few key issues that will make a major difference and are also the subject of substantive uncertainty within the top marketing team. Once identified, the collective *guanxiwang*, plus good market research, can help to piece together the important answers.

Although information needs to be checked and confirmed before one can take it seriously, it only needs to be near enough to make the decision; it needs to be *relatively* accurate. Too often in the West, information is disconnected from its use; in other words, the required degree of precision and the relevance of information depend on what it will be used for. The West tends to seek quality in information for its own sake.

Planning

Planning is important because rehearsing the future can open up more options and develop more skills than waiting to be surprised by daily events. You can practise as many times as you like, at some cost to today, but tomorrow only comes once.

Planning is also learning: learning from the past, from other business units, functions, and competitors and from seniors and juniors in the hierarchy. We need to understand *why* something works, so that we can extend the principles in new situations. Otherwise we can never distinguish context, or simply luck, from good marketing. Most plans are simply adaptations of those that went before. They are evolutionary not revolutionary. What works is extended, what doesn't is cut back. Survival, or Darwinism, in effect, often beats careful, up-to-date analysis – wrongly. Successful behaviour is more convincing than theoretical calculations, but this is no help to those preparing their first-ever plan in China. Should they bring in experts (consultants) with previous experience of preparing marketing plans in China? Perhaps: but having someone on the planning team with previous Chinese experience obviously helps.

Experiential (early) plans are quite different from experienced ones. The latter, as noted above, essentially build on that experience. Where little or no experience exists, then the planning process itself has to provide the best proxy for that experience. For example, the team can debate the likelihood of alternative scenarios. Rather than forecasting exact numbers, they can forecast how big – or how small – they could be. Thus the planning process itself simulates what will happen as best it can.

One essential area for experiential planning is digital because it is all so new and has been developing so fast. It is a prime candidate both for qualitative market research (to experience digital as the consumer does) and for a specialist agency, of which there are several in China. This is covered in the previous chapter.

A plan can also be seen as the minutes of all the meetings, possibly over many months, which went into its preparation. Most Western firms, including those in China, spend far too long working a plan around the hierarchy. They begin before they can tell how the last plan worked out and then finish after the new planned year has already started. They would be better off working twice as hard over a quarter of the time.

By contrast, while the whole Chinese state apparatus, including SOEs, is built around formal planning, few Chinese family businesses, not even the big ones, have any formal marketing plans. What they actually do evolves along Darwinian principles, partly reacting to external stimuli (threats and opportunities in the market) and part based on the firm's own abilities and the nature of its business. Often the development of a Chinese family business reflect the ideas and inclinations of its founder. This leads to some decisions that appear to make no sense – food retailers diversifying into P2P lending, or a car manufacturer into banking – and yet in terms of cash flow and profitability, they often do work. So long as the current approach is bringing in satisfactory amounts of cash, it continues.

Experimentation, trial and error are endemic to market development. One Chinese maker of embroidery machines tried over 100 different products before hitting on one that worked. It was so successful that they were bought out by a Scandinavian firm two years later, each of the original partners making several tens of millions of dollars as a result. In this respect, the huge American consumer products company Procter & Gamble are no different.

Where modern methods do help is in what Sunzi called the 'calculation'. From a range of possibilities, one can calculate which ideas can be tested on the smallest possible scale. One can calculate whether a full-scale model is feasible, for example, the resources needed and the competitive response. And then, when the experimental results are in, one can calculate the best market entry model to adopt – typically more focus on time and place and more specialization. In short, well-managed businesses frequently fail small in order to win big. China has the great advantage of providing plenty of opportunities for failure (as well as success). The question is whether one can learn enough, and survive long enough, to win big.

Reasons why Western companies think it important to write marketing plans down, and traditional Chinese businesses do not, include the following:

- Managers change (average 16 months) in the West five times faster than in [Chinese] family businesses.
- Approvals are needed from different sites, perhaps cross-border.
- The financial (budgetary) system is far more formalized and, in the West, the main purpose of a plan is to gain financial approval. This can be a crucial weakness in those businesses as they end up with plans that can get approval as distinct from plans that will succeed.
- Lack of trust.
- Western intolerance of ambiguity.

Linear Western logic has many advantages, but it also drives out the opportunity for unusual solutions gradually to evolve. Explicit information sharing is given greater weight than implicit.

So where does this leave us in practical terms? I suggest a small cross-functional team is assembled both to plan and to implement the plan. Planning for other people is a waste of time. Notwithstanding reservations about formality, bridging the East–West cultural gap is helped by the written word, so long as the Western side does not give the plan itself too much authority. It is not a legal contract but merely an aide-memoire, indicating the point at which the market learning has been reached. Flexibility and the door to new learning must be left open.

A plan should be developed over three phases and then, if the calculations reveal that the objectives have not been met, it needs to recycle through all three until it does:

- Strategy – does it fit the company's overall objectives?
- *Guanxi* and other aspects of Chinese culture – does the plan fit the Chinese market?
- Calculation – do the plan's numbers add up, and is it affordable?

A bad but frequent practice is to do it the other way around. This starts with the required bottom line, deduces what marketing expenditure will be authorized, and then forecasts the sales needed to balance the books. Since the end result looks much like the previous plan with the date changed, this tends to work quite well, which in turn reinforces the behaviour until something goes wrong. A marketing plan which does not start and finish with the Chinese consumer is doomed to failure.

Good marketing practice begins with the consumers and what they [will] want, or might want in the context of the competitive environment and the company's own capabilities. This is called the E+3Cs analysis (Environment,

Consumers, Competitors, own Company). From this, as we have noted above, emerges the brand's positioning statement (one page or less). The positioning will include customer segmentation and geographic focus.

Having established who the friends and foes are, why the friends will love the brand and how it will kill the competition, we can move on to develop the specifics of building the brand–customer relationship that is the essence of marketing. Who exactly makes up the brand's *guanxiwang*? Draw the network and prioritize those who matter most. Draw the network of the key players and their relationships. Players form nodes and relationship lines. No relationship means no line.

Every brand has many relationships and it is just as important to prioritize time as money. What activities will most enhance those relationships? Why should they want to buy more, more often, and at higher prices?

Understanding and incorporating Chinese culture is at the heart of creating demand, which is what marketing is all about. (Supply, even in China, *should* be easier than identifying and creating demand).

Finally, and only finally, we need to quantify everything thus far. If financial numbers can be assigned, well and good. Quite often, brand equity (the brand–customer *guanxi*) can only be estimated non-financially, and the numbers are very fuzzy. Concepts like awareness, salience, perceived quality relative to the competition, satisfaction, trust, and commitment are important but vague. Nevertheless, these calculations, based on market research, are worth making, using estimates where hard research is not justified. The process of measurement brings focus.

Planning should be fun but it rarely is. It should be fun because it is the annual opportunity to learn, be creative, and play with wild ideas. We only live once (although that is just a majority opinion) but we certainly have the opportunity to rehearse next year's life as often as we like.

Conclusions

Victory in war requires intensive research and understanding of the rival, his strengths, weaknesses, and likely courses of action. In the same way, entering an unfamiliar market (and China is as unfamiliar to Western companies as it gets), and making big money needs good intelligence. Market research contributes crucially to the foundation of corporate strategy and detailed corporate plans. However, given the highly dynamic environment and regional variety, it may soon become outdated and will need to be revised. That said, we need plans since planning is vitally important to learning about this particular world – China. The next challenge, to convert planning into action, is the reason why plans must be constructed by those who will have to execute them – which is why we can save money on consultants.

China has masses of statistics and available research, far more than any company can handle. Many of these data are inconsistent and unreliable. This bothers Westerners more than it does Chinese, who usually look for pictures rather than precision. A fuzzy focus is quite good enough.

To navigate through all this, a Western firm will need to be tough-minded in distinguishing between what they must know and what may be nice to know, but if necessary, can be abandoned. Integrating research needs and the planning process is critical to distinguishing between essential and inessential information. The process needs to be seen as a whole, whereby planning supports information and information supports planning.

Bibliography

Boisot, M. (1995) *Information Space*, London: Routledge.

Hamel, G. and C. K. Pralahad (1994) *Competing for the Future*, Boston, MA: Harvard Business School Press.

Nonaka, I. and H. Takeuchi (1995) *The Knowledge-Creating Company*, Oxford: Oxford University Press.

9 Some key management issues in China

People say that we [the younger Chinese generation] are only interested in money, but that's not true. We want to succeed at our lives, to make the most of the opportunities our parents never had. Westerners think all they have to do is pay us and we will eat out of their hands. But we want opportunity, not charity.

(Anonymous young manager, Beijing)

I want to do something different besides working the earth all the time. If I cannot succeed with my own efforts, then I deserve my failure. But please first give me a chance.

(Bian Chengyu, Sichuanese entrepreneur)

A foreign company operating in China rapidly acquires a Chinese personality, including a name in Chinese, which often may sound in Chinese like the real name of the company. An example is the prominent Chinese household goods company Haier, which modelled its business and its name on the German company Liebherr. 'Haier' and 'Liebherr' each spoken in Chinese sound similar. Not much of a likeness, a Westerner would think, but in China, there it is. The point is that the observant Chinese, who are interested in everything foreign, watch foreign companies in China carefully so as to understand them better, observe how they really work, and learn from them. The image or persona that a foreign company projects in China is very important, because it is difficult to change a bad impression once conveyed and received, and this will profoundly affect the manner in which Chinese consumers, suppliers, and government officials deal with the company and its products. Obviously, the converse is also the case.

What are the values that the Chinese consider when they make this judgement? Integrity and honesty are at the top of the list because those qualities have been valued in China since Confucius, and even before. Chinese people understand very well that foreign companies are just that: foreign, not Chinese. They allow for foreign behaviour being different to Chinese behaviour. But they don't appreciate what appears to them to be national arrogance. Attempts to derogate, or not do full justice to Chinese culture will

DOI: 10.4324/9781003241164-10

damage a foreign company's reputation in China. This rule extends even to the position in China of the Chinese Communist Party and its leaders. A foreigner in China may not like the Chinese Communist Party, but he/she would be completely wrong to think that most Chinese don't support their government. Most do, and the handful that do not keep their opinions private and certainly do not welcome foreign business people denigrating their leaders. It is normal in America and other Western countries to express open views about political figures like Donald Trump, Angela Merkel, or Boris Johnson. But in China, political views should be kept private, even after a couple of beers in the bar.

The utility and elegance of a foreign company's products are certainly important in creating a positive public impression. This is particularly the case in the booming Chinese luxury sector, where European companies like L'Oréal, Hermes, Chanel, Gucci, and Armani have used strong advertising campaigns and large televised fashion shows in Shanghai and Beijing to create strong positive public images.

However, the intangibles are even more important. A partnership with a strong Chinese entity with a good reputation can be extremely helpful in creating a strong positive impression. Volkswagen's long 50/50 partnership (since 1983) with the Shanghai Government has played an absolutely key role in establishing and burnishing the public credentials of the German company in China, which (not coincidentally) occupies nearly 20% of the huge Chinese car market. It was interesting to note at the Beijing Winter Olympic Games in February 2022, that the German ski team wore clothing with large Chinese characters on the trousers, meaning "Germany". Here is a simple, but important example of presenting an image of a good Chinese citizen.

The importance of Chinese Government relations has often been mentioned in this book, but they are such a critical part of success in China, we do not apologize for turning to them once again. The local government in China effectively controls everything and can interfere in everything, in one way or another, whether by taxation or environmental laws, or in some other way. Many successful foreign companies in China employ one or several people just to manage the relationship with the Chinese Government. If the Chinese Government is a customer for the company's products (airplane engines, industrial products, security systems, etc.), then the government relationship has an obvious importance for sales and profits. But even for a consumer products company which sells to Chinese households, the local government officials play an important role. They can provide much well-informed, useful advice: for instance, a good Chinese partner, a good location for a new factory, or an introduction to the relevant ministry in Beijing (where the most important decisions are made). If local officials are glad to have your company in their sector, they will often refer to you in conversations with their colleagues and with other Chinese companies, and they will mention you favourably in their periodic reports to their seniors in Beijing. So, on arriving in China or when starting a new business in China, you need to pay a courtesy call to your local government office to introduce yourself, your key colleagues, and your company and then follow up the contact regularly, because in China, everything is personal, especially business.

Chinese New Year is the major holiday event in the Chinese calendar, and it may be a good idea to invite the local town or city mayor and some of his colleagues to a company celebration. The mayor will probably receive multiple invitations for the same festival day, and will only be able to go to one or two, but at least he (or she) will appreciate the invitation, even if he cannot attend.

What about paying bribes, or involving government officials in your business? It used to be common, even normal, for local government officials at official meetings with foreign companies to drop heavy hints about companies owned by their friend or relative who could provide important assistance to foreign companies. The recent (2020) change in company law in China, which has placed foreign companies on exactly the same legal footing as Chinese companies, has removed many of the opportunities for extracting bribes from foreign companies and, since 2012, Chinese President Xi Jinping's anti-corruption drive has driven most of this activity underground.

But paying and receiving backhanders is a Chinese tradition as old as China itself. As was noted in a recent (2021) survey of the Chinese public, the practice still exists, in spite of a longstanding and much-feared Chinese anti-corruption campaign, with many senior figures who were found guilty of receiving or giving bribes serving long prison terms, or even in a few cases the death penalty. Foreign companies may still encounter subtle and not-so-subtle attempts to elicit backhanders.

Of course, it is easy to say that efforts to extract bribes should obviously be rejected, and even that the people involved should be reported to the Chinese authorities; however, in practice, this could prove difficult. Chinese criminals are extremely clever at thinking of ways to apply pressure and avoid the law. Companies operating in China need to be on the lookout for scams of all kinds, with bribery at the top of the list. Chinese people reading this section of the book may consider that we are overdoing this seamy aspect of Chinese society. They should be reassured that we know that shady activities occur everywhere, including in the United States and Europe, and we are not especially picking on China. Below are a couple of real-life examples:

A Chinese Scam

In 2016, I was horrified to learn about an incident in which a Chinese friend, a professor of high intelligence, great experience, and personal integrity, had been lured into paying RMB 20,000 in cash (about US$ 3,000) into a bank account belonging to Chinese criminals. When the gang involved was rounded up a few months later, it was discovered to be employing about 50 Chinese personnel based in a large secure building in the suburbs of Nairobi, Kenya. It had apparently succeeded in scamming thousands of wealthy Chinese to the tune of hundreds of millions of dollars.

My friend told me that she was contacted on her Chinese smartphone, while she was working in Guangzhou in south-east China, by a credible-sounding man, who introduced himself as a senior Chinese policeman who was investigating money laundering, and who told her that her bank account had been penetrated and compromised. The cleverness of the scam was that it was hard for her not to take this story very seriously. After several days of long discussions over her phone, during which she was advised not to tell anyone, she was persuaded to transfer money from her bank account to another account provided by the 'policeman', in order to 'save her money and help defeat the money launderers'. She discovered later that a senior Chinese professor at Tsinghua University in Beijing lost RMB 17 million in the same scam.

This is an extract from a report in a British newspaper during the Winter Olympic Games held in Beijing, China in February 2022:

> The Winter Olympics' most popular star so far may not be the Chinese freestyle skier Eileen Gu, despite her stunning gold medal win on the slopes in Beijing.
>
> Instead it is Bing Dwen Dwen, the rotund Olympic panda and official mascot of the Beijing Games, who has sparked such a frenzied rush for merchandise that police are taking action to curb price gouging and fraudulent sales.
>
> At least three people have been sentenced to administrative punishment for reselling products of the rotund Olympic panda at inflated prices, Beijing police said, after Chinese state media promoted Bing Dwen Dwen as the cuddly face of the games.
>
> They didn't provide details of the case, but the statement was meant to deter similar acts, which police said "disrupt the normal buying order".
>
> "Please consume rationally and don't buy from scalpers to avoid economic losses," police added.
>
> The official online Olympic store pre-sells an 8 cm tall figurine of Bing Dwen Dwen for 118 yuan (£13.65) to be shipped within 45 days. A 20 cm stuffed doll sells for 192 yuan, but resellers are asking for as much as [and] more than 1,000 yuan on online auction sites.

Scammers are also exploiting the demand. In the eastern city of Wenzhou, the authorities said that a resident paid 3,500 yuan as a deposit for Bing Dwen Dwen products before the fraudster vanished without delivering. In the eastern city of Jiaxing, a resident received a piece of eyeglass cloth after he paid 266 yuan for three small Bing Dwen Dwens and a large one.

Suppliers and customers

Both these groups are strongly influenced by the company's reputation in the Chinese marketplace, whether created by advertising or by word-of-mouth reports from other suppliers or customers. This points to the vital need for foreign companies operating in China to create and preserve an excellent public persona. Fairness, and prompt payment of suppliers (that is, no more than 30 days, preferably less) will go a long way towards creating a loyal and efficient Chinese supply chain, especially when many Chinese suppliers often suffer from very tough treatment from Chinese clients who can take advantage of the extreme competitiveness in most industrial sectors in China. Word of mouth plays a very important role with Chinese customers in a society in which everything is personal.

Recruitment and rewards

Within the company, a critical area for success is the hiring and retention of Chinese managers and staff. Between 2000 and 2010, the main labour problem in China was that the demand for skilled Chinese staff with experience, driven in turn by high rates of growth and the arrival and rapid expansion of foreign companies in China, greatly outstripped available supply. This mismatch distorted the Chinese labour market for foreign companies operating in China.

Today, most foreign companies feel more confident about China's labour market. In the last five years, most Chinese who have visited the United States for further education have returned to China because of the opportunities available. The availability of Chinese professionals, many trained in universities in North America, Europe, and Australasia, has expanded enormously, and Western companies have gained much more experience in hiring and managing Chinese staff. Ask the senior managers of any big company today, Chinese or foreign, if they are worried about the war for talent in China, and they will tell you "not so much"; they work hard and invest heavily in identifying the best talent, have deep pockets, and can offer good career prospects to any ambitious young Chinese manager. But with the top companies creaming off top talent, and others pulled back into family businesses, effectively disappearing from the talent pool, the smaller and less attractive companies,

Western or Chinese, are left with a problem. This calls for a creative approach to recruitment and to people management more generally.

There are virtually no restrictions on recruitment, and the end of many internal travel regulations means most Chinese are free to take jobs anywhere they can. For all practical purposes, China is now a free labour market.

Some commonly used channels for recruitment are as follows:

- Local human resources exchange centres (*rencai shichang*) hold databases and manage job fairs for management staff
- Local labour bureaux (*laowu shichang*) provide a similar service for workers
- Campus recruiting is favoured particularly by top multinational companies, especially for graduates with scientific or technical knowledge and/or formal business training
- Media, especially online advertising
- *Guanxi*: knowing someone who knows someone who is qualified for the job. Often, the best way to find good new staff is by way of references and introductions from Chinese staff already working within the company, because Chinese referees and introducers will not risk the serious loss of face that might ensue when an introduced employee turns out be a disappointment to his or her new employer. By the same token, Chinese staff may not refer their friends or personal contacts to the company they work for, unless they are proud enough of their employer to think that their own prestige will be increased by introducing their friend.

Staff retention

Surveys have shown that China used to have the highest labour turnover rates of any country in Asia.

Various explanations for these high turnover rates have been proposed:

- By providing higher salaries, Western companies were encouraging Chinese managers to become more mobile. Many young Chinese were literally salary chasing, moving on every year or even six months as new, better paying jobs came on the market.
- Traditional Chinese values are breaking down and China is becoming a much more fluid society
- Chinese employees may feel loyalty to Chinese organizations, but not to Western organizations.

Today, the situation has improved, but companies still need to work hard at making sure their valued employees feel committed to the company. In assigning roles Western managers may well cause loss of face, and where that happens the individual is likely to resign. In both recruiting and terminating employees, face is of prime importance.

Although, as mentioned above, Chinese employees at all levels are eager to improve their own skills and make themselves more marketable, Chinese managers are not currently seeing personal career development in the same way that foreigners do. Westerners job-hop too. Firm comparisons are not available and the diminished loyalty by firms to employees has been matched, not surprisingly, reciprocally. Younger managers look to the market rather than their pensions for security. Critics of young Chinese managers, however, suggest that they are doing themselves no favours by accepting the next higher pay cheque that comes along, rather than building a strong career (or CV/résumé, if you wish to be cynical). It is alleged that they move from one job to another with no personal goal beyond that of making money.

The old SOE culture provided housing, education, and health benefits to make up for low wages. However big the salary from the JV, these benefits are hard to make up, especially in areas in eastern China (Beijing, Shanghai) where housing is particularly expensive. Company benefits are, therefore, important. Where housing is particularly expensive, companies can either provide employee housing directly or a cash housing allowance on top of the pay cheque. More important and more widely provided are benefits such as health care. Pensions are becoming increasingly important too, as the state pension system is being 'de-emphasized'. Benefits may amount to a 50% supplement to the base salary. MNC's which offer comprehensive benefits packages and internal chances for promotion have low turnover rates. Those with high turnover rates are usually smaller operations or representative offices. Chinese companies tend to offer lower salaries and large end-of-year bonuses which are tied to profits. Foreign MNC's offer higher base salaries, often with no bonus, or a very small bonus.

Promotion = status = commitment. Before economic liberalization, workers were often restricted in employment assigned to them by the state. They therefore worked hard to work their way up the promotion ladder in their own organization. However, today, not every young Chinese manager wants to climb the corporate ladder. Some young people are looking to become self-starters. They might take a corporate job for a few years to gain experience, but eventually want to strike out on their own. This is particularly true of those who have returned to China after studying in the West. For these young men and women, the chance to learn and gain experience is at least as important as salary.

Foreign companies new to China sometimes make the mistake of not realizing that Chinese staff expect to be treated as well as expatriates working in the same company in China. For industries in which Chinese personnel are key gainers of business, like investment banking or private wealth management, this is not such a problem, and indeed, successful, high-profile Chinese employees of investment banks in China are paid very high salaries. But in luxury goods, where products such as handbags and jewellery designed in Europe or North America depend on their foreign design rather than Chinese salesmanship, this can be problematic. Any sign of second-class treatment of

Chinese employees, whether in terms of salary or something else, will create great dissatisfaction and even anger. In our experience, well-treated Chinese staff return the favour by working extremely hard, showing great loyalty to their foreign employer, and helping to create a positive external impression of the company, which is extremely valuable.

The importance that Chinese attach to appearance and personal respect (or 'face', to use a common description) greatly affects the way they respond to Western managers. If a manager does anything to make a Chinese employee look foolish or incompetent in front of his or her colleagues, then the Chinese person will feel ashamed, and may relieve him or herself of this shame by converting it into anger or resentment against the manager and the company involved. Personal respect is a more vital component of relationships with Chinese people than it is with Europeans and North Americans.

Therefore, if wrongdoing has occurred, or is suspected to have occurred, it is essential to proceed cautiously to establish facts and carry out remedial action. Witnesses and suspected wrongdoers must be interviewed privately, and fair and reasonable treatment must be observably applied throughout.

Training and development

Annual attrition rates of around 10% year in Chinese staff are normal in China, and sometimes the attrition rate is as high as 15–20%. What can keep Chinese employees in place, and persuade them not to start looking to change their job? One solution recommended by bigger Western companies working in China is *training*. Paradoxically, given that recent research suggests that young Chinese do not have planned career paths and their definition of what 'career' means is much more fluid and hazy than in the West, there is also plenty of evidence that these same young Chinese value training and professional development. This is true of many workers, not just managers. Companies that invest in training and development report higher levels of retention than those that do not. There is of course the phenomenon of 'train and run', as workers and managers take their new qualifications and go elsewhere to seek better jobs. This is used by some companies in China as an excuse not to invest in training. In response we would make the following observations:

- 'Train and run' is a two-way street. If compensation packages are good enough, well-trained workers and managers from other companies will want to join too. Also, some departing employees may well want to return to the original business at some date in the future. Training in this sense becomes a case of casting bread on the waters.
- Training is not a unique event. Rather than putting employees into one training programme and expecting them to stay, you should consider developing staged programmes that will last for some years, encouraging them to stay and complete the programme (at least) before departing.

- Nor does training have to mean formal programmes like MBAs, technical programmes, and so forth. Mentoring and on-the-job training can be ongoing, and there is evidence that Chinese employees value both highly.

There are marked differences in education among Chinese employees, depending on the region as well as age group. China's universities are too few to meet the needs of such a large population, and the educational provision and sophistication of western and some central Chinese regions lag years behind. Technical training can be of a very high standard, given the variable technology levels with many hundreds of technical training institutes around the country. In fields like computer science, training is as (or even more) advanced than in the West. In other fields, the situation is more patchy, partly because topics which require freedom of thought and an ability to take different perspectives are hampered by controls in China on what can be said and written, and by the Chinese reluctance to stick their neck out, especially amongst strangers. Where possible, graduates of the older and more prestigious technical schools offer a better quality and more standard graduate.

The top Chinese MBA programmes (China Europe International Business School, Guanghua at Peking University, Tsinghua, People's University, Chang Kong in Beijing, Jiao Tong in Shanghai, Lingnan in Guangzhou) are as good as most of the good MBA programmes in Europe and the United States, and two or three (CEIBS, Tsinghua, Guanghua) are world class, especially for students looking for a Chinese flavour. But, just as in the West, MBA programmes in China are strong profit generators for sponsoring Chinese universities, and virtually every Chinese university has at least one management programme. Many of these are sub-standard, but many of the Chinese students who pay large sums to attend them don't care, because they are paying for the MBA label which they hope will propel their careers in China. Therefore, in China (just as in the West) it is not enough to know that a potential hire has an MBA or technical qualification. Where the qualification came from, and how it was obtained must be checked.

That said, many of China's successful private companies are led by men and women with no formal management education at all. They have grown their businesses through hard work and native shrewdness, using their local networks and the system – though with the environment growing more complex and competitive, they are finding that more is needed. So, many top-level Chinese executives, directors and even chairmen and CEOs are signing up for MBAs and, increasingly, shorter Executive MBAs taken at night and at weekends. With all the caveats on quality above, this trend is helping to create a generation of business leaders who are essentially Chinese in outlook, but who can speak the Western business language and understand the concepts by which Westerners manage. Successful Chinese managers are those who can work in both systems.

In the past, Western companies recruited heavily, outside of business studies, from the graduates of the best Chinese universities, especially but not exclusively from the faculties of science and economics. The rising popularity of law as a field of study also offers opportunities. These universities train people in the techniques of analysis and rigorous thinking, which are foundation stones for good management in every case. For companies wishing to avoid the rat race of competing for MBA graduates of unknown and sometimes dubious quality, other university disciplines still offer interesting alternatives.

Here are some tips for attracting and retaining Chinese staff:

1   Offer the right compensation package. Money is obviously important but not all-important; fringe benefits matter too. It is not always necessary to pay top dollar, or top yuan, to get the best people, but managers are advised to track comparable salaries in their area to ensure they do not fall too far behind. Outside of share option schemes in 'tech' companies (which have made many young Chinese rich beyond their dreams), Chinese employees are generally resistant to the idea of performance-related pay; some Western firms have managed to introduce it, but doing so takes time and careful management.

2   Think carefully about recruiting. Develop a profile of the people you need and invest time and money in their recruitment, then take steps to integrate them into the firm. The orientation process is particularly important and has to consist of much more than showing new managers where their desks are, how to use the phones, and where to make tea. An introduction course of a few days held off site is a good idea, and will be a great help in introducing newly hired staff to each other. Gordon Orr, long-serving director with McKinsey & Company in China, recommends treating orientation as a training programme, helping new managers to understand the new company's culture and history; this being China, the history does matter.

3   Use training and professional development as a retention strategy, as described above.

4   Offer chances for promotion and new responsibility, especially to those employees who are most needed.

All this seems like good advice, but as many Western managers interviewed for the book acknowledge, all this is no more than best-practice HR management in the West. One lesson seems to be that companies that have sophisticated HR policies will have less difficulty in adapting to China than those that do not. Planning and investing in recruitment and retention are becoming ever more important in the West too.

What it comes down to is the need to develop a good relationship between the company and employees, ranging from senior management to shop floor workers. Cultivate and build strong relationships with employees, just as with customers. Building relationships will not eliminate the problem, but, if well resourced and executed, it will be possible to keep turnover to a low level.

Letting people go

No one, except a sadist or psychopath, enjoys firing people. Nevertheless, occasionally it has to be done, either because the individual has transgressed severely, or because he or she is a negative force within the company. When you have decided to let someone go, the first thing to remember in China is that, beyond the material aspects, losing your job entails a serious loss of 'face'. How to address this? If the dismissal involves an element of serious wrongdoing, then lawyers should be involved, and the matter is simplified. In either case, the dismissed employee must be treated with respect. (Of course, any dismissal process must carefully follow a process which involves the HR department and could also involve lawyers – this goes without saying). The one-to-one interview which terminates the employment (not a letter) must fully explain the background and the reasons. Presumably, the dismissal will follow on from a warning period, so the employee will probably not be surprised by the outcome. Patience and gentleness, not roughness and brevity, are the best ways of proceeding. Generous departure terms, including several months of paid leave, go a long way to soften the blow. Chinese employees who are dismissed can be tenacious about using legal means to prolong their employment, so it is vital to ensure that the legal aspects of dismissal are well founded and considered in advance. They may also try to take their revenge by bad-mouthing the company after they have left. This is why a careful dismissal process is important.

Understanding Chinese companies

Hierarchies

Most Chinese organizations are far more hierarchical compared with their Western counterparts, in the sense that the channels of reporting and authority are more formal, if not authoritarian. On the other hand, the distance between the bosses and the workers tends to be shorter, with a few strong leaders at the top, a few managers running around in the middle, and the majority of employees at or near the bottom. The majority of Chinese small and medium-sized businesses are led by a single dominant owner/manager/director. The same is also true of most large businesses, though in some cases there will be a dominant group, perhaps 3–4 directors at most, who are clearly *primus inter pares*. Very often, these dominant directors are also the founders of the business, or joined early in its history. It is quite possible that between them they will have a controlling interest in the company.

Early attempts to segment Chinese businesses into different types focused on two models, the state-owned enterprise and the 'Chinese family business'. Because the purpose of these inquiries was to find business models that actually worked, no one paid much attention to SOEs and the focus was on family or private businesses. These early studies also focused on overseas Chinese communities, where the majority of businesses are family affairs. Hong Kong businesses are most often very family oriented; Li Ka-Shing's son Victor is prominent in Cheung Kong and Hutchison Whampoa, while Peter Wu 'inherited' the managing of Wheelock from his father-in-law, Sir Y.K. Pao. A dominant family member, usually the father, was head of the business; other family members occupied key posts; and employees lower down the organizational pyramid looked to the father and the other members of the family for leadership.

In mainland China the advent of the Chinese Communist Party threatened the Chinese family structure which Confucius had supported two thousand years before. The Party tried to remake society along Confucian lines (or utilize ancient beliefs to strengthen its own position) by casting itself as the 'father' or 'head of the family' to all Chinese. This borrowing of the Confucian family ideal in China by the Party can be clearly seen in Chinese companies which are owned and controlled by the state such as the large banks, for instance, Bank of China and Industrial and Commercial Bank of China, and the utilities, for instance, China Telecom. But the true family unit is very strongly rooted in Chinese society. It has survived the Communist revolution and the purges of Mao, and today it continues to form the foundation of many privately owned Chinese companies, some of whom have become very large. The characteristics of the Chinese business, especially the small to medium-sized family business, have Confucian elements, and Confucius saw the family as the core of Chinese society. Rather than Chinese family business, we could speak equally of Chinese Confucian business.

Whatever label you want to attach to it, the Confucian ideal of the family translates easily and naturally to Chinese business. One of the consequences is that decision-making and power are highly concentrated and the 'power distance' (the barrier sensed by those lower in the hierarchy between them and those who run the business) is significantly increased.

One negative consequence of this is that Chinese businesses can have short lifespans. The Chinese tend to be at least as bad at succession planning as foreigners. In Hong Kong, nearly as many businesses disappear as appear each year. The majority of closures are due not to insolvency, but simply because the owner dies or wishes to retire and does not have a successor. The retirement of a strong man often causes a large decrease in profitability. Not all these businesses simply close their doors, of course; many are sold or merged with those of their neighbours, but for all practical purposes they no longer exist.

The three conclusions we draw are, first, that the Chinese corporate should be seen as, if not a family per se, then a structure similar to a family with similar bonds of trust, responsibility, and obedience. In China, where business and private lives are not so clearly demarcated, this makes sense. Second, the formal structure is developing along the same lines as elsewhere but, for historical reasons, empowerment is some way behind. Third, respect for authority and power is much greater. Chinese managers have a greater need for approval both in the sense of getting permission or instruction and in the sense of positive reinforcement.

Until the new millennium, Chinese businesses, especially Chinese SOEs, tended not to employ specialists. The hierarchies that existed focused on power, responsibility, and salary; they were less likely to be task related. The main reason for this was that state-owned companies were not profit focused, but politically focused, each being an organ of the Party's power and control. In a 1990 Chinese steel mill, for example, individual employees were likely to be notionally capable (though not necessarily trained) to carry out a variety of tasks ranging from stoking a blast furnace, to skimming slag, to sweeping the floor. Traditionally, a work unit was given a production quota to fill; it was up to the members of the unit itself to decide who carried out which tasks.

This has changed, because as a result of the huge restructuring of China's state sector which started in the late 1990s under then Prime Minister Zhu Rongji, even large Chinese SOEs have had to place measurements of profitability and return on capital at the top of their management goals.

Decision-making and leadership

To generalize somewhat: the typical (good) Chinese manager operates in a very hands-on style and is familiar with all aspects of the business. He or she delegates far less than his or her Western counterpart, spends less time in meetings and formal consultations, and more time actually making decisions and implementing policy. Some surveys have suggested that Chinese managers believe that travelling and meetings are the least important aspects of their jobs; they would rather spend more time doing desk work, assessing and evaluating information, and making decisions. It is interesting that in one survey, only 31% of the sample believed that scheduled meetings were an important activity and only 4% believed that unscheduled meetings were important. Meetings are only necessary when something quite serious is happening or about to happen, and because meetings are less frequent they can also be more formal and ceremonious.

Decision-making in Chinese organizations tends to be autocratic and takes place at a high level. In a privately owned company, decisions are usually made by one individual, the owner/manager/director, and in private. The results of the decision are then announced, usually without explanation. It is assumed that the decision has had sufficient consideration before it is made and will be understandable to those people under the influence of this decision.

Western managers, used to a culture where staff are often expected to have input into strategic discussions (even if that input is later ignored or thrown out) can trip up when trying to consult with Chinese employees. Asking Chinese staff what the company should do next is likely to result in a lot of worried expressions. Most Chinese workers don't see high-level decision-making as part of their job; that is what the leader is there for.

They don't want to be blamed later if things turn out badly – it is not their responsibility.

The same applies to soliciting opinion from outside the company. Rather than meeting with consultants, suppliers, and so on to discuss issues, managers prefer short, quick face-to-face conversations or telephone calls. One consultant we know had a client whose preferred time for a telephone chat was around 1 a.m. after the working 'day' had finished. These conversations tend to be very brief, focus on one or two points, and end abruptly.

Challenging a decision once it has been made is often considered a serious offence, because it may cause the superior to lose face. At this stage, workers are expected to keep their views to themselves. There is a saying: 'Honour the hierarchy first, your vision of truth second'.

Management by relationships

Another generalization, albeit a valuable one: Western companies use systems to control relationships, while Chinese organizations use relationships to control systems. Western companies use a legalistic framework of procedures and controls to police relations. One must not exaggerate: both cultures operate both arrangements, but the balance differs. This legalistic and financial control framework is confusing for Chinese managers who feel mistrusted, and do not know how they stand in relationship to the boss. It also tells them something very dangerous: if this is the Western game, let us find out how it works and beat the system. Of course, this confusion is also a function of novelty. Once these systems become commonplace and accepted, the problems should decrease.

Chinese managers believe that one of their key tasks is to maintain harmony within the organization, both between people and between work units. This is particularly the case where Confucian values are strong. When the workers create discord or challenge leaders' decisions, their actions create bad feeling and cause loss of face.

Leadership anywhere in the world operates on the basis of respect. One may not like, or even admire, the leader, but if he or she has established a good track record and observes the main principles laid down by Sunzi, the troops will follow. On the other hand, leaders are certainly expected to develop a relationship with their employees. This is formalized as *wu lun*, the relationship of unequal pairs; each employee should feel a personal connection with the employer or manager, and should feel to some degree dependent on that leader. This relationship gives the employee a claim on the leader as the surrogate father-figure who owes the former protection and help. There are all sorts of stories of Chinese business owners and senior managers being approached while walking in the park or playing golf by employees with problems to solve. A Shanghai manager was once visited at his home by an employee at 11 p.m. in order to help patch up the breakdown of the latter's marriage.

At the same time, management is not just about leadership. One can argue which matters more, but persuading people to follow is just part of the story. A tactical plan needs to be drawn up, practical decisions need to be made, and resources need to be in place – and not diverted. It will be interesting to watch the principles taught in China's MBA schools (from Western textbooks) collide with the practices in their workplaces. They are taught mechanical controls, but operate in a Chinese relationship-based environment for handling risk. The vast majority of Chinese MBA places are part-time; the students are also holding down middle-management jobs. Chinese professionals who are trained in Western business have to know how to operate in both worlds. For them, success is doing this well. What is interesting is that some Western managers working in China, or with Chinese partners, are learning how to do it as well.

The relationship approach to risk management clearly works better in small family businesses than in multinationals, though it has to be said that the mafia, with similar (if criminal and fear-laden) characteristics, seems to span continents without difficulty. But note the need, as with *guanxi*, for close family like ties. Maintaining these relationships requires constant communication – hence the significance of the mobile phone.

Western firms do not need, even if they could, to abandon the control systems that have served them well elsewhere. On the other hand, in China they need to understand why their Chinese colleagues find them awkward, to say the least. They should try to develop ways of managing which combine Chinese principles of 'face', networking, and consensus-building in parallel with Western control systems.

Conclusions

Western companies in China should think of themselves and market themselves as employers who care about their staff, understand how Chinese people like being treated, and are prepared to invest in their employees. The concept of the employer brand is gaining ground in the West and it makes just as much sense here. Status can be attached to working for a particular company (and vice versa).

As part of that process, companies can actively manage employee expectations. Disappointment with salary increases, unrealistic expectations, and general job dissatisfaction are all responsible for job departures. Non-financial incentives also have an important role to play in employee retention. Although the present move is away from the iron rice bowl and full security, many employees value these things highly. Benefits can be a powerful inducement to employee retention.

What is developing in China now is a subtle mix of the best of both worlds – Asian/Chinese and Western. Most Chinese recognize that Western management systems have a lot to offer in terms of efficiency, use of technology, and development of creativity. Thus it is a mistake to see Chinese business culture as 'anti' any of these things. At the same time, to be successful, Western companies operating in China will have to understand and apply the iron rules of Chinese society, of which observing and respecting 'face' is the most important.

Bibliography

Yang, M. Mei-Hui (1994) *Gifts, Favors and Banquets*, Ithaca, NY: Cornell University Press.

10 Adding it all up

In editions 1–3 of this book, this chapter had the title "China and the World". When they were written, one or two decades ago, that concept seemed entirely appropriate, and that was how virtually every foreign company thought about China: we are on this planet and China is on another.

But today, in 2022, there are many large foreign MNCs for whom China represents their largest single country market. Here we refer to companies like General Motors, Apple, Volkswagen, Chanel, and Diageo. It is no longer appropriate or sensible for companies headquartered in North America or Europe (or anywhere else) to think of China as being on another planet to ours, or living inscrutably behind the Great Wall. This is a big change, because for a thousand years, Westerners have thought of the Chinese as driven by contrary beliefs, thoughts, and emotions which are, for Westerners, apparently impossible to understand. The Chinese themselves, with their profound sense of Chinese nationalism and their determination to retain their independence have often deliberately encouraged this sense of being alien.

And it is certainly true to say that differences exist and they are profound. Many Westerners have been brought up believing in a deity of some kind. If they are French, Italian, Austrian, Spanish or German, it is likely they spent a substantial part of their childhood in a church. Many people from all Western countries, whether religious or not, have some kind of conscious or unconscious belief in a benevolent being, to whom, in moments of extreme stress (like, before a battle), they offer prayers.

But, as we have touched on in an earlier chapter, Chinese people come from a completely different place. Ideas of harmony, balance, hard work, family spirit, and duty, not a deity living in heaven, are what most Chinese are raised on. It is more likely that the Chinese person with whom you are negotiating believes that dragons, not God, live in the clouds. Another profound difference with most Western countries is that most Chinese grow up in an intensely competitive environment, where failure does not just mean possible starvation, but loss of 'face'. Most Chinese don't have the luxury of being able to fail. This can lead, for Chinese people, to a hard approach to business, comparable to the ruthlessness of the American and European slave traders and plantation owners of the seventeenth and eighteenth centuries. China's steady economic development may change this Darwinian reality, but the

DOI: 10.4324/9781003241164-11

country's huge size and regional disparities mean that it will take a long time for most Chinese people to adopt the more nuanced view of Westerners to success and failure.

The hardest challenge for foreign companies which hope to be successful in China is to understand Chinese society and factor that understanding into their business plan and execution. This means striving to comprehend Chinese culture and civilisation, because China's culture shapes the mindset and actions of Chinese people. This is particularly important in such an ancient, rich culture as China's, in which every new event which occurs is immediately compared by Chinese people to events from Chinese history, of which some may have occurred a thousand years or more ago. Once a glimmer of comprehension has emerged, then the Chinese environment must be integrated into the culture of the company.

Obviously, this is a challenging requirement, and some companies will fall by the wayside, either because they lack the commitment or the flexibility or leadership to make such an effort. Twenty or 30 years ago, it was common for foreign companies looking at the Chinese market to flinch and turn away at the apparent opaqueness and irrationality of China. The Chinese market in 1995 or 2000 was not large enough to attract chief executives whose eyes were fastened more on their company's current profitability than on Chinese cultural niceties.

In 2022, the situation is different, because for many MNCs, China represents their largest market and/or their largest opportunity. In Germany, VW and Bayer; in Sweden, IKEA, Ericsson, and H&M; in Italy, Ferragamo, Valentino, and Prada; in France, Schneider Electric and Hermes; in the United States, Coca-Cola and Starbucks: these are just a handful of the thousands of foreign MNCs who see China as their big growth opportunity in the next two or three decades, and who are, therefore, prepared to make considerable effort, and undergo the costs needed to incorporate Chinese ways and attitudes into their business.

What, then, are the key qualities needed to make a success of "Doing Business in China"? Number one is 'humility'. No one would admit to thinking that Chinese people and Chinese culture are in some way inferior to those of your own country, but in reality, this sentiment is still not uncommon, as we can see from some of the more extreme anti-China diatribes from the extreme right in the United States. (Of course, it may also be true that many Chinese think that Americans and Europeans are inferior to them. But remember, it is you who are attempting to penetrate the Chinese market, not the other way around). Nor should you expect Chinese people to buy your products because you have been successful in other markets. Look carefully at Chinese people and their buying habits. If there are products similar to yours already in the market, then that is a good start. Sometimes, though, that is not the case. Hermes, the iconic French manufacturer of handbags and other personal items, started in China in 1996 by exporting from their French production base (a network of small and medium-size labour intensive factories spread through France) through a distributor in Hong Kong.

Hermes spent five or six years trying to understand the Chinese market and how Chinese consumers behaved before they moved onto the mainland, and made a major upfront commitment by building their China headquarters building, a stylish French design, in the most fashionable part of Shanghai. Naturally, the Chinese market since those days 25 years ago has developed and changed enormously. Nevertheless, Hermes succeeded, and now the company has a firm foothold as an aspirational product in the minds of wealthier Chinese consumers. Chinese sales now represent the largest single part of Hermes global business. Humility is an essential precursor to understanding and appreciating how China's history and culture affect the actions and decisions of Chinese people, whether they are decisions to buy, or decisions to combine forces in a joint venture, or do nothing.

AT&T

In the late 1980s, when most people in China did not have a telephone, AT&T responded to a request from the Chinese Government to present their fixed-line telephone exchange as a model for China's development of its own domestic telephone network. After preliminary discussions, the Chinese Government asked AT&T to let the Chinese have one of their telephone exchanges, so that investigations could be conducted by Chinese technicians as to the suitability of the AT&T exchange for Chinese use. AT&T complied with this request, the Chinese did their research, and then asked AT&T, prior to contract, to carry out a number of modifications in order to make the AT&T telephone exchange suitable for operation in the Chinese telephone system. AT&T refused, saying that they would sell the exchange 'as is' to China and it was for the Chinese themselves to make any necessary modifications or adaptations. The Chinese then turned to another company which made telephone equipment, Siemens, and went through the same process. This time, though, Siemens agreed to modify their telephone exchanges to meet the Chinese specifications. A joint venture between Siemens and a Chinese factory to design and manufacture telephone exchanges was established, which eventually produced hundreds of exchanges for Chinese use. When AT&T learned of Siemens' success, they offered to make the modifications to their own exchange themselves, but it was too late, because the Chinese had decided to commit to the Siemens telephone exchange technology.

The lesson to be drawn from this story is to be humble, not to believe that your technology is always superior, and try to find a workable solution with your Chinese customer.

Number two is 'commitment'. Although the Chinese economy is much larger than Japan and Germany's combined, it remains an emerging market. Its growth rate is still high, and much of the country is still undeveloped. The market is changing rapidly and is therefore inherently volatile. Chinese sales can disappoint because tastes have changed, new competitors have emerged, or economic trends have shifted. The Chinese Government can change course without warning. In a country in which the Chinese Communist Party controls everything, a change of course can mean radical shifts in profitability for companies in the firing line.

In October 2020, for example, the Chinese Government took offence at public statements made by Alibaba founder Jack Ma in a speech at a conference in Shanghai. Ma was detained and told that he had to change his ways and respect the Chinese Communist Party and the Government. This incident developed into a new campaign, of 'levelling-up', to place limits on the ubiquitous power of the Chinese 'tech' companies, and to reduce the huge inequality which had developed as China grew. The Chinese Government attacked private companies whose products they viewed as anti-social or likely to cause 'disorder'. In the latter category were private Chinese companies which sold financial services online; in the former category were companies which provided tutoring services, because the Government wanted to relieve the large extra burden which out-of-school tuition costs brought to the average, competitive Chinese family. China's government made it clear that the interests of investors came second to the well-being of Chinese people, and second also to the supreme role of the Chinese Communist Party.

This approach was a big change from the previous couple of decades, during which one Chinese tech company after another (Tencent, Alibaba, Meituan, Pinduoduo) had listed its shares on NASDAQ and created another large group of young Chinese multi-millionaires (or billionaires). Many foreign investors complained at the sudden change of direction in 2020 and 2021, but they could not move the Chinese Government. Companies who are investing in, and developing the Chinese market need to be able to look beyond these shocks and stay the course. If you think that your company doesn't have the staying power for China, it is better not to start.

Number three is 'deep pockets'. Success in China needs investment over a period of time which can last a decade and more. Viewing China as a source of short-term profit usually disappoints. There are exceptions, like the founder of a successful mobile phone chain in the United Kingdom who made his first money by buying Motorola handsets from a local British factory, and smuggling them through Chinese customs to resell them at huge margins in China because, in the late 1980s and very early 90s, mobile handsets were much in demand, but few and far between in China. Having one was a status symbol for the local government officials who were about the only people then who could afford them. But this was not an onshore Chinese business – and in China, those kinds of opportunities are few and far between, and usually lead to trouble. A multinational company which is planning to build a substantial, well-founded business in China has to be prepared to invest and reinvest.

Then, it goes without saying that the company's products or services must be attractive to Chinese consumers or enterprises, and that the organization in China must be well led and able to attract and retain high-calibre professionals. We have touched on these elements in previous chapters.

Relationships

We are not afraid to repeat the simple, but essential truth: personal relationships are the key to successful business in China. *Business may flow out of friendship, whereas in the West friendship may flow out of business.* To the Chinese – as to others in the Pacific region – relationship building is a natural part of the environment and doing business. Westerners, who lack the subconscious knowledge that in China, a key personal relationship can outweigh all else, need to plan and track such networks consciously and with great care.

We have discussed corruption in Chapter 4. It is seen by some as an inevitable outgrowth of *guanxi*. That is incorrect and complicates an already complex subject. True *guanxi* – a personal relationship which is built on mutual respect and liking, bringing goodwill on both sides – cannot be bought. Pseudo-*guanxi* may be essential for survival but it can also erode future prospects.

The law

Among the myths about doing business in China, one is that there is no such thing as law, or that Chinese businesspeople do not respect the law. The first is no longer true and attitudes to the second have changed. China has an established and growing body of commercial law and its court system and the legal profession are developing. These are early days still, by comparison to our long-established Western legal system, but certainly no Western company can afford to ignore this development, which is discussed at length by Professor Chao Xi in Chapter 5.

A good Chinese lawyer can be of great value to a business, not just to interpret the law but also to navigate China's increasingly complex web of laws and regulations – one that is filled with conflicts and contradictions. The trick, as in any country or culture, is locating that good lawyer in the first place. Today, however, all leading Western law firms have representation in China, and often their offices in Beijing and Shanghai are very large. As Chapter 5 describes, there are differences between the Western and Chinese legal systems, and there always will be. Understanding those differences and how the Chinese system works is crucial.

Intellectual property remains a hot topic, despite the considerable progress that the PRC Government has made. International rules and standards have been embraced, but enforcement remains difficult and costly, and piracy may still be a cause for concern. Our general advice is to use a multiple strategy when confronted with piracy; legal suits may be necessary to persuade government officials that the matter is serious.

In China, government, the law, and relationships are interwoven and hard to separate. No one 'connection', however good, is adequate. In cultivating multiple connections, remember that they are reciprocal: favours received are, or may be, credits against future favours expected. It is not a bank account, but expectations for the future are created. It is easy to get overloaded, in which case doubts and distrust will creep in.

Establishing ventures

Since 2020, when the law governing foreign enterprises in China changed, it is no longer necessary to discuss the various forms of Chinese corporate structure – primarily WFOEs and JVs – in detail. The question remains, however, as to whether forming a joint venture with a Chinese party is a wise move, or not. The answer, as we discussed at length in Chapter 6, is that 'it depends'. There is no clear rule either way. Some foreign companies, like Procter & Gamble, the American personal products giant, have been very successful in China working on their own; others, like Volkswagen, have done equally as well in collaboration with a Chinese partner. All we can say in this book is that joint ventures in China should never be ruled out, because they can bring great advantages, in local reputation, market understanding, and government relations, but also difficulties, for example with product copying. Establishing and managing a JV is never an easy matter, as one or both partners may lack a clear agenda and/or trust. A *hongniang*, or go-between, can help partners come together, but in the long term, it is the relationship of the partners with each other which will determine the success of the joint venture. The importance of the *hongniang* role is misunderstood by Westerners, just as the need for management consultants is misunderstood by Chinese. In practice, such misunderstandings may cancel out: some intermediaries may be seen as *hongniang* by Chinese and as consultants by their Western clients.

JV negotiations can take years, and the Chinese usually expect commitment to be long term. Many believe going it alone should be the first preference for market entry, but many large and established Western corporations continue to use JVs. We recommend assessing both options and picking the one that works best for the situation.

Marketing mix

Brands are especially important in China because most consumers lack certainty and experience, and need the reassurance which a strong brand, like L'Oréal or Starbucks, can provide. Early leader advantage has more going for it than in other markets. Early sampling and 'name' recognition are important. 'Name' means branding: symbols, colours, and numbers all mean more than Roman letters.

The market in many branded products in eastern and central China has matured. Pricing can be 'confident' because wealthier Chinese consumers often equate low prices with an inferior product.

Representative offices are a must for all but the smallest traders with China. Medium-sized firms should consider sharing with Western non-competitors. The size and regional complexity of China means that distribution issues need more priority relative to developed countries.

The full range of marketing tools is available. The less conventional may be better value, depending on the situation. E-commerce and a strong online presence is essential for every consumer company.

Marketing process

Marketing process includes, at the very least, analysis, planning, implementation, measurement, and both market research and internal analysis.

China has more statistics than any company can handle. It is important to check their reliability. This bothers Westerners more than the Chinese who are looking for pictures, not precision. Fuzzy focus is often good enough for them. To pilot through, a Western firm will need to be tough-minded about what they must know and what might be nice to know but possibly should be abandoned. Integrating research needs and the planning process is critical to selecting, and then acting on, crucial competitive information.

The classic four Ps – product, price, package, place – marketing plan format should be supplemented for China with the strategy *guanxi* calculation sequence. It is not that one should adopt the Chinese format, because such a thing never existed. The point is that planning, as a rehearsal or modelling of the future, should represent the Chinese market in a Chinese way. The essence of marketing is that it is outside-in learning. Absorb the context and build it into plans.

Government

No foreign company can succeed in China without having a strong and productive relationship with the Chinese Government, because in China, The Party, operating through the Government, controls everything. Local Chinese government officials are often highly intelligent and well trained, and many speak English. Getting to know them, and doing business with them is not usually difficult.

Management issues

Chinese businesses should be seen as families rather than as representing modern organization theory on earth. They are more formal and traditional than their Western counterparts, with decision-making concentrated at the top. Consequently, if you want anything done by a Chinese business, you have to go to the top.

One consequence, as most Western companies have already learned to their cost, could be high staff turnover. Smaller, leaner, flatter organizations are less likely to engender staff and managerial loyalty, and staff tend to move on as soon as they get a better offer. We have looked at how Western companies, by managing in a more 'Chinese way', can improve retention and keep costs down. We also examined training, especially for managers, where although there has been a proliferation of management training programmes, many are of doubtful quality. Hiring and keeping the best people requires time and investment.

Conclusion

On the one hand, the world economy is not a zero-sum game. China's growth will help the rest of the world, just as since 1960 Japan has provided immense benefit to us all. On the other hand, we are all in competition with China and with Chinese companies. Relative wealth depends on our relative skills and endeavours. Working hard is being replaced by working smart. This is no longer a matter of how many white-overall clad ladies are turning out how many microchips or plastic toys. That was then. Tomorrow is about the depth of understanding from which creativity and innovation can gain competitive advantage.

China represents an enormous opportunity over the next several decades for a wide range of Western multinational companies. If this book has helped to improve the understanding of "Doing Business in China", then writing and revising it has been worthwhile.

Bibliography

Overholt, William H. (2018) *China's Crisis of Success*, Cambridge, UK: Cambridge University Press.

Prasad, Eswar S. (2017) *Gaining Currency: The Rise of the Renminbi*, Oxford: Oxford University Press.

Shambaugh, David (2018) *China's Future*, Cambridge, UK: Polity Press.

Afterword

At the time of going to press, in mid-2022, foreign businesses are experiencing a heightened level of uncertainty in China business.

One reason is increased anti-China sentiment in many Western countries, aggravated by fears of a Chinese attempt to annex Taiwan. Another is the need to share business data with the Chinese Government, which has become a problem for some foreign companies whose business model relies on data confidentiality.

But the most important reason is the tough 'zero-COVID' policy operated by the Chinese Government controlled by President Xi Jinping, which has required lengthy, severe 'lockdowns' in many Chinese cities. This latter factor has disrupted most companies' China operations and, in particular, has impacted the profitability of companies addressing the Chinese retail market.

It is still expected by most large global multinationals that China will provide between 20% and 30% of global economic growth over the next decade. Most multinational companies wish to take advantage of this expectation, and therefore most are still committed to the Chinese market.

In my experience, which stretches back to the late 1980s, periods of heightened uncertainty and risk occur from time to time in China, but are succeeded by easier times, as uncertainties are resolved, and as China turns from managing its own internal problems to recognizing, once more, that foreign companies bring great benefits to China.

Part of "Doing Business in China" is understanding and managing periods of heightened uncertainty, whether political or economic in nature. Volkswagen is one of many large multinational companies which can bear witness to the good, long-term financial returns to be obtained from taking a patient view of China business.

Index

Pages followed by n refers to notes.

Printed in the United States
by Baker & Taylor Publisher Services